Dear Pitman Publishing Customer

IMPORTANT – Read This Now!

We are delighted to announce a special free service for all of our customers.

Simply complete this form and return it to the address overleaf to receive:

A Free Customer Newsletter

B Free Information Service

C Exclusive Customer Offers – which have included free software, videos and relevant products

D Opportunity to take part in product development sessions

E The chance for you to write about your own business experience and become one of our respected authors

Fill this in now and return it to us (no stamp needed in the UK) to join our customer information service.

Name: Position:

Company/Organisation:

Address (including postcode):

                                         Country:

Telephone: Fax:

Nature of business:

Title of book purchased:

Comments:

- | Fold Here Then Staple | -

We would be very grateful if you could answer these questions to help us with market research.

1 Where/How did you hear of this book?

☐ in a bookshop

☐ in a magazine/newspaper
   (please state which):

☐ information through the post

☐ recommendation from a colleague

☐ other (please state which):

2 Which newspaper(s)/magazine(s) do you read regularly?:

3 When buying a business book which factors influence you most?
(Please rank in order)

☐ recommendation from a colleague

☐ price

☐ content

☐ recommendation in a bookshop

☐ author

☐ publisher

☐ title

☐ other(s):

4 Is this book a

☐ personal purchase?

☐ company purchase?

5 Would you be prepared to spend a few minutes talking to our customer services staff to help with product development? YES/NO

PITMAN PUBLISHING

The Business Publisher

Written for managers competing in today's tough business world, our books will help you get the edge on competitors by showing you how to:

- increase quality, efficiency and productivity throughout your organisation
- use both proven and innovative management techniques
- improve the management skills of you and your staff
- implement winning customer strategies

In short they provide concise, practical information that you can use every day to improve the success of your business.

FINANCIAL TIMES

PITMAN PUBLISHING

the Institute of Management
F O U N D A T I O N
PITMAN PUBLISHING

WC2E 9BR, UK
LONDON
128 Long Acre
FREEPOST
Pitman Professional Publishing
Free Information Service

No stamp
necessary
in the UK

Partnership Sourcing

An Integrated Supply Chain Management Approach

DOUGLAS K MACBETH
& NEIL FERGUSON

FT
PITMAN
PUBLISHING

PITMAN PUBLISHING
128 Long Acre, London WC2E 9AN

A Division of Pearson Professional Limited

First published in 1992

© Longman Group UK Limited 1994

British Library Cataloguing in Publication Data
A CIP catalogue record for this book can be obtained from the British Library

ISBN 0 273 60208 X

10 9 8 7 6 5 4 3

Phototypeset in Linotron Times Roman by
Northern Phototypesetting Co. Ltd, Bolton
Printed and bound in Great Britain by
Biddles Ltd, Guildford and King's Lynn

CONTENTS

FOREWORD

Over the past decade the best UK enterprises have adopted the practice of continuous improvement, and partnership sourcing is crucial to the process. It optimises the benefits to be derived from a total quality culture and enables businesses to achieve 'world class' capability and competitiveness.

Partnership sourcing takes time to adopt and you will need the right systems in place. However, it does not require high cash investment. Like most good ideas the concept is simple; that customers and suppliers working together as a team can drive down total cost, improve quality and speed products to market, far more effectively than the same people working as adversaries. Already many leading companies report tangible and intangible benefits from adopting the partnership sourcing philosophy.

Since Partnership Sourcing Limited came into existence in 1990 we have developed a close relationship with Supply Chain Management Group at Glasgow University Business School, who are at the leading edge of supply chain 'best practices'. I have no hesitation in commending this book to you whether you are a customer, supplier or student of the subject.

Kenneth Cherrett
Director-General
Partnership Sourcing Ltd.

PREFACE

The need for this book arises from a variety of influences.

What is now the Supply Chain Management Group at Glasgow University Business School began, in 1987, to research aspects of managing suppliers in Just-in-Time (JIT) manufacturing companies. Around that time it had become clear to us that the predominantly American multinational electronics companies in Scotland were already taking the path of the perceived Japanese best practice of Total Quality Management (TQM) and JIT. Part of this included significant reductions in the number of supplier companies with which the major companies were dealing. It also seemed likely from our reading of the literature and some contacts with practitioners that the customer companies would behave in different ways to these supplier companies. That original research set out to identify or create a 'best practice' model for customer/supplier relationships based on the experiences of six major customer companies, some of their direct suppliers and a more widely based sample from the electronic and mechanical engineering industries, over forty companies in all.

From that first research project came the prototype of the customer/ supplier relationship positioning tool which is described in Chapter seven, along with a management guide in workbook form which was called *The Customer–Supplier Relationship Audit* (published by IFS in 1989). Shortly after this our second research project engaged Digital Equipment Corporation (who seconded an operating manager to work with us part-time for one year), along with other Original Equipment Manufacturers (OEMs), in a project to investigate local sourcing to Electronic OEMs. In this project we used the positioning tool as a pre-qualification process to locate potential supplier partners from outwith the electronics supply industry. (Both projects were supported by the ACME Directorate of the UK Science & Engineering Research Council.)

Our first contract with the UK Department of Trade and Industry followed. Here we were to investigate the current practice of excellent companies in the UK and research-based work in Europe in terms of Supply Chain Management tools and techniques. We visited twenty-four of the English winners of the Management Today Best Factory Award (we felt we knew enough about the Scottish scene by then). One major finding was the lack of impact of relationship changes back up the chain towards the supply source. The best companies were working hard with their first-level suppliers but nothing much else was in evidence.

Then came Partnership Sourcing: the joint DTI–Confederation of British Industry funded project which has done valuable work to capture case examples and suggested plans of action, and promote them widely and at senior levels. Their high profile campaign has created the common language and the title for this book, but it is our view that the concepts and practice of partnership sourcing need to be in place at each of the links of the chain of supply, from Mother Earth to final consumer, to begin to have the kind of impact on whole business sectors which will transform competitiveness.

Certainly there are short-term benefits, in some cases simply obtained, once we see parties to a business relationship as part of the same team and not the enemy, but the truly amazing gains are realized when all of the abilities of all of the players on the same team are engaged and directed to improving the competitiveness of the whole chain.

Since our research beginnings our team has evolved until we now constitute a joint venture company with Glasgow University to continue to perform academic research in the area and to commercialize the intellectual property created during the earlier research projects.

From our beginnings in electronic and mechanical engineering manufacture we have moved into automotive, aerospace, chemicals, food industry packaging, rail transport, health service and oil exploration.

Our experience convinces us that the generic principles of Partnership Sourcing apply (with some modification for context and language) in most business environments. (Partnership Sourcing themselves have published a booklet for the service industries.)

The demand for conference and workshop production from many different quarters and supplied by a variety of people demonstrates the growing acceptance that in an increasingly difficult, competitive environment it is unlikely that any single organization will have (or be able to maintain) a high enough level of capability to survive on their own. Of course, in the Western economies they might be able to buy their way into new fields but the Merger and Acquisition game, for all its glamour and visibility in the business media, is not noted for its guaranteed success.

Strategic Alliances seem to offer valued alternatives. In major new product introductions and new technology developments, the sheer scale obliges a form of collaborative venture to be created. This offers some similarities to the area we are discussing but our focus is perhaps more operational, but actually every bit as strategic as for example Compaq's decision to ally themselves with the suppliers of their other core technologies (i.e. Intel for microchips and Microsoft for operating systems). Strategic in this sense means having a major impact on company success and survival in the medium to long term. Choosing an organization (either customer or supplier) to Partner with has exactly the same implications.

Some organizations have made significant progress along this road and some examples are quoted later from both SCMG and Partnership Sourcing's experience. Others, to be honest, talk better than they walk. Most organizations, if they are serious about moving to Partnership Sourcing, recognize it for what it is – a major challenge to existing systems, attitudes, structures and behaviours. It is also a challenge to the over-simplistic view that the lowest price in the market is automatically the best possible result.

In this book we will try to pull together theoretical concepts, practical experience and processes of management intervention to help accelerate an evolutionary process.

At this stage in our business development we are challenged by questions about the appropriateness of our well-established belief systems. At least, those of us in Western organizations are so challenged.

Perhaps the biggest challenge is to discard the reliance on simple solutions. The world is increasing in complexity through becoming more inter-dependent. We need to expand our definition of the boundaries of our sphere of activity and begin to recognize that when we decide or act on the basis of imperfect information (as we must always do) then the ripples extend widely in space and time. Businesses, if they are to survive longer than the average half a human lifetime, have to adapt and continually re-identify and implement systems to provide the features which their customers regard as an appropriate product/service package. The better companies understand this need for closeness to the customer very well but looking only in that direction is not enough.

The strategic processes of management literature suggest looking widely at the environment to better position the organization with its strengths and weaknesses to obtain the opportunities while avoiding the threats.

This process need not be, but too often is, still set largely inside the existing organizational boundaries defined in ownership terms. What might it look like if defined in influence and relationship terms?

One of the great benefits of a systems approach to management is that we are free to draw the system boundaries wherever we wish and can expand or contract the unit of analysis to allow different perspectives and different amounts of detail to emerge or be subsumed in 'larger' issues. As will be discussed, the systems approach also uses the concept of system effective-ness as more important than any sub-system's local efficiency. Systems' thinking also recognizes the dynamics of the business situation and recognizes that time delays and feedback loops add to the complexity.

All of this supports the approach advocated in this book that the competitive world of business is not actually peopled by cowboy-like figures drifting into town for a quick shoot-out before riding along to the next frontier. Businesses have roots, histories, family connections, obligations to communities, desires for survival, renewal and meaning. They are living organisms which either grow or decline.

The thrust of this book is to highlight that building mutually satisfactory relationships in the business world is both more effective and inherently more satisfactory for the players in the game.

Nothing that we describe indicates that making the transition from a focus on the short-term quick hit of the 'pure' market transaction to a long-term commitment is easy. However, it can be done, and we will suggest ways to help that change process. The will to change has to be there and this book is intended to provide support to managers embarked on an exciting journey to a new way of business life.

The book is structured in four parts.

Part One   New Market Demands and New Supply Understandings, sets out the changing requirements in the market place and the ways in which the basic business deliverables can be provided.

Part Two   Theory and Practice, looks at the theoretical and practical aspects of Supply Chain Management, Partnering and Strategy and the ways in which Partnership Sourcing can be translated into new organizational forms.

Part Three   Making the Change, proposes a model of the change process and examines in more detail approaches developed by SCMG along with very many managers from a variety of organizational settings.

Part Four   Summary, completes the discussion with a little exercise to orient your organization on the road to full partnerships.

The final chapter provides a case study which can be used in your organization, or even with your partners, to give a flavour of how it might feel to be faced with the real strategic implications of being a Partner or not. There will always be the choice of doing nothing but the likelihood is that making that choice is actually to choose not to be a player in the future business game. Many of the other sides' teams already play this way and the need is to at least come level and then allow the power of an integrated approach to innovation to distinguish between success and failure. At the moment we are competing with at least one of our hands tied behind our backs. We are not sure that our eyes are fully open either.

There have been many people who have influenced this book, many of them participants in research studies or public and in-company workshops and too numerous to mention individually but we thank them for their various contributions. Our sponsors will know better than we if they received the expected value. Many of them have stayed with us for some time now so perhaps we can believe that our attempt to put into practice what we preach is bearing fruit.

Internally Martin Murphy of SCMG has added greatly to our efforts in many ways while Jill Woelfell's contribution to all of SCMG's activities is very significant. Graeme Macbeth worked long and hard to get the manuscript together and is due much thanks.

We continue to learn from and with John Carlisle, Richard Lamming, Peter Rushmore, Harry Troute and Gary Smyth amongst others but we accept all responsibility for the sins of commission and omission contained within. It is after all part of a learning process and continuous improvement is needed here as elsewhere.

Finally our thanks to Ken Cherritt and Neill Irwin and the team at Partnership Sourcing Ltd for the sterling work that they are doing to raise the profile and awareness of the issues discussed here. Much remains to be done and we hope that this book will contribute in a useful way to that process.

Douglas K Macbeth
August 1993

INTRODUCTION

Partnership Sourcing, co-destiny supplier partners, strategic purchasing, supply chain management, external resource management, value-adding partnerships, quasi-vertical integration . . . The list goes on, but the phenomenon being discussed is one which organizations are beginning to recognize as one of the more strategic issues of recent years.

As the manufacturing world woke up to the emergence of excellent Japanese companies onto the world stage in industry after industry, the managerial panacea generating brigades of consultants, academics, government advisors and practitioners all began to create employment in the new industry of the 1980s – the Japanese 'Best Practice' factory tour. As might be expected the messages came back about different bits and pieces of the overall jigsaw. In no particular order, we had robots, Quality Circles, Total Quality Control, Statistical Process Control, Computer Integrated Manufacturing, Kanban, Kaizen, Toyota Production System and Just-In-Time. At the same time a similar set of experts was examining industrial culture, industrial policy, decision-making processes and financial support and industrial structures. All of this within the context of a highly competitive home market place with an initially undervalued currency and barriers to imports.

Almost without fail these panaceas on their own failed to be successfully replicated in the West although the underlying principles, particularly of Total Quality and Just-In-Time began to be more carefully implemented, often with significant results. The relative failure was, in our view, the result of too narrow a focus and expectations that miracles could happen overnight. When they did not, the whole exercise moved on to the next flavour of the month, with last month's initiative being consigned to the waste bin along with all the other failures. Worse still, the excuse came to be that the Japanese industrial process was so bound up in the collective culture of Japan that it could not be exported. The view was that it was culture-bound and geographically limited, and thus the complete system could not be used elsewhere.

The better companies went ahead during this time with operational improvements to their manufacturing processes which paid handsome dividends and in some cases allowed the organization to continue as a competitor although often less competitive than the best-of-class companies globally.

Then came *The Machine That Changed the World*[1] at the end of the decade and this shattered a number of myths. Here was an academically sound piece of research written in user-friendly form which slashed through the concept of a culture-bound approach. While the best manufacturer was still Toyota in Japan, the second best was a Ford plant in Mexico (albeit with a little help from Ford's alliance with Mazda). Here was the proof that it was the management system, not the country's culture, which made the difference and it was exportable. In fact by that time it had been exported as the Japanese moved offshore, initially to the USA and then to Europe.

The other key message was that this system was not just about efficient factories but was a business solution aimed at increasing customer satisfaction, in which whole lifetimes of successive generations of products were managed through from conception to use and replacement in the market, with competitive measurements at least twice as good as anyone in the industry. Womack et al coined the term 'Lean Production' to emphasize both the minimal use of input resources for greatly increased output and the fact that the complete system requires coordination of all internal customers and suppliers with their external counterparts and that this is done in ways where innovation, involvement and response are at much higher levels than traditionally.

Richard Lamming's work on the supply chain aspects of that study and his subsequent book have been important contributions, although we might disagree with his chosen title for the book.[2]

The automotive industry is the leader in this field but electronics is not far behind and many of the same precipitating factors were present there as well.

As we all tried to understand the generic principles which underlay this newly discovered approach, it also became clear that the basic business relationship was founded on a different principle to that currently obtaining in Western organizations. This is one part of the Japanese history and culture which we in the West did not generally share but which was often displayed to some extent within subgroups of friends, family, social, political, service collectives and societies. This principle is mutual obligation, which it is expected will balance itself out over time.

Once we accept that we owe an obligation which we are honour bound to repay, we immediately change mindsets from a short-term focus on 'taking advantage' to considering the possibility of repaying the debt by some constructive action in the future.

Mutual obligation also implies interdependence in which one party's continued survival not only depends on the survival of the other party but also on the actions each takes towards the other to improve their chances of success.

This understanding emerged as some of us were looking at ways of making JIT more effective and widespread. To others it came as their internal quality improvement projects had to break out of the organization's walls to really influence the end results.

We therefore have a convergence from the practitioner side and as we shall see later (in Chapter Four) from the academic, theoretical viewpoint as well.

What these streams of events have demonstrated, amongst other things, is that the business need is a multifaceted one where the complex interaction of many participants in different organizational groupings all have an impact on the eventual outcome. This complexity forces us to raise our vision from our immediate surroundings to see the business in a much wider context. We call this the supply chain to capture the idea of linked activities (within and across organizational boundaries) from raw materials to final consumer. Managing the supply chain in an integrated way will not guarantee success, but it can provide an opportunity to compete more effectively with other supply chains in your particular market place.

In our view, therefore, the new requirement is to put mutual obligation relationships into place in each of the links of the supply chain.

This is likely to be with fewer organizations since the trend in the reducing total supply base any organization deals with continues. A survey (in 1993) of manufacturing attitudes in the UK, confirmed a move to fewer suppliers and more partnership relationships, with 63 per cent of engineering firms looking to reduce suppliers. This is largely a board-led trend![3]

The name for these relationships and the integrated supply chain approach they imply has come, in the UK at least, to be known as Partnership Sourcing. This is largely as a result of the creation of a company of that name by the UK Department of Trade and Industry and the Confederation of British Industry.

To provide a starting point to our discussions let us quote from Sir Derek Hornby's introduction to the first of the Partnership Sourcing booklets.

> Partnership sourcing is where customer and supplier develop such a close and long-term relationship that the two work together as partners. It isn't philanthropy: the aim is to secure the best possible commercial advantage. The principle is that teamwork is better than combat. If the end-customer is to be best served, then the parties to a deal must work together – and both must win. Partnership sourcing works because both parties have an interest in each other's success.
>
> Like all the very best ideas, it is a simple one – though it demands considerable

work, commitment and patience – and its rewards can be immense.
Partnership sourcing can help you:

- achieve world-class quality standards
- cut lead times and increase your flexibility in response to market fluctuations
- slash your stock and administration costs and bolster cash flow
- plan better through long-term, information-rich relationships with customers and suppliers
- reduce production down-time and boost capacity
- cut your 'time-to-market' – the time-lag between identifying a market and introducing a new service or product to that market.
- innovate through better information from customers and suppliers, and access to the technical resources of both.[4]

What has also become clear is that this is needed because the internal operational improvements we hinted at earlier (and discuss later) are not enough on their own. This is emphasized by the report from the Manufacturing Futures Project centred for Europe at INSEAD. This found that the 108 large European companies in the survey had 'largely absorbed the principles of customer-driven manufacturing such as total quality management or just-in-time-based flow practices. The results are there, in particular in terms of the improvement of inventory turnover, or ontime delivery or perceived quality. These are improvements in physical terms measured close to the factory floor or the customer. But these improvements have not led to an improvement in the competitive position of European manufacturing. No doubt the current economic environment contributes to the fact that manufacturing improvements did not get translated into profits or increased market shares. But perhaps there is a more structural reason. All manufacturers worldwide have adopted similar improvements and are fighting on a level field. If this is correct we need to find out what comes after "lean manufacturing".'

The answer proposed is the 'Virtual Factory' which 'gets its task of transforming materials and components into value for the customer done by using resources outside the manufacturing function proper. Resources with the supplier, marketing and sales, engineering, even the customer, have to be mobilized and leveraged in order to carry out the manufacturing task.' These tasks '. . . get carried out by networks of resources inside and outside manufacturing. These networks will not emerge spontaneously but require manufacturing managers to pay attention more than ever to the relations with their peers and partners and to the management of interfaces.'[5]

The virtual factory in our terms is the supply chain and as we have clearly indicated it is not restricted to manufacturing. We do however agree with Arnoud de Meyer in believing that Partnership Sourcing as part of an integrated supply chain approach offers the opportunity to create distinctive capability and strategic advantage, and the reported benefits arc significant.

> Domino Amjet reduced their supply base from 260 to 100; reduced response time from 16 weeks to 4 weeks; moved ontime delivery from suppliers from 45% to 90% and reduced factory lead time from 16 weeks to 2 weeks. All this when output rose 74% but done with 33% less floor space and the cost of bought-in materials in the period 1990–1993, below the rate of inflation.[6]

It takes them two years to form effective partnerships and Nissan and ICL expect full benefits over all their partners to take ten years. This book is intended to reduce that learning time.

For the moment, let us look at some more examples to whet your appetite.

DEMONSTRATED BENEFITS FROM SUCCESSFUL APPLICATIONS

The document produced by Partnership Sourcing Ltd. (1990) provides some very useful case materials from

- *Laing Homes (Quality specifications, total acquisition costs, and supply chain integrated action with Palgrave Brown and others)*
- *IBM (supply of services with Thomas Cook)*
- *Kodak (quality improvement and long-term contracts with Croda Colloids)*
- *Nissan (Supplier Development Teams and Kaizen processes in Hertford-shire BTR)*
- *Tesco (product development with Moy Park)*
- *Heath Springs using Partnership Sourcing as a marketing weapon with Lucas Heavy Duty Breaking Systems*
- *Glaxo with Courtaulds and others in a consortium to develop a new drug dispenser system in a five year deal.*

Each of these carefully chosen examples draws out some of the difficulties and successes of the approach and is certainly recommended reading.

From a variety of involvements of SCMG in this activity we have also created a list of examples. These tend to fall into two categories, i.e. short-term operational and medium-term strategic.

Black & Decker (B&D) and McKechnie Plastic Components (MCP) agreed to move, over a period of time, to a position whereby MCP's desired margin would be achieved on all part numbers, at a unit price acceptable to B&D. As a first step, an analysis was carried out of the prices and margins on all part numbers supplied by MCP to B&D. Where more than the desired margin was being achieved, the selling price was cut and the reduction then applied to a part number where the desired margin was not yet being achieved; volumes were also taken into account. The actual financial volume of business being done did not change significantly, yet there were considerable psychological effects. B&D no longer felt they were paying over the odds (being screwed) on some part numbers, and MCP now felt they could afford to be open, and honest with B&D when submitting/discussing quotations.

Storage Technology traditionally carried out the whole of the hardware installation for their customers. They took delivery of the storage devices from their sister company in the US, and they bought in cables from a supplier in the UK. StorageTek's engineers then installed the hardware and cabling at the customers' premises. As one of the results of a joint StorageTek/supplier team suggestion, the cable supplier's staff now deliver the appropriate cables to the customer's site and carry out the cable installation. This releases the (more expensive) StorageTek engineers for other, more appropriate, highly skilled tasks.

StorageTek's decision to appoint a courier firm to restock and control the inventory of spare parts through the UK has resulted in substantial customer service improvements. Minimizing customer downtime was a key factor of StorageTek's customer service policy, and to do this they held spares at 133 locations throughout the UK, that their engineers could call upon, yet the system didn't work very well. The solution has been to identify and then work with a firm of couriers who were prepared to offer a nationwide service. Spares are still provided by StorageTek UK, but the courier firm takes responsibility for delivering them to seven storage locations nationwide, manages their storage, and then, on StorageTek's instructions, delivers them, not only to a customer's site, but to the hands of the StorageTek engineer there. Under this new system, 95 per cent of spare parts are delivered within two hours. The courier company has agreed to dedicate staff and vehicles to StorageTek, in return they are guaranteed all of StorageTek's business.

The companies have identified a need to change the appearance of the couriers; they are now representing StorageTek and will have access to clean/smart working environments. They need to convey the correct image. StorageTek have identified a need to educate the courier company's management team in customer service issues. Since the supplier is paid on a contract basis rather than per job both companies can forecast costs/income accurately. The courier company monitors its own performance in areas considered important to StorageTek, and the results are fed back to

StorageTek.

John McGavigan and Co. Ltd.'s expertise in membrane switch technologies for Information Systems customers was re-developed to provide a safe steering wheel car horn switch which was capable of rapid and safe fracturing as the driver air-bag inflates from the centre of the steering wheel. McGavigan's existing facia display customers now have new technology support to a marketing (i.e. safety) thrust.

Fullarton Fabrication started as sheet metal workers producing boxes and cabinets for IT customers. As they progressively added more facilities/ capabilities and technologies they moved to become system integrators (up to 85 per cent of a cash dispenser machine) and to produce complete assemblies (keyboards and monitors). Their company growth has been dramatic in personnel and turnover. When they learned of the shortage of local plastic injection moulding capacity for their IT customers from discussion about their customers' future plans, Fullarton invested in six state-of-the-art machines – but without an order to fill them – then!

Dewhurst plc. provides metal key-pad controls to NCR's cash dispensing machines as the worldwide sole source. Their capability as supplier to NCR has caused NCR's competitors to approach Dewhurst to try and persuade them also to supply these other customers. Dewhurst decided (without discussing it with NCR) that it was better for the relationship with NCR not to become suppliers for that kind of product to companies who might harm NCR's prospects. Nevertheless partnering has proved a marketing opportunity for Dewhurst.

These examples also demonstrate an often forgotten aspect of such changes, that they have innovative potential. By freeing people from the grind of adversarial and defensive positioning they are enabled to think more creatively about better ways to do the business. Apart from any other benefits it is more fun this way.

It is not without its own form of pressure however since the expectation is that innovative thoughts will continue to be generated as we will see later in a Toyota example of braking system suppliers. The stress tends to be more internally generated so as not to let the partner colleague down. It is no less real however.

True partnering is not a 'cozy' relationship, but it can be very beneficial as this report form the *Financial Times* indicates:

AES, a supplier of machined castings and other parts to Toyota, Honda and Rover, provides one of the most vivid examples of the cultural adjustments a British supplier, with its roots stretching deep into the old, adversarial traditions of the UK industry, has had to make en route to its goal of becoming a world-class supplier.

A year ago AES was part of Beans Industries, a former British Leyland subsidiary which, among other things, was churning out reconditioned engines for the Unipart group. Unipart bought 80 per cent of AES from Beans, with an option to acquire the remainder shortly, purely because the company had contracts to supply seven components to Toyota.

Unipart Industries – the group's components manufacturing arm – had already learned much about quality from Honda. In a benchmarking study of 17 Japanese and UK components firms carried out last year by Dan Jones – co-author of 'The Machine That Changed the World' – and Anderson Consulting, it was the only UK company to match the best Japanese companies on quality. But the study showed it was unable to ally quality with Japanese productivity. What better way to try to close the gap than to supply to one of the most efficient of all Japan's vehicle makers?

Despite his previous experience of working with Honda even Frank Burns, AES' managing director, was shaken by Toyota's reaction when asked for its approval of the Unipart move.

'We said we wanted to acquire the business and why – and did they have any objections? They said 'we don't mind but please hire these 20 people' and gave us a list of individual names. We did, of course, and that gave us an early insight into the incredible detail with which Toyota tackles everything it does.'

Burns and David Nicholas, managing director of the parent Unipart Industries, had no problem persuading Beans employees to cooperate, and were able to offer the inducement of improved staff status and other elements of the Unipart package.

'They all wanted to join the "new world", despite there being no recognition for unions,' recalls Burns. (Unipart derecognised all unions two years ago, although there is no ban on membership.)

AES remains a small company, employing 40 now and an expected 50 by the end of 1993. It is divided into two main areas, one working for Honda, the other Toyota. The Honda area, which has been running for a year, is well advanced, refining the team working systems brought from Premier Exhausts, another Unipart subsidiary, as the combined experiences of working for Honda and Toyota are absorbed.

Training is top priority – to achieve quality and to address the productivity issues highlighted by the benchmarking study. Fifty per cent of team members can perform every operation on the 13-machine Honda sector; 60 per cent can perform 80 per cent of the tasks and the proportions are climbing weekly.

That the training bill is currently one half of the wage costs also illustrates one of the key influences of Toyota still alien to a vast swathe of UK industry. AES invested in all the necessary systems and capacity before production began. Eighty per cent of the contract's cost base was built into the opening phase of manufacture – a proportion likely to be the norm for all future business.

'It means,' says Burns, 'that we have the right machines, quality standards, manning levels, training etc. so that costs fall rapidly as production gets under way. The classic Western approach is minimal initial investment, rectifying mistakes and putting in more investment as production builds.'

Three months ago, Burns went to Japan to take part in Toyota's latest production system course. He found himself looking anew at areas where he had thought he already had a lot of the answers. He is teaching the course to AES' employees and later the whole group.

The insights about waste, he freely admits, left him initially incredulous – notably the proposition that up to 85 per cent of employees could not be working at any one time.

'They said that around the factory you normally find 5 per cent of people visibly not working. But then a further 25 per cent could be waiting, even if briefly, for deliveries or for a machine to finish its cycle. Then you could have a further 30 per cent building inventory. Toyota regards that as not working because there is no immediate contribution to the manufacturing operation. Lastly, they figure that up to 25 per cent can be working to method and requirement – but the method itself is not efficient, involving wasteful movements, for example.

'I got back; we checked, and found those numbers weren't far off. The problem is that UK managers tend to focus on the 5 per cent visibly not working and possibly those waiting – and totally ignore the rest.'

The benefits arising from Toyota's unrelenting attention to detail have led AES to adopt U-shaped production cells, in which one operator can move easily from one machine to another, rather than operating just one machine.

Initially, each machine required an operator to press two centrally mounted buttons and watch the process begin. A visiting Japanese engineer suggested replacing the buttons with Toyota's flap-type switch mounted at one end of the machine that the operator could hit with the flat of his hand at the start of his tour of the machines.

Burns acknowledges it sounds trivial. 'But they are an integral part of the Toyota Production System (TPS). And in saving one second they equate to 64 man-weeks on the seven lines. We reckon we can save 2–2.5 per cent of the labour bill a year – that's the entire training bill for some companies.'

The switches indicate the different philosophy required for TPS. 'The natural, British management response when the suggestion came about moving buttons was "£25000 – 'just for moving buttons!" And on that ground, in the past, it would never have been done.'

The Japanese visitor produced 185 kaizen (continuous improvement) suggestions. And AES' teams have come up with half as more(sic) again.

The application of TPS principles is already showing in productivity. On the Honda flywheels line, four men were producing 750 flywheels a week on two shifts. Introduction of U-cells and related improvements, plus a third man lifted output to 1000 a week. The third man has now been redeployed but output remains at 1000 a week.

Premier has also introduced the Toyota U-cell system, with reported productivity gains of 30–40 per cent. Perhaps warning other European components groups about the cost and quality benefits deriving from such close links with the Japanese, one leading European vehicle producer is switching to Premier as its exhaust systems supplier.

In the next chapter we will begin to look at these issues in more detail.

Part One

NEW MARKET DEMANDS AND NEW SUPPLY UNDERSTANDINGS

1

RE-THINKING THE REQUIREMENTS OF THE MARKET

In this chapter we will

- examine the changing nature of consumer demand and the implications for manufacturing businesses

- describe the pre-requisite technologies which must be employed to make it economically possible to survive in these markets

- discuss the new operating principles employed by world class manufacturers to enable them to be effective competitors.

INTRODUCTION

Awareness of the importance of Supply Chain thinking is based on a realization that traditional approaches to the needs of global market places are not going to be good enough.

These changing customer expectations are forcing a re-appraisal of basic technological approaches in manufacturing and organizational principles. We will examine each of these in turn.

CHANGING CUSTOMER EXPECTATIONS

Increased quality and reliability

Quality is a moving target and what was once regarded as adequate soon becomes inferior as competitive products overtake it in the quality stakes.

This is not simply a customer perception issue, important as that is. Increasing technological complexity in products, especially those integrating different materials and sub-systems, requires very high absolute levels of quality. This is demonstrated by the progression in quality measurement scales from percentages to parts per million to parts per billion.

Such a search for perfection might be seen as unreasonable but can be argued for from two viewpoints. Firstly, if we consider not the correct results but the potential errors and their effect we realize very quickly that perfection is not only good to have, it is actually essential. For example, at even 200 parts per million (i.e. 99.998 per cent) levels of quality this would imply, for American data: 380 newborn babies each year dropped by doctors; 320 lost pieces of mail per hour; 400 incorrect drug prescriptions each year; 100 incorrect surgical operations performed each week; 440 cheques deducted from the wrong account each hour; your heart fails to beat almost twice per day! Note however that in very many situations quality is measured in percentage terms so a 99 per cent level of quality would be 500 times worse than these figures! In certain safety-critical products such risks have been historically reduced (but not eliminated) by extensive inspection processes. These add cost to provide the safety margin required but are inherently a waste since they do not provide real value.

The second viewpoint is that quality levels can provide order-winning criteria as long as your competitors cannot match them. Any company that complacently accepts current quality standards in the market, runs the very real risk that a competitor will capture some of their market with a better quality offering. The attitude of mind is also important. A company that constantly strives for improving quality levels has to challenge existing practices, attitudes, systems and behaviours. At some levels this will impact product quality in the market place, but more fundamentally this company is likely to be incrementally improving its business competitiveness in other ways which could re-define quality from the customers' point of view.

One particular aspect of Quality is Reliability which puts a duration on the length of time a product or service is expected to satisfactorily provide the desired function to the customer.

Both Quality and Reliability can be difficult to define in the absence of detailed specifications from customers. This is not always forthcoming since customers can take the view 'I don't know what I want, but I'll recognize it when I see it'.

Like the more general concept of Quality, Reliability will also have base line levels which 'qualify' a product/service for a market. In like manner customer expectation is for this to be both guaranteed and improving in real terms.

The acceptance of Quality and Reliability as both fundamentally important and moving targets is one of the main indicators of companies who both understand their markets and are seriously planning to be major players in those markets.

More choice in existing product ranges

As customers become more discriminating they tend to expect to be able to influence producers either directly or indirectly to provide a more 'perfect' fit between their needs and wants and the company's provision. An increasing variety of product offerings is difficult for manufacturers to manage, but it is well recognized that the costs of finding new customers are at least ten times greater than the costs expended in retaining existing ones. Advanced companies go to great efforts to keep in touch with their customer base to track how their needs are changing and to predict future requirements. This is not just impersonal market research, it is in fact a different view of the supply chain where the links with customers are continuing to the mutual satisfaction of customer and supplier.

In order to satisfy these new demands without a major cost penalty, manufacturers will tend to design their products as part of a family which is more or less consistent within itself and ideally offers a progression path through various levels of need and sophistication. Obvious examples are in motor vehicles where global producers cover every type in many ranges, or historically where Digital Equipment Corporation's initial range of computers utilized completely common architectures such that expertise and software applications would never become redundant. As this process proliferates, major producers effectively become capable of efficiently manufacturing for niche markets. In fact one of the many interesting results of the 'Lean Production' book[1] is that in volume and variety terms Toyota actually produce shorter runs in lower volume than those European producers formally regarded as specialist, niche producers.

More choice through new products

The last example should perhaps be better used in this section because the very best producers also manage to change substantial proportions of their componentry as new product versions come to market. That is, it is not simply a styling exercise producing this year's version of an old standard.

As well as extending or filling an existing product range it is also necessary to develop completely new products for existing and new customer segments. As long as this is done in an effective manufacturing way and the associated marketing and sales effort brings customer and product together as well, then this provides real growth opportunities. It also provides barriers to entry for competitors not able to match the product range. Managing the increased diversity creates its own challenges however and the balance needs to be made between variety for customer satisfaction and focus to make the management task achievable. It is interesting however that in the latest recession that even the Japanese are asking if they can justify such wide ranges when the pressure for short-term profits is raised.

More customization

Both of the above approaches provide increased variety of product offering in a slightly impersonal way. That is to say that while the product definitions are supposed to take customer need into account, the actual purchaser of the finished item is not known in advance and is not directly involved in specifying the precise nature of the finished product. Customization addresses this issue in that it explicitly welcomes customer input and modifies product design as appropriate. Having customers in direct contact with the manufacturing system changes the nature of the business in a whole range of ways. The extent of customization, over what timescales, become strategic decisions and as we shall see later, the balance between the demand lead time allowed by customers and the extended time to design, procure, manufacture and deliver can more or less determine the degree of commercial risk a company is exposed to.

Getting close to customers and reacting positively to their needs is one of the underlying principles of partnership sourcing and so we should welcome such moves and organize accordingly. In the limit, customer involvement provides the best of both worlds, the customer obtains precisely what was desired and the supplier has a guaranteed sale with prospects of repeat business with a satisfied customer.

Faster satisfaction of need

While not every market requires speedy response it is another of those areas where all other things being equal it is possible to create a differentiation in customers' minds if more rapid response is possible. There are many possible time wastes in total lead time and elimination of these is triply beneficial. Increased customer satisfaction and reduced supply investment risk are local benefits while at the same time life is made more difficult for the competition. In such cases the prudent tactic is to offer a reduced response time that you can comfortably attain since the new value will soon become expected. Any failure against the new target is still a failure even though it may be better than previous average levels.

Speed is also important in that new innovations can be incorporated more quickly thus maintaining a technological lead.

It will also often be the case that it is in non-manufacturing areas that much of the lost time will occur. Reducing these highlights the effects of taking a holistic view of the business system. Thus direct and indirect areas can lever each other to increased performance levels.

Freedom to change late in the order cycle

A further flexibility niche to have is the ability to vary the detailed product specification late into the product manufacturing lead time. This can only be possible in products where the final order is for a particular configuration of components, sub-assemblies, software, etc. as an integrated package. Radical re-design will not be possible within the order cycle lead time.

In order to accommodate this the design must be sufficiently modularized such that the unique specification allows for the rapid substitution of one constituent for another. Here again, if this is not to be facilitated by massive stock holdings then rapid response and production change-overs will be needed. The design and manufacturing process must also aim to produce the maximum commonality of parts until the latest possible stage where the complexity factor of variety impacts only the later stage of production. (In Chapter Three this is best shown by a 'T' configured plant.)

This kind of flexibility is difficult to manage in many businesses since it requires a full understanding of production capability and a system that welcomes a constrained range of customer choice. In businesses where this is not well thought out there can be a tendency for sales people to allow customers this flexibility without a full understanding of what impacts this will have both internally and externally through the supply chain. The critical path of sequential activities along the supply chain constrains the freedom to change, therefore using this as a conscious strategy in the market place can only be safe when the whole supply infrastructure is very responsive. (The pipeline inventory measures introduced in Chapter Three are relevant.)

Increasing levels of customer service

The final area of change expectation recognizes that often customers are buying not merely a product but in fact a whole mix of product and service. In some cases the after-sales support and the continuing maintenance activity is already expected and valued. Obviously too, a company offering to customize a product must necessarily become closely involved in understanding the details of a customer's requirements and translating them into the unique product.

Progressive companies aim to capture customers and retain them as loyal to the 'brand name' throughout their lives. This is done by involving them in new product trials, data gathering and in some cases by anticipating their future product requirements according to the expected life-style changes. For example Japanese car salespeople will track the growth of a family and bring the large 'family' size product to their notice, unasked for, as a further service.

To summarize this section it is clear that the market demands are for a more personalized, rapid response to customer requirement through real and apparent product and service innovation and it is to this challenge that each member of the Supply Chain must respond. In order to do so we must also recognize that there are requisite changes in technologies and organization.

PREREQUISITE TECHNOLOGIES

Statistically capable technologies

Any manufacturing process is inherently unable to produce output consistently to a single target value. In reality there is variation which tends to fall into a normal distribution shape whose precision is defined by its measure of spread or dispersion called standard deviation or sigma.

This value is set by the process operating for a given product at given values of equipment setting. Within the process two things can go wrong. Assignable causes are those that are recognizably discrete and can be recognized, modified and perhaps removed. Random variations are just that, random, and their unpredictability makes them more difficult to control. Improvements in these areas often require continuous incremental effort and close monitoring and control.

This basic capability is matched against the specification tolerance as decided by the design function. The tolerance is the acceptable range of values within which the product must lie. The balance between these two are demonstrated in Figure 1.1 and is related in two measures Cp and Cpk. Cp is process capability and is defined as

(upper specification limit − lower specification limit) / 6 sigma.

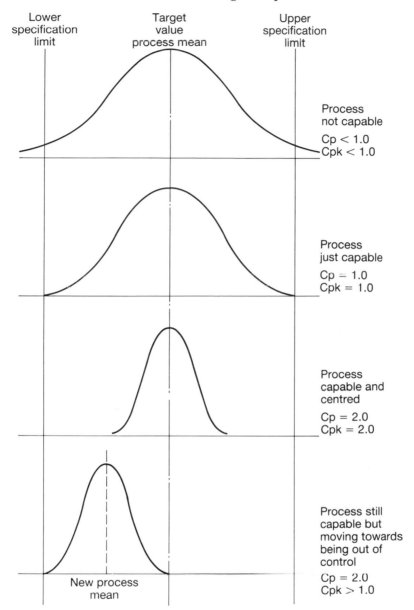

Lower specification limit

Target value process mean

Upper specification limit

Process not capable

Cp < 1.0
Cpk < 1.0

Process just capable

Cp = 1.0
Cpk = 1.0

Process capable and centred

Cp = 2.0
Cpk = 2.0

Process still capable but moving towards being out of control

Cp = 2.0
Cpk > 1.0

New process mean

Figure 1.1 Process Capability and Specification Limits

As long as Cp > 1 there is a possibility of controlling the process through statistical process control charts such that the chances of creating reject materials are managed to an acceptable probability level. Once we have a process with less spread than the tolerance band the location within the range becomes important. It is here that the more critical Cpk measure takes over.

Cpk = smaller of (Upper Specification Limit − Process Mean)/3 sigma

or (Process mean − Lower Specification Limit)/3 sigma

As long as Cpk > 2 the factor of safety is regarded as acceptable since the distribution's centre would have to move a substantial amount to create probable reject materials.

Thus a prerequisite of effective statistical control is that the process capability indices are appropriate. Notice, however, a corollary to this concern. Action for improvement can take either or both of two directions. The process variability can be reduced, i.e. moving more towards a point value rather than a distribution. Alternatively the specification tolerance can be increased making the target easier to hit. Ideally the process should be improved to make it more precise since according to the Taguchi Loss Function any variability is an inherent waste and ultimately a cost to society.[2] There may however, be real limits to possible improvements which are technically established. Thus in semiconductor technology the wave length of the light source constrains the closeness with which microchip circuits can be packed. There is also a tendency not to fully question why certain tolerances have been specified. Often custom and practice or an excessively conservative approach produce tolerances tighter than actually required for product integrity. It is therefore important that both specification and process are critically examined.

The important message remains however, that without processes capable of being effectively controlled within the defined limits then quality at source is impossible and the only alternative is to recognize that defective products will be produced and to inspect out the bad items. This adds cost and not value and does not support continuous improvement which can only come from more fundamental investigations.

Flexible processes with simple change-overs

Flexible production comes in a number of forms and can be real or potential. Flexibility dimensions include product, product mix at any point in time and volumes demanded. To this must be added the extent of the range of flexibility within each of these dimensions which can be effectively catered for and finally the response in both time and resource needed to effect a flexibility change.

Defining the market requirement for flexibility types is an important strategic decision. Such a decision is also constrained in that major technological innovations in product or process technologies or in materials technologies can radically affect the utility of a given manufacturing system choice.

A 'flexible' assembly line for mechanical turned parts and sheet components which also involved robotic spot welding and mechanical setting was made obsolete by a complex engineering plastic incorporating glass fibre reinforcing which is moulded complete and ready for subsequent assembly in a fully automated injection moulding process cell.

Unless a full understanding of the business need and projected developments in product, competitor and supplier markets is in place, the tendency to go for the fancy, big, production machine seems to be overwhelming to many technical experts. Such 'big' technology requires major investments which then are prone to the overhead recovery argument. This takes the form 'that machine is costing £xooo per year in depreciation and other costs so we better keep it busy to generate output to cover its overhead'. If such decisions are made in isolation we might simply be activating the machine and producing work-in-progress inventory which complicates the management task and actually costs money. Only if material can be sold through incorporation into finished goods should it be produced. Otherwise, such inventory is not an asset but a liability.

Big machines can be difficult to use flexibly. If we design one machine to cope with lots of variety it often means that when actually in operation much of its designed capability is not being used. Multiple smaller machines covering the same range of flexibilities might make sense and reduce the big machine activation syndrome. Multiple machines can also permit volume flexibility through varying the numbers of people operating the machines. These smaller machines might also tend towards the situation where their function is limited and they can be switched from one product to another for little response cost. Larger machines, in order to produce flexibly, will need to be changed over from the production of one version of product to another. The change-over time and effort is the resource cost which, if too great, can constrain the degree of effective flexibility attainable. Historically this cost has often been taken as fixed and production batch sizes increased to distribute the effects of this cost over a large number of units of output. Thus was created the concept of 'Economic' batch sizes. Best practice conversely is to see change-over times and costs as wastes which must be reduced in order to reduce the waste of over-production through large batches for which there is no immediate demand.

Using basic industrial engineering methods of analysis and human creativity, often from the operators of the machines themselves, the times to change over or set up the machines for the next batch can be progressively reduced. In a number of companies the management team have handed over a video camera capable of split second timing to a work group to aid their own improvement activities. The camera and the studied work is agreed to be the property of the work group and the resulting video can only be seen by permission of the work group. This avoids the historical problems of industrial engineering or work study where the 'one best way of working' was determined by management, imposed on the work force with little or no consultation and regarded as exploitation. A self-directed improvement effort where the work group takes ownership of problems and opportunities and makes effective changes is a much more positive approach, and begins to capture the hearts and minds (and not just the hands) of the workpeople.

Effective communication and information processing

Information technology is undoubtedly a powerful tool to assist many business tasks. Technology can operate in a variety of ways however. It can be used to replace human effort (either manual or intellectual) or it can be used to enhance or extend effort. Unfortunately there is also a potential to engage the technology for its own sake without thinking through the validity of the apparently precise technological solution. At a simple level this is the concern with school children operating calculators for mathematical problems without checking if the resulting answer makes any sense in direction or value. At a more complex level this could be the recognition that a computerized production planning and control system based around Material Requirements Planning (MRPI) or Manufacturing Resource Planning (MRPII) is so dependent on accurate data that extensive shop floor recording equipment is installed to automate the stock and material information movement.[3] Thus complex solutions to the problems of complexity breed further complex problems which are 'solved' with yet more complex technology. The underlying problem is not tackled in this approach. Essentially the need is to gain control, simplify where possible and give the information generation, control and usage back to the people who need it.

Communication is a two-way process. These are easy words to say but actually difficult to put into practice. In most communications it is not the actual words, intonations, body language, ambience, etc. which is key, but the other party's perceptions of what is being communicated that is the differentiator between success and failure. Remember also that, especially in a communication requiring the other party to do something, it is natural for the other party to ask 'what's in it for me?' What's in it might simply be the avoidance of future pain or discomfort but if we have thought through the recipient's frame of reference and can communicate that these effects are recognized and compensated for, then the likelihood is that the communication will succeed. Even better if the communication is supportive of behaviours and actions which the recipient would personally choose to exercise in the given circumstances.

We must also recognize a dynamic in the business causing many of the associated factors to vary over time and circumstances. With such a personal and variable transmitter and receiver in communication it is no surprise that we get it wrong.

Expecting technology on its own to 'solve' such situations must be unrealistic (at least with current technologies). Thus Electronic Data Interchange (EDI) has the potential to drastically reduce the wastes of time and resource involved in many more traditional communication channels. In practice, however, it often speeds up the transmission of garbage and has been abandoned by some senders until they clean up their own data validity mess. In similar fashion receivers will tend to ignore the electronically produced production/delivery schedules when frantic telephone calls from the sender countermand at short notice the previously sent details.

Communication needs understanding before it needs technology.

This is true between communicators inside the organization and is even more true between organizations. The dynamics discussed earlier also suggest the need for ongoing effort to keep a personal level of contact going to monitor and adjust for changes at either end of the link. If this effort is put in regularly at non-crisis times then a speedy understanding can be achieved 'over the wires' when a crisis does occur. Building up the personal relationship is also important from the very obvious point that getting to know someone personally makes it difficult to treat them impersonally. Thus customers and suppliers form faces, personalities, names and friendships and no-one likes to let a friend down. They will automatically consider how the 'friend' will react to a change and try to help them accommodate the change with minimum disruption.

This basic principle should underlie all communication but *must* underpin Partnership Sourcing communications. Once established, however, we must build an information processing system which supports these principles. Like any other process it should be designed to be capable, flexible, effective and amenable to continuous improvement. The Partnership Sourcing communication system will need to provide audit trails perhaps, but simplicity should also be a target.

One issue for customers not willing to permit high levels of dependency with their suppliers is that of compatible equipment and multiple standards. If a supplier company installs EDI equipment for one customer will this be suitable for their other customers? If not, and duplicates are needed, this is another non added-value waste in the chain that someone (everyone?) pays for. A prime example of this was the vehicle assembly company who decreed that a supplier must have compatible Computer Aided Design (CAD) equipment to their own or else they would not be considered for future work. Within a few years the definition of compatible was revised to being one of only two customer specified systems. This was due to the slowness of developing and agreeing standards for data transmission between CAD systems.

Information technology has the potential to close-couple a customer's and supplier's production planning system (i.e. MRP talks to MRP) but there are big issues of confidentiality, access control, data manipulation, etc. If it could be made to work to mutual satisfaction then truly could we talk of 'managing the external factory'.

Perhaps such a scenario is not actually consistent with the partnership of collaborators ideal that we are aiming for and implies that yet again the customer organization 'knows best' and is imposing its will on the supplier. Perhaps it will be better to keep a human collaboration in the feedback loop to agree and commit to the new requirements.

We have been talking here about links from customer to supplier. Equally the supplier must make efforts to develop understanding and exchange information with the customer. Often the customers will be the drivers in this process simply because of history and perceived power, but suppliers can also realize market advantage by demonstrating a capability to work closely with one customer and to use this to offer a differentiated service to other customers.

In this section we have demonstrated the attitudes to technological issues that we must have developed, but there are new organizational principles at play here as well.

ORGANIZING PRINCIPLES

Customer satisfaction

'The Customer is King'; 'Total customer satisfaction and delight is what Total Quality is all about'. These are phrases that capture some of the current guru messages. A number of points must be made. The obvious first one comes as no surprise. It is satisfaction of all of the customers along the chain that is the route to success. Companies can, however, go bankrupt satisfying their customers, so this has to be balanced by the caveat that it cannot be satisfaction at all costs, but should be customer and supplier satisfaction against agreed and understood requirements and performance standards. We must also provide a mechanism which allows the supplier to say 'Yes, but . . .' to a customer request. (The Relationship Positioning Tool process described in Chapter Seven is just such a mechanism). Making promises which cannot be fulfilled is not customer service even though at first sight it might be seen as being customer focused.

Absolute process control

This is the goal of quality management since it is only by control at source that waste can be avoided. We discuss this later but it is important to recognize that the national and international standards BS 5750 / ISO 9000 / CN 29000 are not about manufacturing process control but about managerial process and paperwork control aimed at eliminating the onward transmission of defective items, based on inspection and segregation approaches.[4] As such there is no forced requirement to avoid creating defect materials, no required continuous improvement methods and above all, it does not help reduce the total cost of non-conformance (Total Quality Cost). It is possible to go bankrupt operating to these standards, since poor process control creates the need for more and more inspection, reduced material throughput, increased material and labour usage and failure costs.

The standards mentioned can produce a degree of assurance to customers that their incoming material is 'controlled' in number of defect terms. They do not of themselves demonstrate that a qualified supplier is actually good enough to justify devoting attention and resource to them.

Avoidance of waste

This lies behind all attempts at improvement. It is worth highlighting that while manufacturing (broadly defined) typically creates a cost of non-conformance or Total Cost of Quality of some 20–30 per cent of revenue the belief is that perhaps 70 per cent of that is accounted for by indirect areas where traditionally quality measures have not been in place. One difficulty about measurement can be resolved if we consider not only the number of errors found, for example, in paperwork, but also calculate the potential number of errors as an evaluation of service performance. Thus an invoice clerk could have actual errors compared with number of invoice transactions per period to provide some data for trend analysis later. The more advanced companies with well developed manufacturing quality programs are extending their efforts into the offices to spread the message and aim for the significant improvements expected in these areas.

People involvement in control and improvement

We have already described how work teams can be involved in improvement activities with the aid of some education, minimal equipment and support. Japanese companies often have limited numbers of private offices but will have meeting rooms close to the shop floor where teams can discuss, chart and display issues, possible solutions, etc.

The purpose must be to encourage everyone to question the current practice of all they do; to ask if the activity adds value in sufficient quantities and to consider ways of providing the same functional requirement but in different ways. The very best companies encourage suggestion or improvement schemes which generate thousands of suggestions per employee per year. While some of these must be trivial or nonsensical, nevertheless it demonstrates the capability of the proposers to question and evaluate different methods. Such questioning demonstrates the realized potential for continuous improvement.

Involvement in control is also a different mind-set. After the time of Frederick Winslow Taylor and *Principles of Scientific Management*,[5] the principle of sub-division of labour has suggested that there are managers, doers and inspectors as well as a variety of janitorial, secretarial, maintenance, etc. experts to be called on or requested. This 'overhead' resource is being severely questioned now as work groups of practitioners meet to evaluate new information and suggest and plan for modified courses of action.

Response time is the issue here. When things go wrong any delay simply compounds the problems. If that delay is because the batch size is so large and/or produced far in advance of need then the source of the problem may no longer be evident so no permanent fix can go in. Similarly a machine failure which causes a production stoppage until a qualified maintenance person becomes available makes no sense if the machine operator is trained and competent to effect a suitable repair or replacement.

Being given the right to stop a production line on their own initiative, having done their own evaluation of the seriousness of a quality fault, is a powerful recognition both of the worth of the individual but also the importance placed by management on getting quality right even above making the output performance numbers.

Simple, visible controls at low levels in the structure

Part of the implementation of people involvement is a back to basics approach on the production floor. Here visible process guides become the responsibility of the people in the area. They will have been part of the team defining the process instructions and now will be responsible for changing over process description sheets when products change. Cross training matrices will be visible to demonstrate the developing multi-skilling capabilities in the work team. Output performance will be visible either by white boards manually updated or by overhead TAKT time indicators which show the shift target, production to date and the rate needed to work to, to hit the target by the end of the shift.

Very visible will be quality control charts and problem identification lists while, as already discussed, in a meeting area close by, will be visible evidence of the improvement effort going into the process. This will demonstrate everyone's training in problem solving and the basic tools of analysis associated with Total Quality approaches.

Good systems demonstrate the effects of analysis of the total process and while the human effort is not trivial it is not obviously chaotic. A normally experienced visitor should easily understand the flow of material through the process; should recognize certain of the performance indicators and see people going about their business in a controlled and effective manner. There should not be the frantic dash and confusion seen in some plants with piles of inventory obscuring people's view and obstructing passage of people and communication.

Good plants do not rely on high technology to produce 'management' reports. The results have been planned, the controls are in place on the factory floor to allow the people to monitor that plans are being accomplished and management's responsibility is to 'walk the job' and be interested and visible on the line to confirm that plans are being achieved.

One of the cultural changes UK managers discovered early in the life of a Japanese transplant was that rather than reporting a production problem up the organization as it were and being dependent on information transmission from the site, the expectation was that the operating manager had visited the problem area, gathered data for analysis as to possible causes and potential solutions, implemented an immediate quick fix and was simply reporting these actions while alerting the rest of the operation to the need for wider scope investigation and changes to put more comprehensive, permanent fixes in place.

This kind of information processing and action oriented behaviour is difficult if not impossible when working at a distance through a computer terminal into the corporate mainframe. For all the power of computing there is a basic illogicality in thinking that problems can be solved in this way. By definition, current operations in the computer system have been designed assuming a certain pattern of operations. Problems occur in practice because these patterns do not gather or process the new problem information so that the solution is unlikely to be found inside the captured 'old thinking' of the computer programs.

Managers have the opportunity to do the forward thinking when continual firefighting is no longer needed but when real problems occur they need to be part of the concerted attack called down in support of the line to develop improvements which all will share in developing and implementing and where no blame was attached to the perceived failure. Hiding in management meetings is not acceptable. Enabling and supporting problem-solving at the lowest level close to the seat of the problem ensures both speedy response and employee involvement in, and commitment to, the solution. Pitching in to help also demonstrates team commitment and the kind of authority that comes from contributed and valued expertise.

Common destiny equally shared and important

One would normally assume that there would be a different perception between internal personnel and customer and/or supplier personnel. Unfortunately, not many companies offer lifetime employment opportunities and even the best of them in the West sometimes have to renege on their intentions, e.g. IBM. If people or other organizations believe that the relationship can be terminated at short notice by the other party, it suggests that certain risk management strategies will be put in place. At the internal personnel level, employees may not commit their all for the good of the company. Rather they may spend some of their time both inside and outside work, building expertise which will permit them more easily to transfer their employment.

In an analogous situation a supplier company faced only with a purchase order for parts for the next two months may fail to invest in new equipment for future work which is not in any way guaranteed to become available. Even if they do invest, the cost will probably be allocated over the short time of the actual orders rather than the possible life time of the continuing supply contract, thereby increasing the notional unit price.

Belief in and trust of the other party: collaboration not conflict

Trust takes a long time to build and one stupid action to destroy.

Trust depends on behaviours not words. What we do tells others much more than what we say. Trustworthiness is demonstrated (or not) by the actions of everyone in our organization over an extended period of time. It is tested when big problems occur when the tendency to revert to former bad practices is very strong. It is at this point that the resolve to operate in a partnering mode is most at risk.

A major electrical appliance manufacturer was three years into a partnering programme with key suppliers when the cash position of the customer company was briefly exposed. The corporate finance people wanted to impose an extension in the payment terms for supplier invoices from 30 days to 60 days from receipt of goods.

The Procurement people won the argument that to do so would so poison the atmosphere of trust being developed that all the gains (and a bit more) would be lost. They won the argument but it was a close decision. As it happens by talking to their partner companies they were offered and accepted some easement in payment terms to see them over their short term difficulties.

All of the new manufacturing techniques are naturally more 'fragile' than former systems with in-built buffers of inventory at various stages. Partners in the chain are vulnerable to each other's action or in-action. Our colleagues, John Carlisle and Bob Parker, put it very well.

What Partnership means:

A trust that both parties will do what they have said they will do.

A willingness to become vulnerable to the other party supported by a firm belief that the other party will not take unfair advantage of that vulnerability.

A sensitivity to each other's needs, and an active dedication to seeing that both party's needs are met so far as that relationship can meet them.

A high level of clear and candid communication which leaves neither party in doubt about the feelings of the other towards the relationship and the understandings within that relationship.[6]

Being the kind of business partner described in these words is certainly not easy and does not happen overnight. On the other hand, if we can make this happen, and good companies are doing so now, then the nature of the work environment changes dramatically. We no longer have to fight to gain short-term advantages; worry about the aggressive intentions and new lines of attack from 'supposed' partners; when problems occur they are shared and multiple levels and sources of effort are devoted immediately to solving them in a way which guarantees that such a problem cannot recur and above all, there evolves a 'can do' attitude and a belief that together we can shape the future to our mutual satisfaction.

It is not surprising therefore that the best companies begin to behave and think as if they are part of an extended family. Perhaps these will retain vestiges of paternalism with the big customer company being more influential. After all, the Japanese Keiretsu (see Chapter Five) is in effect just that with shareholding and former customer staff in supplier companies and elements of cartelism in their dealings with other Keiretsu. In these and the evolving Western model, partners cannot guarantee being *equal* – they should however aim to be *equitable*.

SUMMARY

- **Customers expect high levels of Quality, Reliability, Variety and Response.**

- **For any supplier to have a chance of satisfying these new demands, they must employ statistically capable processes and be able to cope with more rapid changes of product mix.**

- **The traditional skills of industrial engineering can support improvement processes by the shop-floor experts.**

- **Communication is important but people come before technology.**

- **Basic organizational principles underpinning the satisfaction of the market need include: process control and waste elimination processes driven by people involvement in a highly visible way.**

- **A common destiny for all of the customer–supplier links is the key to new ways of working.**

In Chapter Two we will look at ways in which organizations can react effectively to provide satisfaction of these more demanding market requirements.

2

THE BUSINESS
DELIVERABLES

In this chapter we will

- examine the nature of competitive advantage and the asociated concepts of order winners, qualifiers and order-losing sensitive features

- examine the nature of the importance and interrelationship of the business deliverables of innovation, quality, delivery and cost.

COMPETITIVE ADVANTAGE

Competitive advantage can be defined as those features of a product/service package that persuade customers to deal with a business because it is differentiated in some unique way that other businesses cannot exactly replicate. This definition points to a number of key issues.

The first is that customer perception of uniqueness is the important measure. Secondly, it is a mix of product components and service components in the overall package that is bought and sold and this mix may be different with different customers.

The final phrase in the definition suggests another key factor which is time. Competitive advantage can be very temporary and while replication in the short term may not be possible, in the longer term it will be. Of course, in matters of trademarks and patents there are legal protections for given periods of time but not every country operates these rigorously and even if they do, competitors may well try to reverse engineer the products or design around a patent. Competitive advantage from these sources might therefore be shortlived. One way adopted in sectors of the Japanese business world was to have very rapid new product introductions so that in a demanding market, competitors had little market to attack because tastes had changed by the time their catch-up product was available. This was fine as long as the financial backers of the business were patient and recognized that a growing market share would in the longer term provide an adequate return on the investment. Following the rapid loss in asset value associated with reductions in property values which occurred at the start of the 1990s the pattern in Japan changed so that the companies are now looking for better profit margins more quickly and this may be sufficient to slow the rate of new product introduction. Competitive advantage will have to be sought from elsewhere in these companies.

Order winner, qualifier and order-losing sensitive features

Terry Hill has contributed much to the development of a common language between marketing and manufacturing in strategic discussions.[1] He asks that marketing establish (over a suitable time scale and recognizing the dynamics in the market) those features which most persuade customers to buy from one company in preference to competitors' offerings. These features he calls order winners and in the Japanese market we discussed recently, the rate of new product introduction was an order winner. Qualifiers are simply tickets to play the game. They provide qualifying standards in the same way as pre-Olympic trials sort out the top competitors from the merely adequate. Order-losing sensitive features are qualifiers where the unacceptable standard is very close to the qualifying one and where any underperformance can quickly cause customer dissatisfaction and alternative purchase decisions. These need to be monitored very closely but do not of themselves win orders. These features again are highly dynamic and a source of competitive advantage in themselves if we can so influence the market to move to order winners more suited to our operation than competitors'. Conversely order winners can soon become qualifiers as the competitors all get up to speed. We firmly believe that in most markets quality of the product is becoming a qualifier.

These concepts work against traditionally viewed means to gain competitive advantage which are built around the idea of a trade-off. In technical design questions the trade-off is real and must be accommodated. For example in designing an aeroplane to carry four hundred passengers in comfort across continents the designers explicitly rule out the aeroplane's ability to undertake a combative role for example. To some extent this is also true of business systems but is becoming less true as we consciously question whether the constraints we once believed insurmountable were so only because of our own lack of imagination and effort.

Wickham Skinner's seminal article about manufacturing strategy listed a whole series of the trade-offs then extant in manufacturing of which the classic is probably that between quality and cost.[2] Until we understood quality better we all believed that the law of diminishing returns applied, in that greater levels of quality could only be achieved through the increased spending of resources to guarantee quality. This however was based on a wasteful approach to quality achievement and as soon as quality at source was implemented it was clear that high quality could actually mean lower cost.

In a similar vein strategists like Porter have argued that there are generic choices in business competitiveness and that companies have to decide on which of these four strategies they will base their competitive offerings.[3] These four are: price, quality, innovation and volume/ variety flexibility. Like most stereotypes there will be circumstances where these will still apply but the lesson of good companies is that they cannot afford to only use one of the available competitive dimensions. They have, as Ohmae[4] would have it, to generate strategic degrees of freedom and actually offer customers all of the above generic features, albeit they may be at different stages of the order winner/qualifier transition, backwards and forwards.

What we must recognize however is that there is a preferred sequence in the creation of the business deliverables. That is to say that suitable innovation in all things all of the time can keep an organization healthy and responsive. Thereafter the sequence of quality, delivery and cost then becomes a virtuous cycle in which ensuring quality at source and reliability of delivery (to all of the customers both internal and external to the organization) enables cost reduction to be achieved.

Let us now look at each of these in turn.

Innovation

New product design and development

Innovations are of two main types, those we can describe as incremental and those which are so dramatically different from previous practice as to be regarded as a breakthrough. Both can occur in product or process technologies and in the service delivery process as well. We cannot afford to focus on one without recognition of the contribution to be made by another. In some ways incremental innovations can be seen as allowing the re-qualifying of the business for the market place since without it we are soon uncompetitive. Complementary to this is the reality that sufficient small steps of improvement can be used to outdistance the organization from the competition, thereby providing a competitive gap which these competitors will then have to do something dramatically different to overcome. This is almost the paradigmatic description of the Japanese manufacturing success story causing the West to play catch up while they move on to new competitive areas. Breakthrough innovations on the other hand occur by definition less frequently but can create a much wider impact, totally transforming the industry recipe. Successive electronic chip generations are like this and have impact on the basic economics of manufacture as well as design.

The implications of looking for innovations of both types and in both product and process results in the need for skills at both the new product design and development stage as well as during manufacture. Traditionally Western companies have not staffed these areas with the same skill levels. The importance of design has been partially recognized but the manufacturing areas have received less attention. The allocated skill patterns would also have tended to be different in the different functional areas as shown in Figure 2.1.

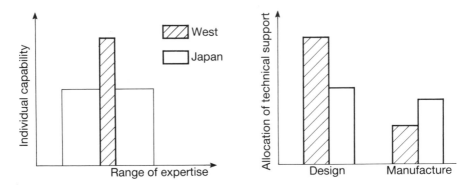

Figure 2.1   Skill allocations in Western and Japanese Organizations

For example, line managers or supervisors in the UK tend to be more people oriented and less likely to be technically qualified than the equivalent people in Japanese companies. As a result industrial engineering support to UK manufacturing lines is needed whereas in Japan the supervisors would be more capable of problem solving themselves. This lack of technical training and capability limits the improvement activities which truly can be said to originate at the shop floor in UK companies.

In the product innovation literature there is discussion about the driving force for ideas. Von Hippel has demonstrated that customers are major sources of suggestions about what might be done to improve products or develop new ones.[5] In other ways as well, market pull can be seen as demand is recognized by explicit request or informed speculation about future needs. Such approaches will tend to build their future vision around known technology and current awareness of need but some innovations are so dramatic that existing customers are not always the right people to evaluate them. History is replete with examples of inventors having a hard time convincing people of the merit and future market potential for their invention. Photocopying must rank in the top league for this and the rate of acceptance of telefax astounded most forecasters. In these cases there seems no alternative to the inventor championing the invention against all the received wisdoms and vested interests. Technology push of this kind is more likely to produce the breakthrough innovations which can be so important. (In the UK a postal strike at the early stages of the new product introduction for telefax is regarded in retrospect as the best possible marketing exercise for business awareness and rapid acceptance as technology push turned to market pull overnight.)

Breakthrough innovations are however more dangerous in business terms than incremental ones and more difficult to cost justify in investment appraisal terms since obviously there is no history of success, no current demand and no technical appraisal except by the already (over?) committed inventor. In strategic considerations one less risky approach is to let others make the initial breakthroughs and then to copy or re-engineer and beat them to the growing market. This requires a special kind of organization both in terms of scanning the environment for new opportunities and in the skills and systems to follow the technology lead fast enough.

The problem of checking if a new product is actually going to sell in the required quantities is one faced by all organizations in the market place, and while market research has techniques to test possible customer reactions, the future is inherently unknowable and therefore the results from customer evaluations set in surrogate and essentially artificial markets are more or less unreliable. How much easier then if the manufacturer could operate a 'produce and try' policy, i.e. introduce the new product anyway and if it is accepted as a good product concept (even if not fully developed to full reliability or potential) then learn and apply the lessons to the rapidly following stage two product. In essence this was how Sony introduced the audio walkman which they admit was launched onto the market with inadequate battery support. The customer reaction was so positive that the problems of power consumption and supply simply had to be solved but at least they then knew that if they were, the market would be there.[6]

There is little doubt that the home Japanese market has assisted this type of market testing through the attitude of conspicuous consumption and limited life product usage. Such high turnover of product variety, whether created by the manufacturers or supported as a reaction to a real customer need has proved very effective in accelerating the rate of technological development. It has not always proved possible to make much of a short-term profit margin in such markets however and as already discussed, the final years of the millennium might cause this policy to be reappraised.

Without such a home market other companies have to address the same issues and may have to adopt more traditional market testing approaches. Here time to respond to a successful trial launch will be key. For example in fashion clothing the manufacturer who can actually modify production schedules in time to catch the popular lines as they sell above forecast will have generated a significant competitive advantage over their competitors who have to decide on fabrics, styles and colours, and size mixes, six to nine months ahead of the actual season. Benetton have managed to make this work in knitted garments and importantly their supply chain or value adding network solution is instrumental in making it possible.[7]

Reducing Time to Market

For competitor organizations in essentially the same environment, identification of customer needs and future requirements and perhaps to a lesser extent the technical capabilities to satisfy them are signals to be received. What will then distinguish between success and failure is the speed and competence with which the base information is translated into effective product/service offerings which satisfy the requirement. The measure of elapsed time from new product idea to market introduction, i.e. time to market is now a real indicator of how well an organization has got its complete act together since without integrated action on all fronts the product launch will inevitably be delayed. Delay at this stage is never recovered and while other types of failure will be expensive, perhaps only a major safety-critical failure resulting in liability litigation and concomitant adverse publicity will so adversely affect the ability to earn a return on the investment.

For organizations structured along classical Tayloristic 'Scientific' or even Adam Smith-based division of labour principles the design process is a serial one where each functional area does its bit to the concept before 'throwing it over the wall' to the next function. This particular supply chain has the usual wastes and delays but is further disadvantaged by the simple but damning fact that cost and complexity are defined early in the sequence but actually incurred later when the costs of modifications to recover from unforeseen interactions or errors is multiplied by all of the ripple effect changes which then also have to be made. This also points out the crucial importance of good design both to create a quality product but also to create a product capable of cost-effective manufacture.

Since we are in the design situation the trade-off reappears but it becomes even more important that all interested parties have an input to the thought process earlier enough to avoid the later problems.

The new principle is parallel working with overlapping stages not serial ones. This approach is well known in both production control where it could be called batch splitting or operating with different transfer to process batches, or in network planning terms where the activities not on the critical path (which must be serial) are done in parallel with the critical ones. If we stick with the network analysis example it is worth noting that the total elapsed time is completely specified by the length of the critical path and therefore reducing the activities on that path must reduce overall project time. The intention is to limit to the bare minimum the activities which will form the critical path and allow as much parallel activity as possible. Breaking into the functional stereotype helps this since in the old way, all work in each functional area had to be complete before any work would be passed on to the next stage or department.

The best practice examples from Japanese car companies described in *The Machine That Changed The World* also point to different organizational and career structures.[8] There the design team boss or Shusa has a complete dedication to a product family following it through to the market place before starting again with the next generation. His hand-picked team owe their advancement prospects to their contribution to the project more than to their original functional allegiances. This is in marked contrast to Western norms where the functional specialism is the career route and typically people will rotate into and out of project teams with little time or inclination to build up either project specific expertise or team spirit.

Traditionally one functional group excluded from these considerations until the very end (and therefore much too late to cause other than trouble and cost if they requested changes) is the set of supplier organizations which have actually to manufacture according to the definitions agreed in splendid isolation in the customer's design offices. One major piece of parallel working desperately needed is to get early supplier involvement in the design process since their impact on the manufacturability considerations will be mutually beneficial.

Chapter Three discusses aspects of this as well. We talk there of the need for a degree of risk sharing in such arrangements but there is another associated concern and potential waste which must be recognized and due allowance made for. If we have parallel working in place it is quite possible that because of different lead times it will be necessary to make decisions about downstream investments before all of the upstream design decisions have been completed. After all, this is the benefit we are seeking through time compression of the total process. The design and development of production tooling is the best example of this concern where the material-forming tool shapes are specified by the precise requirement of the finished product shape. This may be subject to evolutionary development but in the meantime the toolmaking activity has to be initiated. Since tooling can account for a large proportion of the product change cost and takes time to procure, there may be circumstances where a late design change causes large modification or re-creation costs in the tooling. The possibility of such costs has to be recognized at the start and an agreed method put in place to account for the cost of the changes which may involve some risk sharing, at least where there has been some shared responsibility for initiating the late changes.

Innovation in all of the other areas of activity is equally as important and some aspects are discussed later. From the innovation area we move to more operational but no less important deliverables.

QUALITY

There are of course a variety of definitions of quality but the following covers most of the points: 'the totality of features and characteristics of a product or service that bear on its ability to satisfy stated or implied needs' (BS4778, ISO 8402).

Externally this must be the minimum acceptable level since without meeting at least these needs, customers are dissatisfied and may take their future business elsewhere. Note however that in the terms we have already used quality is becoming a 'qualifier' to be considered a player in a market and so we should be aiming a little higher than the bare minimum to gain that extra edge through delighting the customer. Note also that this will often be in non-manufacturing aspects of the product/service package.

This is emphasized in the following list of quality features.

Performance – is possibly the most obvious attribute visible to consumers and relates to the detailed functions performed by the product or service.

Closely associated with this are a range of features which could be regarded as subsets of performance but are worth highlighting individually.

Features – relates to those additional aspects of the product or service which differentiates it from the competitor offerings. These could be ease of use features in the product (for example in-built tutorial teaching tools in computer software systems or self-diagnostic fault finding in photocopiers) or could be associated more with the service aspects (for example, replacement vehicles when car servicing is under way or on-line help desk support for computer systems).

Aesthetics – might be regarded as a special feature which appeals to the artistic leanings in the customer and like many others is subject to variability through the influence of fashion.

Reliability – is an indicator of the length of time during which the product can be expected to function without failure.

Durability – is associated with reliability since this specifies the time dimension over which it has to be reliable.

The following group relates more directly with additional contact with the providers when in some way function is lost or degraded.

Serviceability – recognizes that some ongoing maintenance might be required and makes this easy to do through quick change modules or automates it perhaps by on-line interrogation of the equipment and the automatic scheduling of repair teams.

Response time – relates to the delay between trying to make contact, establishing what is to be done and actually completing the process. This could be as little as the time to answer a telephone inquiry to the non-availability of replacement parts in the repair team's mobile maintenance vehicle.

Personal treatment – this is what Schonberger calls humanity and relates to the way in which the customer–contact people behave when customers contact the system.[9] People need to be trained to interact appropriately and this should vary with the client and is often variable across cultures, especially in regard to personal space.

The next two are more associated with internal aspects of quality whose effects customers will perceive only indirectly.

Flexibility of the production system – to respond to changes in customer requirement. One aspect is covered in response time above, but here the whole collection of flexibility types and dimensions (discussed later) are evaluated by customers as they consider the quality of the product/service package.

The next category used to be regarded as the catch-all in manufacturing terms especially but the above list has demonstrated that it is simply not enough.

Conformance to specification – highlights the minimum need to at least satisfy those criteria which have been capable of precise quantification usually at the design stage. If customers could articulate their precise needs and this could be transmitted into detailed specifications for all activities then this might catch enough to be adequate but the list above provides better understanding of the complexity of the issue. Seen in simple engineering terms conformance can be limited to physical dimensions and miss out on the perceptual and human aspects of quality.

Value – is the essential counterbalance to all of the above and is part of the process customers go through in evaluating whether the delivered quality justifies the price they are paying for the product or service. Value is a difficult concept more easily ranked against similar market offers than measured against an absolute scale. This of itself highlights the competitive aspects of quality and the ways in which it can quickly switch, from being good enough to differentiate in the market as an order winner, to being simply good enough to remain under consideration as a qualifier (but not for long).

Perceived quality – this recognizes that it is not always direct experience that permits customers to evaluate quality. Often it is word of mouth recommendations from friends or family along with consumer reviews and reports in the media. These perceptions create expectations if a purchase decision is made and in any event can extend over a long time period. Branding is a process which tries to capture this by building on a history of experience to justify a customer's perceptions and make a repeat purchase easier as well as support new market offers.

This final category demonstrates that quality must be seen from the customers' perspective. They are the final arbiters and without their continued support there is nothing.

Customer requirement and definition

It is often difficult to precisely define what customers want. After all, if they could do that they could choose a supplier to fit their needs exactly. The task is more subtle. As suppliers we have to understand and integrate a variety of information inputs in such a way that when the final good or service arrives with the customer they recognize it as the embodiment of their interests and desires, which they might have rather imprecisely specified.

The marketing research literature and practice is full of ways of trying to obtain clear definitions of requirements from customers and gauging the success of prototypes and samples prior to final product launch decisions but there are more players in this game than marketing and customers. If we are serious about the 'totality of features' definition then all of the supplying business areas have an interest in the final product definition, including those external to the business in the supply chain whose contribution will be every bit as important in final customer satisfaction.

There would seem to be different cultural traits between West and East in the ways in which these activities are organized. In the West the individual focus and narrow specialization of the 'macho' manager means that his job satisfaction largely comes through firefighting (predominantly a masculine practice), whereas in Japanese society the concern for the group, duty and harmony (*wa*) means that he (since few women are career managers as yet) will spend large amounts of time simply in discussions aiming for consensus or at least acceptance of the final decision. Figures 2.2 and 2.3 are from two sets of data produced by Sullivan[10] and show Japanese and US examples but the rest of the Western business world is believed to follow the same pattern.

The allocation of people resources shown in Figure 2.2 is important but the real message is in Figure 2.3 which shows the effects of the different distribution. In the best case the larger cross-functional teams have surfaced

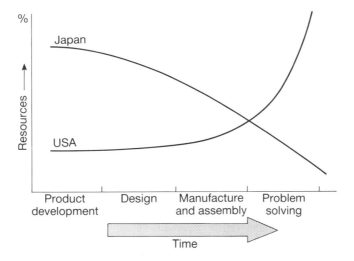

Figure 2.2 Quality Effort by Activity

Source: Sullivan LP, 'The Seven Stages in Company-Wide Quality', *Quality Progress*, June 1987, 77–83

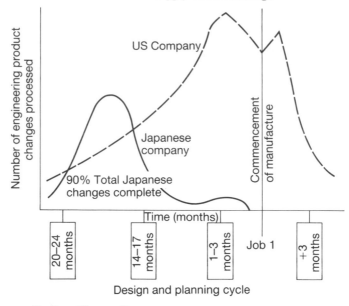

Figure 2.3 Design Change Patterns
Source: Sullivan LP, 'Quality Function Deployment', *Quality Progress*, May 1987, 39–50.

more of the difficult design choices early enough so that all can think through their implications. As a result fewer product design changes need to be processed late in the development cycle. There is a little peak before product launch to tidy up the remaining problems but nothing like the mass of activity in the US companies as they attempt to stabilize things long enough to launch at all, and then have to recover dramatically afterwards.

Data reported in *The Machine That Changed the World* demonstrate that getting this right both reduces time to market and allows better quality levels since the better design with reduced panic measures means that the disruption effect of the new product launch is reduced and that high quality levels are regained much sooner.

Putting the effort in at the design stage makes sense empirically since the American Suppliers Institute has published data showing that in terms of quality improvement the leverage from improvements made at the production stage is only 1:1; during the process design the leverage moves to 10:1 but at the initial product design stage the leverage moves up to 100:1. It is also clear that the cost of making those improvements works in the reverse direction.

The process which seems to work naturally in Japan needs to be systematized and labelled in the West and so the attempt to do the constructive thinking up front and to consistently carry the wishes of the customer through all of the business processes is called Quality Function Deployment (QFD).

The American Suppliers Institute defines this as: 'a system for translating consumer requirement into appropriate company requirements at every stage from research, through product design and development, to manufacture, distribution, installation and marketing, sales and service'. As we can see in Figure 2.4 the systematic approach is captured in a chart somewhat house shaped and hence the use of the term 'House of Quality'. The overall process is also a demonstration of two key supply chain concepts, i.e. that everyone is both supplier to and customer of the next link in the chain; and that the way to ensure that the final consumers' requirements are met is by cascading their requirements through each of the supply chain links.

QFD does this by cascading the data from one chart down to the next level of detailed requirement as input to the chart at that level. The overall process of working on these charts brings together people from all disciplines who have inputs to decisions that all can commit to. Although the chart looks complicated it is in fact little more than the gathering together of lists of features and their relative importance and mutual interaction along with a degree of competitive product evaluation. By weighting the values of requirements and technical solutions the detailed definitions can be made ready for the next stage definition.[11]

The most important of the quality houses is possibly the first one where the voice of the customer is translated into language which the product and process designers can understand and it is in design that quality is enabled.

Taguchi methods[12]

In the design area we also are recognizing that the balance of design specification and tolerance, and process capability is a factor which can permit quality at source to be a meaningful concept. We discussed this in Chapter One but now we should turn to another of the insights produced about quality by the work of Taguchi. The two major contributions from him are linked and relate to the costs of variability and the design process to be employed to minimize the effects of this unwelcome factor.

According to the Taguchi view any deviation from a nominal required value is wasteful and should be reduced. His approach is to impute a quadratic 'loss function' to this variability and he argues that there is a cost to society from this lack of precision. In a sense this is taking the quest for perfect quality to its logical conclusion but he also suggests approaches to help us live with imperfections in the meantime. His approach is to design

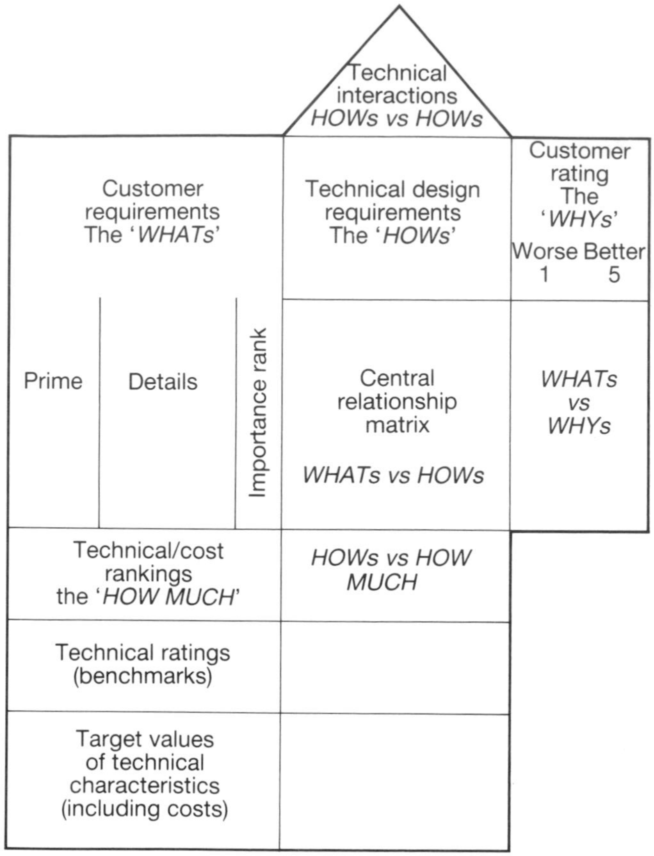

Figure 2.4 The House of Quality

Source: Oakland JS, *Total Quality Management* (2nd edition), Butterworth-Heinemann, 1993, 50.

into products from the beginning a degree of robustness in that the effects of environmental influences, which cannot be removed, are nevertheless limited in their impact. In order to do this he has adapted well-known statistical investigation approaches (called design of experiments) to produce faster (but theoretically less precise) ways of experimenting with these factors (called orthogonal arrays) to identify interaction effects and their sensitivity. At the end of such investigative processes the designs and tolerances can be adjusted to insulate the design from these interfering factors. Such designs are robust in that they can now operate in their desired environment with reduced probabilities of failure or degradation. However the environment should include other players in the supply chain since the variability they may introduce into the calculations may be as important as any internally generated factors.

Prevention-based systems

Types of quality costs

QFD demonstrates one of the major new understandings of how to enable good quality and supports the leverage argument which was discussed above. This suggests that rather than wait for problems to occur and then attempt to fix them it is both more effective and financially sensible to prevent them occurring in the first place. It is also supportive of the continuous improvement ideal in that we should be looking for ways in which to make any fixes permanent and thereby create a virtuous spiral of incrementally more secure performance.

In any quality system, cost is incurred in four main sets of activities associated with prevention, appraisal and internal and external failure. The last two categories are clear enough and usually relatively easy to quantify. Appraisal covers any activity needed to establish the current performance levels and again is usually easy to quantify. Prevention covers all activities intended to avoid creating quality problems and is often less easy to quantify since so many in the organization will be generating costs which could be correctly allocated to the consideration of quality. Traditional cost accounting systems are often not sophisticated enough to do this accurately but Activity Based Costing (ABC) approaches are more likely to capture the data in a useful manner. The series of Quality Function Deployment activities could provide a sound basis for gathering this data for of course the whole purpose of QFD can be seen to be prevention based.[13]

External failure is so potentially damaging that traditional approaches concentrated on sample inspection processes to avoid, if possible, any possibility of faulty products reaching the customers. Any inspection process (especially a sampling one) guarantees a measurable probability of inaccuracy and is subject to the effects of diminishing returns in that increasing levels of quality require ever increasing inspection resource allocation and consequent increased cost. By refocusing the effort to the front of the decision sequence and increasing the effort devoted to the prevention activities it is possible to both reduce the overall failure rate and the overall cost incurred across the whole organization.

This does not eliminate the need for inspection but it changes the nature of the exercise. No longer can a separate department be 'in charge of quality' accepting or failing batches of product based on a sample from the batch and an off-line inspection. Now every customer is in effect inspecting the quality of their immediate supplier – not to punish but to improve. With such a close coupling the supplier feels a real commitment not to let the customer down with a failure and so concentrates on getting it right first time. In itself this is a powerful argument to reduce the batch sizes in order to reduce the reaction time between identification of problems and the resultant fix (a permanent one we hope!).

In Chapter One we discussed the prerequisite technology of having available statistically capable processes since without these there is little possibility of producing the correct design in a controlled way. A concept that highlights this is the $n=2$ sample size. If a process is statistically capable and the product design has been carefully analysed and if process controls are in place then this argument says that all we should have to measure is the first item produced to check the process has been properly set and the final item to again check that nothing unexpected has happened.

Motorola's six sigma quality programme works on the basis of highly capable processes working well within the tolerance limits such that the probability of a result being outwith the specified limits is only 2.4 parts per million even allowing for the movement of the process average by up to 1.5 sigma in either direction. (Note that this means that if the process mean does not move the quality level is 2 parts per billion reject or 99.9999998 per cent acceptable.)

Baldrige quality award[14]

Following the experience of the Deming quality award in Japan, which put quality as an issue firmly in the consciousness of that community, the American equivalent award indicates the degree to which our understanding of the importance of prevention-based quality has progressed. (Note also that the European Quality Award is informed by similar lines of thinking.)

The Baldrige award is founded on the following core values and concepts: customer-driven quality; leadership; continuous improvement; employee participation and development; fast response; design quality and prevention; long-range outlook; management by fact; partnership development; and corporate responsibility and citizenship. The overall framework of the evaluation criteria is shown in Figure 2.5.

Like any such award process much benefit can be gained just by using the framework as a set of improvement directions for businesses to start an improvement process even without applying for the award. One key lesson that it demonstrates is that quality has to be a business solution and is not

Dynamic Relationships

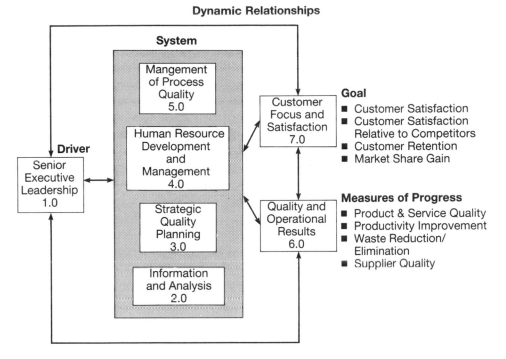

Figure 2.5 Baldrige Award Criteria Framework
Source: *The Malcolm Baldrige National Quality Award*, ASQC, 1993.

limited to one functional area. The partnership development core value is for internal as well as supplier and customer partners and reinforces the messages we have been discussing here. It has also been our experience that organizations that are serious about quality are also those that realize how much of their own quality efforts are enabled or constrained by their external partners. In this way partnership development soon assumes great significance both for its own sake and to push the Total Quality effort along.

Measurement and improvement

Later in this chapter we are going to discuss the problems of traditional cost accounting but here we also have to recognize that to try and capture the different kinds of quality costs, discussed above, can be very difficult. Apart from the obvious wastage costs of poor quality we have replacement material and labour costs, management time costs (especially schedule replanning and progressing) and all of the hassle costs which are really difficult to quantify. Nevertheless it seems to be widely accepted that in direct manufacturing areas the costs of getting it wrong multiply up until costs in the order of 30 per cent of sales turnover are accumulated. It is also widely believed that in indirect areas the contributory costs of 'unquality' may be even higher. These produce fantastic amounts of money thrown away all the time by organizations who work by traditional means. Competitive companies are making serious attempts to capture the real cost of quality and use it as a benchmark of their improvement actions.

Quality cannot actually be free since some cost must be incurred in prevention but certainly the downstream costs should be reduced dramatically and often without significant capital investment. Quality in this sense is all about working smarter not harder and can release working capital for other purposes.

The real need is for much greater levels of measurement in all areas of activity to provide a base point from which we can target improvements. We must always be careful however to choose the appropriate measures since people will perform against the measurement criteria. In a relationship change project this is a most important consideration since without changing traditional performance measures new behaviours will not survive.

Improvement tools

To enable employee involvement in continuous improvement it is required that they have training in some aspects of creative thinking for problem solving and in basic processes of data gathering and analysis. In Chapter One we described how these processes are made very visible to visitors to best practice organizations, not simply to impress them (although it will) but because it has become part of the way that things are done and is part of the operating culture.

Improvement suggestions from operating groups (often in process set-up and change-over procedures) will often show up aspects of basic product or process designs which could be re-engineered to make a repeat failure impossible, i.e. the process of failsafing. Whole books are devoted to simple devices to make it impossible to assemble parts incorrectly or to operate machines when they are malfunctioning or when parts are not available. These become permanent fixes and product re-design or initial design can be used to make it easier to do the correct thing than the potential error.

Here again the message of wide consultation early in the design process is reinforced as a prevention tool.

In Chapter Seven we will describe the SCMG approach to measuring the partnering relationship as an aid to improvement planning. It has many of the same features of initial benchmark measurement, the creation of teams of relevant parties and joint actions to improve and monitor. In this the Deming cycle of plan, do, check and act to improve and re-test, also applies.

Delivery, reliability and response

Figure 2.6 shows the relationship between the amount of time available between a customer placing an order and receiving delivery of the completed order – the demand lead time, and the accumulated times involved in the supply side – the supply lead time.[15] This latter measure is akin to the pipeline measures discussed in Chapter Three but in this diagram we are looking at the single firm boundaries. In supply chain terms there are of course a series of such diagrams extending along the chain. The crucial point highlighted in the diagram is that all the investment incurred prior to the gaining of a customer order is inherently at risk. It must also be noted that in certain cases the demand lead time is effectively zero, i.e. customers will not tolerate any delay between placing the order and receipt of goods. This is the retail supply 'off the shelf' situation. If there is an appreciable demand lead time to play with, the trick is to try and reduce the supply lead time until it is at least equal to the demand lead time and ideally less than it to minimize the investment risk. This of itself is a powerful justification for attempts to reduce the wastes in the supply chain pipeline to provide the reduced investment risk, reduced real investment and increased ability to respond in a reduced time scale.

It is worth noting that simply to offer a reduced lead time as a marketing

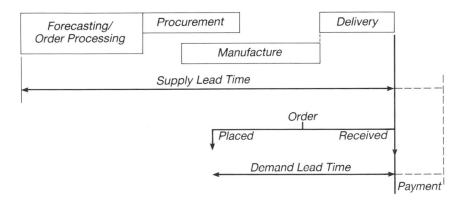

Figure 2.6 Supply Demand Balance

Source: Macbeth DK, *Advanced Manufacturing: Strategy and Management*, IFS, 1989.

ploy actually increases the amount of investment at risk if no other actions are taken and so such a strategy requires careful consideration. Once the lead time becomes established at the reduced value it is likely no longer to be an order winner but a qualifier and in consequence will increase the pressure on the operational system to continue to perform to the enhanced standard.

When above, we talked of the effect of serial working in the design process we recognized the need to look for parallel activities where possible but there is another implication of the supply chain critical path. On any critical path any delay to any activity will produce the same delay to the overall project. Thus it is on our supply chain critical path. This is why there is a preferred sequence in the delivery performance measures. Any failure to deliver precisely as agreed to any of the customers along the chain causes the performance of the whole chain to degrade. For this reason the absolute commitment to reliable delivery to agreed timings is the drumbeat for the whole chain to march along to. Once reliability is guaranteed then we can begin to think of ways in which the total time could be reduced by improvements in one or more activities but we must remember the lessons of the demand and supply lead time balance and only move to a shorter delivery lead time to customers if we can comfortably guarantee that we can reliably meet it. In some markets the ability to flex the delivery due dates promised to customers is an order winner but there are other kinds of flexibility which should also be considered.

Nigel Slack for example discusses four types of flexibility, i.e. product, mix of product types being produced at one time, volume of individual orders or production runs and delivery lead times, each of which has both range and response dimensions.[16] For example, product flexibility relates to the available variety of product types in the range of products being offered. The response dimension relates to the time, ease and minimum cost involved in actually changing from producing one product type to another. Modifications to the dimensions are possible but usually over different timescales, i.e. response is more of a day to day action but range will tend to be changed only in the medium to longer term.

In supply chain terms Slack's observed subdivision of the drivers for flexibility between, dependability on the supply side, productivity inside manufacturing and availability on the demand side, of a company demonstrates the tendency to sub-optimisation we also discuss elsewhere. The real need is for the whole chain to agree what forms of flexibility, in what magnitudes, need to be available, at which points along the chain. Once decided the task is then to ensure equitable treatment for all parties since it may well be that at the flexibility enhancing node the apparent cost is increased yet others reap the benefits.

This has happened in practice in JIT supply in the automotive sector. Here the car assembler demanded that the suppliers provide materials to stock a factory-side warehouse. The assembler than pulled stock from the warehouse on an hourly basis but only paid for the materials if and when they were pulled. The suppliers were carrying the inventory management costs of the warehouse and its associated logistics system while the car assembler appeared to have lots of flexibility with no stock. This of course is nonsense in supply chain terms (and especially in relationship terms). No wastes were removed from the chain in this 'improved' situation – they were simply shifted to a different node in the network, perhaps with a reduced overhead charge to some extent but without making significant or fundamental improvements. The car factory looked better however but was in reality playing the old adversarial game to look good internally and to support their own customers' fluctuating demands. A major strategic opportunity was overlooked since a more enlightened investigation of the whole chain may have provided the same or improved levels of customer service by building real flexibility into the system without the inventory buffer at the warehouse. That could have been a real WIN-WIN result.

COST

Cost accounting began in times when direct labour was proportionally a much larger part of the total manufactured cost of products. It thus made sense to allocate the residual costs or overhead against the labour hours incurred in production. This was always a simplification to avoid the need to accurately monitor and allocate actual resource usage against each individual transaction but for many years fulfilled the needs of business. As fixed capital investment replaced labour and incoming material cost increased (along with the tendency to reduce the levels of vertical integration by increasing the proportion of materials sourced from outside suppliers), so the allocated overhead began to rise as a proportion of the much reduced labour cost. It is now commonplace to see overhead allocation rates of more than 500 percentage points of labour cost to spread the overhead over the few parts of the remaining business that are actually adding value. This process is bad in itself but its really insidious effect is to distort investment decisions particularly of the make or buy type. With such allocation regimes it is quite likely that a decision to source from outside looks to be cost justified but only because the overhead burden carried by the part makes it uncompetitive. Of course it may be that this actual part does not use as much of the overhead activity as it is loaded with but the system has no way of recognizing this. A decision to outsource on this basis is therefore likely to make matters worse since there is unlikely to be a reduction in overhead commensurate with the reduced production activity (after all how would we know what it was?) and so the unchanged overhead is now allocated over even fewer items making more of them uncompetitive.

It is recognition of these problems that leads to consideration of those factors which actually cause cost to be incurred, i.e. the cost drivers and to the Activity Based Costing (ABC) approach. This devotes effort to identifying those activities impacting the cost drivers and therefore builds up a more realistic account of the overhead actually utilized by any activity. It should also be possible to identify more correctly the actual cost of quality using the ABC method than in traditional systems where only a certain few obvious resource costs can be separated out from general overhead.

Traditional cost accounting and inventory control methods, particularly if computerized in a Material Requirements Planning system, works by recording transactions. That is, every time a part moves from location to location around the business then that becomes a computer transaction (sometimes recorded by bar-code readers or similar technologies), and the computer system then has to arrange for the information data base to be updated to recognize the changed state of play. While computers are fast machines they also have processing rules and sequences and with thousands of transactions for thousands of parts and activities the overhead effort in the computer to make all this happen becomes significant. Add to this the tendency to reduce the batch size processed at any point in time and we multiply up the number of transactions needed to run the system. If we now add in the effects of more frequent deliveries from suppliers in smaller quantities to a system which is producing at a much higher throughput rate than historically, we begin to describe a system that cannot cope.

To get out of this problem we must return to first principles and ask why all of this transaction recording was necessary. Often the answer will be that we simply did not have adequate control over the system so that we always needed to be able to cross check where everything was and what we needed to do next. If we paint a different scenario where we are in control of quality performance and in control of the logistical flow of materials, then we do not need such internal controls over each transaction. If there is no wastage and no queues because our production supply chain is coordinated and working to our delivery drumbeat then all we need to know is that a certain number of items completed processing and were passed on to the next stage in the chain. Without built-in failure, what goes out must have used the planned amount of input resources and so rather than record each resource change we can simply explode the information from the final delivery schedule.

Thus our internal inventory position will be known and can be verified on an audited cycle counting routine and we can pay our supplier invoices by exploding the dispatched number of parts by the bills of materials which the parts must have consumed.

This backflushing process can be advantageous to the supplier also since no detailed invoice is needed for each delivery and payment comes regularly and automatically. If the throughput speed is sufficiently rapid the next customer in the chain might pay before the agreed time to pay the suppliers' invoices. Care needs to be taken with this however since delayed payment from large customers to smaller suppliers seems to be endemic, in the UK at least (other countries have legislation to prevent this abuse of buying power). In the retail supermarket sector the benefit from an out of synchronization condition in invoicing and payment suggests that the supermarkets are acting as banks and earning a return on the suppliers' investment in the goods supplied. This is not something they have as yet been prepared to share with their partners but this sector has historically been one where relatively few major buyers dictate terms for hundreds of suppliers in a very competitive market place playing according to traditional, adversarial rules as described in Chapter Five.

Earlier in this chapter we discussed the preferred sequence of control over quality and managing the delivery performance to create control over cost. In this sequence cost is an outcome of doing the other things correctly and in this sequence the concept of the trade off does not apply. If we attack from any other direction the dreaded trade off appears with a vengeance. For example if we try to reduce costs as an input we often find that either or both of quality and delivery is adversely affected.

We must also recognize that cost is an internal measure of resource use. The parties with which we trade will want to know what price we are asking for our goods or services and will want to understand our internal costs in so far as it indicates capability and potential improvement possibilities and may ask for details as part of an open book costing operation in a partnership sourcing investigation. Cost is, in the main, a way of keeping the internal score. Much more fundamental is the need to understand and improve on the processes which create this score.

There is no doubt that cost overall should be reducing but the route to that desired outcome is not to apply a cost saving by *dictat* but by continuous improvement efforts along the supply chain to take out non-value-adding wastes. To do this, attention will continue to be focused on issues of quality and delivery performance to lever the improvement out in cost terms.

An issue that presents itself in this scenario is the one of sub-optimization where, if the viewpoint taken is too narrow, a local optimum decision can produce a system-wide situation less than it might have been. The corollary to this is that in order for the bigger system to obtain an optimum solution it may be necessary for a local decision to produce results less than the locally derived 'best' solution. In supply chain terms where ownership of all parties to the chain is not in single hands this principle can mean that one link in the chain has to do something which appears wasteful to the local viewpoint. Under conditions of market competition and self interest such behaviour is not logical and will not happen. The challenge for the supply chain is to recognize these decisions and so reward the chain-supportive decision so that the locally sub-optimizing manager is not penalized for doing the 'correct' thing.

This raises the difference between efficiency and effectiveness. In the terms of the discussion so far a locally efficient decision can produce a less than satisfactorily effective supply chain solution. The dispute between effectiveness and efficiency occurs inside the operational units as well and is another outcome of traditional accounting thought processes. If we are under pressure to make some contribution to the bloated overhead charges the tendency will be to work our resources to the full. Thus people are under pressure to produce and machines have to be kept running. This is sometimes in spite of the fact that there are no immediate demands for output. We need to differentiate between being busy and being usefully employed. Part of the Just-in-Time and Theory of Constraints approach is that in certain circumstances it is actually better for the total system if a resource is not activated since often to do so would only increase the amount of inventory to be stored without any prospect of making a sale based on that inventory.[17] This need not mean that the time not now used for production output cannot be put to good use in other ways. In relation to people this provides training, development or improvement time and in relation to machinery could allow preventive maintenance, set up reduction or failsafing modifications to be made.

Thinking in this way is yet another of the challenges facing managers as they adapt to the new competitive environment but like many other things discussed in this book the changes are interrelated and require a system-wide change programme to make them effective.

SUMMARY

- **Qualifiers are features that allow you to play in the game but order-winners positively discriminate in your favour. These are dynamic and can be influenced.**

- **Trade-offs are not set in stone. The best organizations try to do it all.**

- **There is a preferred sequence: Innovation in everything; control of quality at source; manage the delivery heartbeat to all customers along the chain and cost reduction follows as an output of doing everything else correctly.**

- **New thinking (alongside fundamentals not properly understood) can impact each of these deliverables.**

In Chapter Three we will examine the nature of the supply chain, where wastes can occur and what can be done to make its operation both more coherent and effective and less painful for the participants in the chain.

Part Two

THEORY AND PRACTICE

3

SUPPLY CHAIN CONCEPTS

In this chapter we will

- examine the nature of the value chain and how value can be added

- examine the ways in which wastes are created and how they can be eliminated along the extended supply chain

- describe the nature of the non-material flows and technology transfers in the supply chain and the ways in which this changes when organizations apply Partnership Sourcing principles

- discuss ways in which innovation can be encouraged and applied.

FLOW OF MATERIALS

Added value chain

One of the new guiding principles which was discussed in Chapter One is avoiding creating waste, which is a cost to the business. A different way of thinking about this is to recognize that in order to justify charging customers some premium over the input cost to us, we must in some way add some value to the good or service for which the customer is prepared to pay. This is on its own a powerful concept since it reinforces the view that value is defined by the customers' perceptions and not our own. It is therefore consistent with our new understandings about quality. Such a definition should also help us measure value since we can now examine each aspect of our business from the customers' viewpoint. Those activities contributing to the added-value process and which move the organization along its chosen strategic path are to be retained and developed while those merely adding cost with no appreciable quantum of added value can be critically examined with a view to removal or re-development.

How is value added? There are a number of categories which are fairly obvious and which constitute the basic types of business provision. These are varieties on the theme of transformation.

All operating systems transform some amount and mix of input resources, add appropriate value and 'deliver' the output results to the customer who may or may not have been present during each transformation stage.

- *Manufacturing* consists of physical transformations to a physical, tangible product.
- *Transportation and distribution* systems provide a desired re-location of goods, services and/or customers. In the case of distribution there can also be added value by re-sizing or re-packaging goods or in performing the value-adding function of collecting together disparate items into a coherent 'shopping list' for onward delivery.
- *Information provision* organizes and delivers data in a way suitable for use by customers but with no other involvement.
- *Education and training* use base knowledge information along with learning process knowledge to modify customers' thought processes and action choices.
- *Entertainment* can have elements of the previous group but usually more subtly presented with the aim of providing both intellectual and psychological challenge.
- *Psychological* and *physiological* value can also be added by food/drink

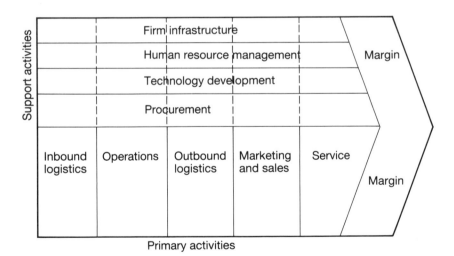

Figure 3.1   The Value Chain

Source: Porter ME, *Competitive Strategy: Techniques for Analyzing Industries and Competitors*, The Free Press, 1980.

sectors as well as by the medical services although in the latter case, as well as adding positive value they can also be involved in reducing negative value through damage recovery and waste minimization.

- Some aspects of *financial services* provide products to manage/control/ improve customers' finances but they are also in the business of providing comfort through a belief that the impact of future possible and expensive events will be reduced.

To some extent all value-adding operations provide similar perceptions of comfort to customers along with that of being important and being cared for by the supplier. A further related aspect is that to some extent the supplier provides a 'guarantee' of suitability that the product/service is fit for the customers' purpose. All of these aspects can be supported and enhanced by provision of information packaging around the product/service offering.

Along any supply chain elements of many of these value-adding transformations are observable.

Value chain model

If we consider the model of the value chain presented by Michael Porter we see a generic description of any organization.[1]
In the diagram Inbound Logistics relates to all of the activities involved in organizing a reliable source of supply of all of the input materials used by an organization. Operations perform the required transformation. Outbound Logistics of delivering product to the customer is next in sequence followed by Marketing and Sales and finally Customer Service. Overlaying these are the support services of: Procurement of input resources; Technology Development which can be of product, transformation process or of organization processes; Human Resource Management and the general organizational infrastructure of legal, financial, internal planning and external liaison.

This model tries to emphasize the flow of the adding value process from supply side through to satisfied customer. As such it does not conform to traditional functional hierarchical organization structures, which often work across the pattern of flow and while having some utility, were seen to need complementing by Deming in 1950 when he was advising the Japanese on ways to improve their manufacturing quality practices.[2] The Deming flow diagram is shown in Figure 3.2.

Value networks

The above model serves to illustrate useful concepts but takes as its

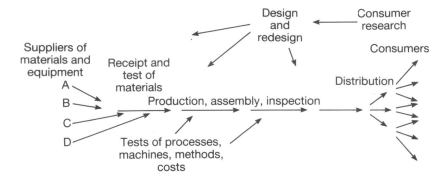

Figure 3.2 The Deming Flow Model
Source: Deming WE, *Out of the Crisis*, MIT Press, 1982.

boundary the limits of the given organization's ownership structure and of course the real world is more complicated. Each organization can be seen as demonstrating one of the value chain models but organizations exist within a complex and shifting pattern of interactions with their environment. At one end they interact with their supply infrastructure while at the other they will have at least one, and can have many thousands of customers. Each separately identifiable supply or customer unit will have its own value chain model even if sometimes single individuals cover all of the roles normally separated in larger organizations.

In effect we are describing a network of value chains where one unit's output is another's input. It is simple to conceive of these as linear and unidirectional groups of related chains but here again reality is more interesting for few businesses deal with single products or services. In many cases someone who is your customer for some things is your supplier for others. Even worse, a supplier might in a different part of its organization be one of your serious competitors and thus the relationship questions become ever more complex; even more so if organizations take a financial stake in other members of the network. Any investigation into the alliances, joint ventures and supply chain linkages of global industries like automotive, aerospace and electronics shows a complex network with criss-crossing links resembling a plate of tangled spaghetti.

If we sit in glorious isolation imagining ourselves to be at the centre of such a web of potential chaos, how can we conceive of a way to make the right decisions? What constitutes success? To what extent can or should we try and maximize our benefit at some others' cost and which other(s), for how long? Who is the most important member of the network?

Let us address the last question first. Like all living organisms our organization wishes to survive. Therefore we have to be the most important part of the network. All in the network will have the same wish to survive.

An impartial, omnipotent overseer of the network might take the view that for the network to survive particular individual members should be sacrificed but in free markets there are few such supra-network powers. The closest the business world comes is in the various regulatory authorities, licensing agencies and legislatures and all must operate with more or less imperfect information.

Some have argued that the final paying consumer should be regarded as the most important. This is in a sense true but not completely. It may in fact be possible for such a customer to be completely satisfied but for our organization's survival to be threatened.

Apart from this aspect why is the final customer at the end of a long chain, in which we occupy one of the early nodes, more important than the customer next in line to us with whom we have trading relationships of some kind? In effect the way in which it is feasible to have the final customer drive the chain of supply is through each of the customer/supplier links all the way back up the chain to Mother Earth. This theoretical ideal can only be achieved if each of the participating organizations wants to operate in this way and believes that their long-term future is more secure by so doing. This is perhaps more of a contractual point. In terms of information input to decisions it is perfectly feasible to try and link all of the companies into a great information network such that upstream suppliers can access company requirements a number of levels below them in the flow of materials towards the final consumer but this aspect is only now being considered in limited circumstances.

The key drivers in this scenario are demand and effectiveness. Demand is defined in terms of customer requirement, but of all of the customers along the chain, both internal and external to our organization. Effectiveness reflects both an improvement goal (new product/process and service offerings) and improvement in waste reduction throughout the whole chain. Done correctly the demand side is constantly delighted and developed while the supply side is increasingly more capable of meeting new challenges.

Transformations of goods downstream

While the next section uses manufacturing examples there are comparable examples from other sectors where for example it is information which is transformed rather than physical entities. In essence the concept of flow of materials is as of a river flowing down from the hills to the sea. This is already apparent from our use of upstream and downstream to indicate relative positions. It is nevertheless a transformation process in which different patterns of flow can be discerned for different market situations. The primary distinction is whether items are progressively removed or added as we go downstream.

A physical reduction process could be the production of a pure chemical from a complex feedstock. An example of a different kind could be the process of editing for the newsmedia where extended reports are progressively reduced to bare essentials often being captured in a punchy headline or sound-bite.

Adding processes can be associated with what can be referred to as I-V-A-T analysis where the form of the letter suggests the pattern of material flow.

Note that in all of these we are describing the predominant flow pattern. In reality the 'stream' can have extra tributaries and might even loop back on itself thereby defying gravity in our analogy.

The I-shape is the unidirectional, unvarying production of multiple identical items or of a continuous material as in our chemical example earlier. Because of its uniqueness and inflexibility this pattern is less of a problem in supply chain terms since the decisions are limited (once the system is designed and operational) to when to switch on the flow and for how long.

The other shapes are more complex and interesting. Note that we are viewing the letter shapes as if they are superimposed onto a flow of material such that the direction is from the base of the letter to the apex. Schematic diagrams of these shapes are shown in Figure 3.3.

A V-shape has the following characteristics:

- limited raw materials at input stage
- wide variety of finished products
- generally diverging pattern
- product variety determined early in the transformation process
- parallel streams with similar processing capabilities.

This type can be found in textile manufacture, metal fabrication and chemicals. From different sectors we could cite a graphic designer or financial advisor.

While offering a capability of variety of output, in supply chain terms the problem comes from the need to define actual final product early in the process and a general concern that with so much going on the management of response to changing orders or customer requirements becomes more complex.

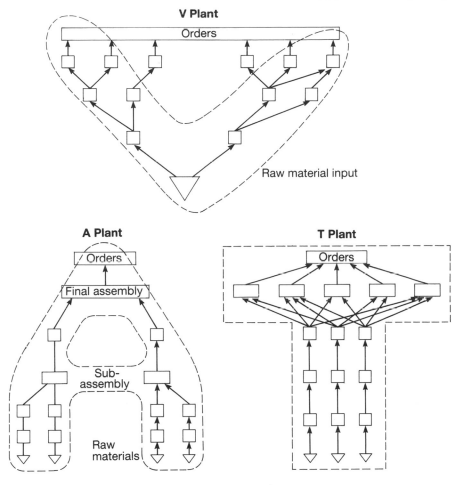

Figure 3.3 V, A and T Plant Configurations

An A-shape has the following characteristics:

- numerous raw materials at input stage
- limited variety of finished products
- generally converging pattern built up in a hierarchy of sub-assemblies
- different streams of component parts using different facilities.

This type can be found in aerospace, make to order and in major assembly businesses like civil engineering. From different sectors, interior decorating and fast food stores as well as retail distribution exhibit similar characteristics.

Like the V-shape the supply chain problem here relates to when a demand has to be made firm to allow for the long path from start to finish.

A T-shape tries to keep a simple flow path until the latest possible moment before suddenly branching out into a wide variety and has the following characteristics:

- wide combination of products from a restricted number of component or sub-assembly parts
- final process stage can be driven by actual customer demand
- holding of part-finished items can be large and forecasting effort is directed here
- labour intensity at final stages to be able to react quickly.

Examples of this type can be found in electronics, garden and household appliances while à la carte restaurants are somewhat similar.

If the problems related to the vertical part of the 'T' can be solved this shape is potentially very attractive in supply chain terms since the decision on final product specification can be delayed and thereby offer fast response to customers.

Each of these patterns has its own features which help or hinder a more integrated view of how organizations can help each other to satisfy the market requirement. Some effort to recognize the operational logic of the other party's flow pattern will help to understand their problems and needs particularly in relation to the timing of information requirements so that the needed performance has a reasonable chance of being achieved.

Transmission of requirement

As we have previously mentioned the supply chain concept of ripples of information going back upstream from final consumer through each of the customer–supplier linkages is the basis of the supply chain message.

This must be driven by customer base requirement, informed by supplier interaction and improvement suggestions and delivered by supplier performance. Customer delight can be the main goal but all in our particular network have to be comfortable with the actual outcome or we are simply storing up trouble.

Of course it may well be the case that the transmission of requirement is acceptable but the requirement is inadequately defined. Thus information gathering can sometimes extend across supply chain links, bypass the formal routes and might be interactive. This can raise interesting legal, contractual and intellectual property-related concerns about the range of interactions in the network.

It is evident that information flows (direction, frequency, mode and communicating parties) are multidirectional and crucial to the effectiveness of the chain. This is examined in more detail later. For the moment it is worth considering another role of information.

Information is power

Information is certainly power but the way in which it is used is also important. Information as a commodity is different from many others. Normally a transfer of a resource from one party to another causes the ownership, control and physical realization of that resource to also transfer. The resource of information is different in that giving another party some of our information does not prevent us continuing to use it. In this situation it is less a case of transfer of a resource as it is an increase in the spread of the resource (without any diminution) across a wider area of activity. This sounds eminently sensible but not if we are in a competitive situation with those parties we are talking about. When this occurs, information becomes something that becomes closely controlled, rationed or even manipulated into disinformation. In this mode the power of information is as a limiter of competitive freedom to the opposition. Note that in many organizations the so-called enemy or competitor may be the next department or function and that some managers have built careers on creating their own information gathering and limiting systems. In these situations the power of information is at best to enhance the prospects of some few individuals/organizational groups or organizations but is actually corrosive of real progress. Such practices in Total Quality terms are wasteful but it comes as no surprise that to change the behaviour of such managers is not easy or swiftly achieved.

Conversely, information shared between collaborating groups is enabling, allowing others to add to the sum of knowledge by contributing their own information and ideas. Used in this way information becomes the power to permit the network to collectively benefit through a process of sharing. There is however a big caveat and that is that we will not share information with those we do not trust. If we believe that the release of information will be used against us in some point-scoring exercise, the worst of which is the market place, then it is understandable that we do not release that information. That, unfortunately for us and fortunately for our competitors, is precisely what has been happening in most of our Western business sectors.

Part of the new operating practice is thus to engender and build on the basis of mutual trust and responsibility but trust is a fragile thing. It is developed over extended demonstrations of open, sharing and caring actions (not merely words) and yet it can be destroyed or fatally damaged by a single thoughtless act. Trust is also highly dependent on the actions of individuals in organizations who may not do as the 'organization' has dictated or because they simply did not understand the significance of their actions. Thus while we will discuss information flows between organizations, part of the learning process is actually internal to specific organizations as they ensure that information is used constructively between the internal customers and suppliers.

The philosophical difference in information usage is that in the first, control is exerted by a few on the many (often to the benefit of the few) through selective use of information whereas the second is based on the belief that by providing full information to all, control will be exercised by each to the mutual benefit of all.

DELAYS, DETOURS AND SPILLAGES ALONG THE WAY: MANAGING THE PIPELINE

Types of wastes

Toyota are widely credited with categorizing the following seven forms of waste:

- waste from over-production
- waste of waiting time
- transportation waste
- inventory waste
- processing waste
- waste of motion
- waste from product defects.

Over-production has been a traditional approach to the management of uncertainty in the business world. If we are uncertain as to what kind and size of demand we can expect we can choose to over-produce and store output in anticipation of that demand. In similar fashion if our products are easily substituted we may have to guarantee instantaneous availability, i.e. off-the-shelf supply to capture the sale. In an uncertain world over-production can buffer or insulate the operations area from the full effects of demand fluctuations. We now realize that this is a flawed solution to the problem of a mismatch between the rates of change in the market and the capability to track that change in the operations system. Rather than tackle the real problem of operations response we have chosen to ignore it and compensate by investing in inventory.

An internal factor tending to support over-production is the belief in recovering a capital investment by keeping the facility in production to contribute to total overheads. The overhead recovery argument is equally flawed since over-production contributes nothing and accumulates costs until it can be sold. In fact the indirect costs of having excess materials around the system, while difficult to quantify, can be very significant. In supply chain terms if every link in the chain is regarded as independent and the supplier perceives an unpredictable demand pattern and buffers against it, it is no wonder that levels of work in process inventory are so high in many companies.

A further internal problem relates to batch sizing. The economic order quantity approach suggests that there is a balance between the costs of initiating an action and the costs of storing the output from that process. In manufacturing terms this argument is about the size of the batch to be produced against the costs of setting up the process to run the batch. With long and expensive set-ups we would choose to incur this cost as infrequently as possible and therefore minimize the number of times the batch is run by producing large batches, i.e. over-production. The correct approach is not to take the set-ups as given but to target improvement activity to reduce them to insignificance thereby making it economic to produce in 'batches' of one, just as the customer requires them. Set-up reductions greatly increase operations' flexibility and by avoiding the need for large batches (which force us to forecast demand further ahead in time), we actually make our environment less uncertain and therefore need less over-production as protection. This is another of the examples where good practice actually is positively reinforcing to other aspects of competitive activity.

Waiting time or queueing time is another function of large batch sizes. If for example we have a process which takes one minute to complete and we have chosen a batch size of 100, each part will be waiting for a total of 99 minutes either for processing or after processing until the rest of the batch is complete. Immediately we have changed a process which should have a lead time of 1 minute to one with lead time of 100 minutes but the value-adding time has not altered at 1 minute! Of course we do not have to wait until all 100 are complete before transferring items to the next process. If we moved them onwards as soon as the process had finished on each one the average lead-time would reduce to 44.5 minutes but we might now incur additional transportation wastes, i.e. 100 journeys to the next process instead of one as a complete batch of 100.

Another problem of allowing large batch sizes and queues to build up relates to the requirement to react to panics that are likely to cause interruptions in the original sequences, as the critical items jump the queue to gain access to the processing resource which must then be set up to cope with the special item. This increases average lead times for the delayed parts, increases set-up costs and the blood pressure of all concerned. This story is as much a feature of office systems as manufacturing ones but here the set-ups relate often to the thinking patterns of the process people rather than the technical systems they work with.

Transportation can provide some geographical position value even in operations systems which are not explicitly involved in geographical transformations. In many cases however the transportation does not really add significant value as seen from a customer viewpoint which is the important one. After all, a customer is not interested if a sales order has to travel between three departments covering 1500 metres and taking three days to action. They will be interested in what this does to responsiveness and quality, not in the details of the transportation itself. Transportation does however add significant cost through material handling equipment, indirect labour and command and control systems to know when and where to move things and how to avoid damaging or losing them in the process. One real indicator of factories which have got it all wrong is when there is a whole fleet of formula one fork-lift trucks zooming all over the place being busy and essentially useless.

Thinking in terms of effective flow paths through the organization can challenge existing transportation procedures often to immediate effect.

Inventory as discussed earlier can have a function in buffering and smoothing out fluctuations in the external environment but by definition inventory is not being worked on and is simply waiting, either for the next processing stage or for a customer to appear. Traditional cost accounting counts such stock holding as part of the current assets of a business but in reality they are liabilities until they are sold and actually cost a lot of money just to look after them properly until the happy day when the customer takes delivery.

All businesses should aim to reduce to a minimum, inventory held for purposes of operational supply. Inventory holding for reasons of speculation are a different matter and of no interest here. Of course in some organizations output cannot be stored and the idea of inventory is less relevant for core products or services. Inventory of consumable and support items will however still apply.

Processing waste can be a natural outcome of certain transformation processes but the danger is that because it is to some extent expected, the reasons for its existence are not challenged often enough. There is also the danger that a given sector has a recipe of received wisdoms which insiders find difficult to question. In many cases the expected wastes are not predetermined by the technologies in use but actually result from managerial and operational practices.

A company printing polymer facia panels for the automotive industry expected to waste 100 sheets every time they set up with different ink colours and screen prints. To ask these traditional printers to run a batch of 100 was regarded as too stupid but under protest they did it and by treating every sheet as if made of gold they ran a successful batch. Now they have to find a way to do it repeatedly and consistently.

Waste of motion harks back to the times of the Gilbreths and early motion study.[4] At that time of F W Taylor [5] and Scientific Management, the belief was that the one best way of working could be defined by industrial engineers for work people to adhere to rigidly. Now we say that the work people are the process experts and they should be helped to continually improve the work patterns such that they can work smarter not harder. In this the basic rules of ergonomics and motion economy for individuals and teams working in conjunction with the physical processes, are little changed from the early decades of the twentieth century. In any repetitive process, detailed analysis of avoiding, combining, rearranging and reordering patterns of movement to remove strain and non-essential moves can pay dividends. This spills over into aspects of workplace layout, material handling and production planning and can be used to redesign the set-up processes as previously discussed.

The waste of product defects is an obvious and potentially hazardous situation. Effort has to be redirected to the design stage to ensure that defects are less likely because of the prevention thinking put in at this stage. Part of this should be the use of failsafing devices in the processes such that foreseeable errors, in assembly for example, cannot occur. Much of this is simply applied common sense and a little engineering ingenuity and here again the experts are the process people who can see the problem sooner than anyone else and often can suggest ways to remove the problem. They do need management support to make the changes however.

Protection factors and second guessing

The danger of the above wastes is that they are taken as given. If we assume that these wastes are going to happen then to protect our business we are likely to build in protection factors. Thus a supplier contracts for a three-week lead time when normally one week will do. This is believed to give sufficient moral and perhaps financial protection against the normal panic requirements on a Friday night for a change in next week's scheduled deliveries. Such a customer creates in the supplier a recognition that their forecasts are of little value and an exercise in creative second guessing takes place where the supplier in effect overrides the communicated demand in the expectation (often realized) that the real demand is going to be different. This pattern is true of internal customers and suppliers especially across the cultural boundary of manufacturing and marketing. In many cases the pressures of sales bonuses and targets creates a belief in the sales team that certain market penetrations will be achieved. If this is then sent as a production output plan to manufacturing but the optimistic case is unfounded who gets the 'blame' of excess inventory?

From the other point of view a customer anticipating problems of supply availability might ask for materials earlier than is actually needed thereby increasing pressures on an already struggling supply infrastructure. They might then compound the error by placing multiple forecast orders on different suppliers. This message is relayed back upstream slightly out of time phasing and modified by any minimum batch sizing rules in place. In this way whole industries come to believe that the world is doing one thing when the reality is different.[5] Silicon chip production is a classic example of this going rapidly from boom to bust as the inflated order patterns melt away when the real demand is experienced or more correctly not experienced.

Here again the multiple linkages in the supply chain provide a multiplier effect which Forrester's Industrial Dynamics work years ago demonstrated could rapidly produce unstable fluctuations in output and inventory in a simply linked serial chain.[6] This is shown in Figure 3.4 which shows the effect of a single 10 per cent step change in retail sales producing wide amplifications, spread over an extended time-scale.

This is the perfect situation where information shared across all of these boundaries about the real demand could avoid this complicated and fundamentally flawed guessing game.

Testing not trusting

Another fundamentally flawed game is that known as goods inwards inspection.

When customers contract with a supplier for the delivery of a given item there is in theory sufficient information available to the supplier so that there can be no doubt in their mind about the level of quality and quantities expected. The supplier has also been adjudged sufficiently competent, else why did they get the contract? It is also to be expected that the supplier has some form of quality control in place and yet when the goods are delivered the customer inspects them! The only reason can be that the customer does not trust the supplier to do what they have contracted to do.

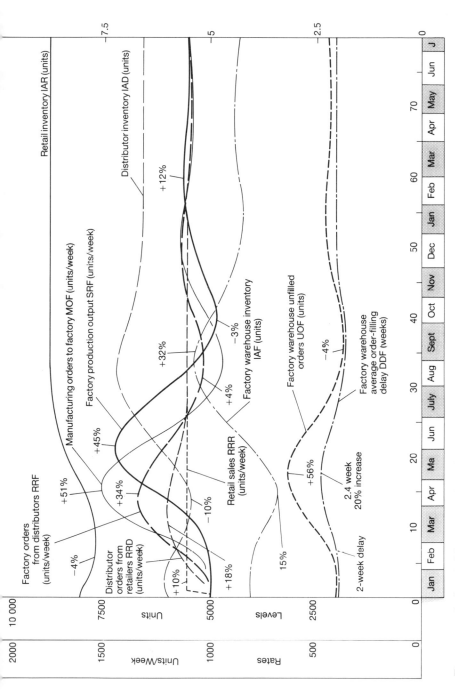

Figure 3.4 Industrial Dynamics Simulation Results from a Serial Retail Distribution Supply Chain.

Source: Forrester J, *Industrial Dynamics*, MIT Press, 1961.

This is the worst kind of avoidable waste tying up resources for no value added to the customer and sending messages back upstream which will not engender trust since none is being displayed. It can also be counter-productive since if the supplier knows that inspection at the customer end is taking place they can ease off on their own quality effort and simply fight it out with the customer when the time comes. Other stupid behaviours take place where customers reject goods and they are sent back to the supplier for rectification, repair or replacement. The supplier can simply repackage them and send them back hoping that a different sample does not show a problem or that a different inspector will interpret the standard in a different way. This little game again wastes resources often taking so long that Production, under pressure for output, accept the disputed batch in order to keep working. Another game then takes over as the two sides argue about financial recompense for the problem. In all of this the needs of the final customer are all but forgotten.

To change this will not be quick but both sides have to recognize their own contribution to this nonsense and work together to demonstrate that the alternative is both desirable and feasible.

Failure costs and effects

Direct/indirect costs

Like all quality related costs the wastes through ineffective supply chain management break into two main categories, i.e. those which are relatively easily identified and those where quantification is either impossible or traditionally difficult. The direct consequences of an actual visible failure can often be counted in terms of the immediate resource allocation of people and equipment to sort the problem, at least in the short-term reactive mode. Even in this case however what can be more difficult to measure is the effort needed to produce a persistent longer term fix to the problem which is likely to involve many more functional areas and decisions as the impact of changes ripple through the organization. If these aspects are difficult in apparently obvious areas how much more difficult will they be in those areas where the waste is no less real but is much less visible? The goods inwards inspection area is more obvious once thought about and is often among the first to be targeted for improvement but here the knee jerk reaction to simply eliminate the activity will in all probability create the opposite effect to that desired. A long period of operation according to 'old' thinking infects not only our own organization but that of our supplying one also. Goods inwards inspection provides a buffer against an uncertain external environment. Simply removing the buffer without modifying the environment or our ability to react to it is a recipe for danger. Similarly, influencing the environment takes time and resource which has to be accounted for somewhere and should be put in the balance against the waste reduction benefits to be accrued.

Unless the organization really understands what their business needs for customer satisfaction demand of them, the resource allocated to waste removal of this kind can be seen as a cost and not an investment since the resource is expended in the short term and the benefits will accrue in the medium to longer term. When survival is the issue, time horizons become frighteningly short.

When we now consider more opaque areas of potential waste through some of the second guessing activities for example it is quickly apparent that the information to evaluate the scale of the problem and the benefit achievable, is more difficult to obtain. Often the organization structure and practice will make it difficult to gather meaningful data. This can be because the boundaries in the structure make access difficult across these boundaries and because of the sub-system tendency to the sub-optimum solution. Here the organizational measurement and reward processes encourage someone in the sub-group to make a decision which provides a local maximum in some indicator while, when considered from the total system viewpoint, the more effective decision is actually to reduce the level of that indicator to enable another indicator to provide a better overall result.

These are problems that fast-flow, 'Lean' manufacturing companies have recognized as they try to understand the Total Quality message and to create meaningful values of the Cost of Quality. In recognition of this and to cope with aspects of investment appraisal which can undervalue the merit of investments in new advanced technologies the approach of Activity Based Costing is being promoted.[7] In simple terms this identifies those factors which actually drive the creation of costs rather than simply allocate a global lump of overhead cost across an increasingly meaningless notional direct workforce. If we can allocate realistic costs and also single out activities which can add value and not merely cost then we can really begin to target improvement actions more effectively. Here again the difficulty is to raise our vision from the immediate and parochial to focus more on the overall effectiveness of all of the parties who contribute to our competitiveness in the market place.

In order to do this it can be useful to construct ways of diagramming the materials pipeline to identify all of the players and their relative contributions in reality or potential.

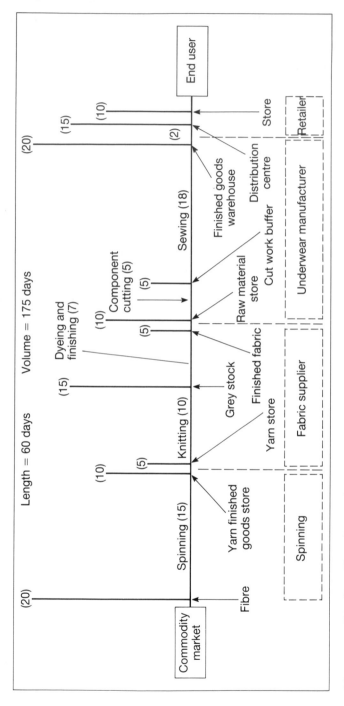

Figure 3.5 Pipeline Chart for Underwear Manufacture
Source: Scott C and Westbrook R, 'New Strategic Tools in Supply Chain Management', *IIPD & LM*, 21.1, 25.

Charting the pipeline

One approach advocated by Scott and Westbrook[8] is to map the pipeline of materials as shown in Figure 3.5.

In the diagram horizontal lines represent the average time spent in the processes indicated while vertical lines (drawn to the same scale) show the amount of waiting time in the queues for each process. This creates two useful measures. Pipeline length is the sum of the horizontal lines, i.e. total process lead time and indicates responsiveness to a demand increase within the same stock constraints. Pipeline volume produces a value for all of the inventory in the system by adding the vertical and horizontal lines together. This volume takes time to 'drain' out of the system and is therefore an indicator of the time taken to respond to decreases in demand given the same rate of manufacturing throughput.

A different representation of the same kind of thinking is presented in Figure 3.6 Here the value added at different parts of the inventory pipeline is mapped against a time scale. Here horizontal lines indicate a period of non-value add, i.e. inactivity and are therefore equivalent to the verticals in the other diagram. This diagram however, by indicating the amount of money committed in the pipeline, allows an evaluation of the cost impact particularly when volumes demanded from suppliers are being reduced. This is a major consideration for those customer companies who have entered into supply agreements such that they are liable for schedule changes within an agreed procurement lead time.

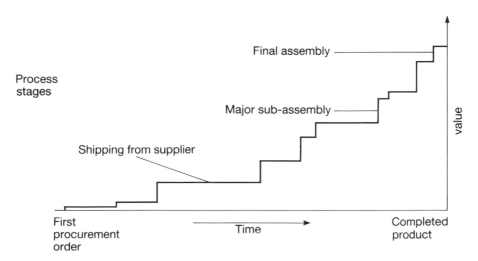

Figure 3.6 Value Added Pipeline

Another way to consider the pipeline effects is in relation to the organization shapes we have already discussed (i.e. IVAT) since each shape has a different impact on the degree to which change late in the product production process can be accommodated. The T-shape is the most friendly in this regard.

In each of these approaches the purpose of the exercise is to create a priority agenda for improvement actions. By targeting the queue or delay times in the overall process and looking for improvements in these, overall pipeline delays and wastes can be reduced to the ultimate benefit of the supply chain participants and their customers. Often these will highlight the second-guessing holding of stock at parts of the chain as protection against another party's lack of consideration or communication and can become an obvious target for joint improvement teams.

This aspect leads nicely into our next section which considers the role of information in the supply chain.

INFORMATION FLOWS IN BOTH DIRECTIONS: CALLS TO ACTION OR CREATION OF CONFUSION?

Technical, involvement, business, and people

Best practice companies take very seriously their requirement to communicate fully and competently with their opposite numbers but communication has three aspects. Firstly there is the sender, then the message and means and thirdly the receiver. Faults or sources of intermittent noise in generation, transmission and receipt are often not immediately obvious but when the desired action is not forthcoming only then might it be realized that the communication process was at least partly to blame for the difficulty.

Supply chain communications are a means to relay information which should inform decisions and instigate appropriate responses including the signals to produce or deliver. They can also be important means to build understanding and trust and develop interpersonal relationships which will reduce the need for formal communications later. This latter aspect in particular is typically not well developed in many companies and in fact can raise questions about 'consorting with the enemy' or being 'too cozy' and not demanding enough. The latter view is often expressed by those who only perceive the 'law of the jungle' philosophy of business behaviour or are disciples at the altar of 'competitive market forces'.

The opposite view is the one we subscribe to. That is, if you deal with your opposite numbers as friends and colleagues in a common venture then you will try very hard not to let your friends down. You will also be more tolerant and understanding with your friends' idiosyncracies and reluctant to throw away the investment made in the relationship, preferring instead to expose your concerns in a constructive, developmental way and hopefully guide an improvement in a non-threatening way.

With these general principles in mind we have found it useful to break down the range of information flows into four major categories which are the same for both customer-to-supplier and supplier-to-customer information flows. The details of what is communicated do vary between directions however. Overall the intention is to create a flow of information which provides the basis for effective supply and the sharing of knowledge and ideas.

The *Technical* category covers the detailed specification of what is to be supplied in an up to date and preferably early and accurate medium. Early involvement in design is a key factor to support market responsiveness. The customer organization has a responsibility to share their view of future developments to engage the supplier's brain power in the debate on solutions. Operations problems must also be communicated early, even if solutions are being implemented, since a degree of forewarning allows contingency planning from the partner. Capability changes must also be communicated pro-actively, again to allow full consideration of the implications by the other party. Innovative improvements should be sought and benefits shared on both sides while the supplier has an obligation to gather and confirm quality performance data.

The *Involvement* dimension accounts for measurement and feedback processes on performance and the degree to which one party is involved in the other party's decision-making processes.

Business communications cover aspects of relevance to the other party but not immediately key to current activity. It is however very much future oriented. For example planned new products or projects which the partner could become involved with; end market projections and possible scenarios and the degree to which each is willing to open their books to scrutiny by the other party. After all, if your suppliers are not making sufficient margin to invest they will not be able to follow you into the new opportunities you are planning. Suppliers similarly have to be open about their suppliers, cost information and availability of resources.

The *People* aspects recognize the need to signal personnel structures and changes and role changes. Since effective one-to-one interactions help build effective relationships it is important that this is properly managed. There can be many touch points as interfaces between organizations and the consistency of the messages and perceptions is very important. This is a difficult thing to build and also to maintain but our colleagues Carlisle and Parker have a process to evaluate how well this is being managed.[9] It is also recognized that actually encouraging a wide range of personnel to visit the other party's premises also helps the process of understanding and commitment.

Much of this requires physical proximity – the touch points have to touch hands sometimes. Increasingly technology is being used in this area but not always cleverly.

Effect of electronic data interchange (EDI)

There are undoubtedly major wastes in many paper-based communications systems. The explosive rise in the use of telefax machines is testimony to that truth. At a primitive level this can be used to trigger a delivery note or schedule change but the goal of full EDI is to have one information system exchanging real time data to the benefit of supply chain response times. Unfortunately the Garbage In Garbage Out syndrome is present here also. If EDI is seen simply as a technical fix the true potential will not be realized and what can result is even more frequent transmission of impossible demands in which the other party has had no involvement, no agreement and often no capability to perform. Thus the speedily transmitted but ultimately useless communication called for action but instead created confusion leaving the other party to ask 'which of these impossible tasks do I try to do first?'

Of course the future is through EDI but only once the organizations have collectively decided and developed the appropriate channels of communication and commitment so that the desired result is achievable. As in many other technologies the managerial and organizational aspects take much longer to develop than the technical but perhaps this is because we do not think about those issues in the same structured, problem-solving way.

Sharing the risk of failure

Any investment made in anticipation of future sales is inherently at risk and the longer the total pipeline length, the greater the accumulated risk. This is why the mapping discussed above can be very important. It is often required to book supply capacity well in advance of actual customer order and customers will sometimes agree to fund such purchase commitments within an agreed proportion of their order cycle. Any deviation from the forecast order pattern has impact on this commitment and has to be carefully analyzed. In the computer industry the optimizing of the pipeline for different order fluctuations is an ongoing exercise. In this example the customer takes at least some of the hit when demand fluctuates but perhaps in our Partnership model a greater degree of risk sharing between members of the supply chain should be a feature, particularly if all were party to the market projections and agreed the opportunity the chain was aiming for. In major capital projects in automotive, aerospace, power generation and construction this has been a feature to some degree for many years. Historically such arrangements were constructed in legal contracts which were used mainly to recover liquidated damages on failure by some party. Apart from the lawyers involved it is hard to see who benefits from this approach.

Concurrent or Simultaneous Engineering could be constructed on the basis of a simple market contract to deliver design support to a customer but will be more effective when entered into as part of a shared destiny approach but here the future expectations need to be clarified up front (we will discuss the intellectual property rights aspects later). Who pays for development costs? Are the production orders guaranteed to follow the development contract? Where in the chain should protective inventory buffers be held? How should this cost be allocated?

It is worth noting that defence procurement changes aiming for better value for money actually complicate the situation here since the follow-on contract for production goes out to tender and another supplier's low bid might win the day, but since they cannot know as much about the design as the originators, problems may emerge which will be less adequately dealt with. It is a moot point whether the defence agency in this situation actually does achieve better value for money over all the project stages. Here perhaps is another example of sub-optimization.

Promises and commitments

It is a basic tenet of the partnership model that close relationships create conditions where a customer will choose to put new business in the way of the preferred supplier. Thus companies offer supply agreements for the life of the product or for as long as the customer remains in that line of business.

At one level this can appear to be anti-competitive and akin to cartelism and the EC competition directives would seem to be forcing companies in the opposite direction. The EC Directives on public contracts include the Supplies Directive on supplies of products; Works Directive on building and civil engineering; Services Directives for non-physical supplies (for example data processing) and their associated Compliance Directive. Covering the utilities there are the Utilities Directives for supplies and services and an associated Remedies Directive.[10] Generally, there are three procedures in use – open, restricted and negotiated. The first is the most obviously fully 'competitive, open market concept' and anyone may tender for the contract. The restrictive operates for tenderers who have passed a pre-selection stage where the selection criteria were made public. The negotiated procedure might fit more precisely with the Partnership model since two additional features make this acceptable (apart from a failure to find suitable suppliers using the other approaches). These factors are if there are technical or artistic reasons for choosing a particular supplier or a particular supplier has exclusive rights to the product or service needed. In our Partnership supply chain with supplier involvement in design, assigning proprietary rights to the design might fit into this category. The second factor applies when the nature of the work makes it difficult to calculate the overall price at the outset. This may well be the case with risk-sharing relationships.

Invoking each of these could be seen as an attempt to circumvent the intent of the Directives but as in the defence procurement example, perhaps we have a situation that imperfect understanding of total supply chain costs supports well-intentioned political actions to increase value for money for taxpayers and promote market fairness but results in counterproductive directions in practice.

What is also clear is that Article 85 of the Treaty of Rome 'prohibits agreements and concerted practices between undertakings (economically independent enterprises) which *may affect trade between Member States* and which have the object of or effect of preventing, restricting or distorting competition between the common market'. However, practices which may appear to contravene Article 85 'may be relieved or set aside *by the Commission* where the restrictive agreement or concerted practice in question 'contributes to improving the production or distribution of goods or to promoting the technical or economic progress, while allowing consumers a fair share of the resulting benefit', but does not go beyond what is necessary to achieve its objective or afford the contract parties a possibility for eliminating competition'.[11]

We have argued that technical and economic progress is at the heart of partnership agreements and also that the real cost should be reducing thereby allowing reduced prices to consumers. From these points of view exemption might seem possible. The issue might then emerge of how to demonstrate to regulatory agencies that the partnership sourcing model is in fact economically justified through quantified cost reductions and increased international competitiveness against other supply chains. There will still be some disquiet perhaps that new suppliers have major barriers to cross to break into existing supply chain relationships but in terms of global market places there is no alternative – the serious competition already work this way by nature of their normal business structures and history. Free market politicians might find this a particularly difficult pill to swallow.

TECHNOLOGY TRANSFER – THROUGH TRAINING, PEOPLE AND EQUIPMENT

Getting suppliers up to speed

The thrust of SCMG work is that improvement in relationships takes a considerable effort no matter which side of the customer–supplier divide one is currently on. Nevertheless larger customer companies are more often exposed to competitive actions and world class exemplars than their possibly smaller suppliers. It is also often the case that suppliers are more often reactive to new developments. Hence the belief in customer companies that 'they' will have to change and catch up with the other runners in the race. In the supplier company the eyes roll as yet another new fad is pushed at them by their customer contacts to make them look good to the corporate seagulls who inspect progress towards the new panacea.

More understanding customers recognize that it is in their own self interest to operate with equally capable suppliers and take steps to help that process along. Many Japanese inward investor companies take representatives of potential supplier companies across to home base to expose them to new ideas and equipment and to begin to generate a more coherent picture of the requirements to which they will have to perform. This is no more than the UK's Marks and Spencer retailer has done for decades with their supplier manufacturers. They will work with such companies and support their development for as long as there is real evidence of a willingness and ability to manage to evolve as required for the changing needs of the business. In fact the major reason why a customer should walk away from a supplier is if they cannot or will not change. Given a willingness to change and some time and effort most things are possible.

The support provided takes many forms but will often include general sharing of learning opportunities about new systems, techniques and opportunities. This will often be in mixed groups of customer and supplier personnel. As such it is at most a marginal cost to the customer who is training their own people anyway and also provides opportunities to begin to build the friendship bridges so important later. These training sessions will range from basic awareness to full competence development sessions. In many cases the driving force originally has been through the effort to improve quality and the first courses were around the themes of Statistical Process Control and Total Quality.

This formal approach assumes that the customer company has skills to share but sometimes the flow is different.

Business clubs

Toyota dual source, not for reasons of playing one supplier off against the other for price reduction purposes, but to capture the spirit of a competitive striving for innovation and improvement. Interestingly however each supplier must share new innovation experience with the other supplier but might be rewarded with an increased share of next year's business. This process can be extended into more extensive clubs of suppliers to a common customer which meet a few times per year to share experiences and to look for improvements in the way they do business. Here again the Japanese transplants in the UK have demonstrated that this approach is equally effective at generating an identification with the idea of an extended industrial family.

The issue of proprietary intellectual rights remains however and it may well be that the real communication is less than complete.

Other business clubs of otherwise unassociated companies also fulfil the needs to share and learn from each others' experience. The Scottish JIT Club has for example existed on an essentially cashless basis since 1986 and has been instrumental in transferring learning among its participating managers on a wide variety of 'best practice' approaches. In similar fashion Quality-focused groups and meetings of professional institutions can help spread the message as can government awareness programmes and open conferences.

In most cases however the presence of an important customer articulating a vision of the future requirements is an important motivator for supplier managers to make the effort to attend and try out the theories in practice. If they also know that others have travelled the road before them and are willing to help this is real infrastructure support. In the case of the Scottish JIT Club this has been possible even between companies that are nominally competitors in the market place. Perhaps they see the real threat not being each other but the newcomers to their industry from the Far East. They are also sufficiently mature enough to recognize that in the end all industries need a healthy industrial community in which to do business either as customers or suppliers, thus keeping such approaches secret may pay short-term benefits but is damaging in the longer term. The companies who will succeed are those who can learn from the best wherever that best is and put the improvements into place faster than their competitors. Such an organization will have at its heart such a questing for knowledge and understanding that it will initiate actions innovative of themselves to create a new best practice and thereby get the best of both following and leading developments in different activity areas.

Exchanging resident experts

Many major customers have supplier development teams which are often multi-skilled to help bring their suppliers up to speed. As we have discussed this is often based around improving the levels of quality produced but Hewlett Packard for example have had teams of engineers helping out with design and manufacturing problems in the supplier companies. In this case however there was no restriction as to which customer's order was in trouble. The HP engineers would help the supplier regardless. This is real commitment and a valued resource for the suppliers. Of course this kind of support should not need to go on indefinitely. The aim is to so develop the supplier that this support will no longer be needed and performance will continue as anticipated.

One of the dangers in this approach however is that such resident experts might be perceived by the parent organization as having switched allegiance and identifying too closely with the interests of their temporary hosts. Thus these programmes need careful management.

Particularly in cases of new product development, expert exchanges can be for long periods of time to coordinate and liaise between two or more in-house teams. The mandating of such experts is a big issue so that there is no doubt in anyone's minds about the acceptable range of decisions such people are empowered to make. Even after their return to the parent organization such people can have an important role to play as a conduit of communications between the parties. There is however the issue in typical western companies of 'management churn' where people move on a regular basis from job role to job role and often location as well. The relationships built between people therefore have to be built between systems as well or the messages being sent will not be perceived in the same way and responses may be degraded.

On the supplier side 'fixers' can be transferred for trouble shooting purposes and for joint improvement activities.

A Japanese company in England produces video recording equipment for a German customer. Following a telefaxed complaint of a quality problem a volunteer from the experienced assemblers was called for and was on a flight to the customer the same afternoon to inspect the products and ensure some continuity of supply. This assembly person was accompanied by a technician who carried out investigations of possible causes of the problem. Various ideas were faxed back to England before the root cause in one processing operation was identified. Within 48 hours the customer had a full technical report recording the situation, the measures taken to remedy the immediate fault and more importantly the longer term design and manufacturing modifications put in place to guarantee that such an event could not recur. In this way what could have been a disaster for customer–supplier relations actually demonstrated both serious commitment to customer service and also command of an effective recovery and improvement process.

Transfer of process and/or test equipment

As part of a general move to outsource more of the non-core business activities there can be a tendency to do this on the basis of inadequate strategic and financial analysis. The financial difficulties of inappropriate overhead allocation processes are well understood if insufficiently acted upon. Choosing to buy rather than make because the delivered cost is less than the manufactured one through the allocation of hundreds of percentage charges on the operational labour hours is only justified if the overhead is reduced in line with the reduced number of manufactured parts. All too often this fails to keep in step and we have a progressive reduction of manufacturing's ability to justify making anything as the overhead is allocated over fewer and fewer parts.

There is a real danger in this process that core technologies are in effect given away in the name of a spurious short-term cost saving. Most organizations rightly regard their design knowledge and technology as core to their business but innovations can come from sources outside of the design office. In fact many incremental innovations have their origins in manufacturing and from customers asking for minor changes. These aspects are more associated with process skills and if we have decided to outsource these then we could be cut off from development in that technology and from the learning effects which come from regular use of these technologies. In such cases what is transferred includes actual equipment along with the knowledge of how to operate it. If we decide for good strategic reasons that we no longer wish to actively participate in any technology where once we had expertise it is important to build into any supply contract an obligation from the other party to permit us to track the technology as it evolves. One way to do this is of course to have that supplier's experts as part of the product development process with our own design team so that they can interrogate them and understand the implications of any new developments.

In electronic systems the expertise of writing the software to drive system test equipment is so wrapped up with the processes of design that there can be real danger in assuming that another test equipment supplier could build sufficient sophistication into their test equipment without gathering an understanding of the inherently proprietary design philosophy and architecture of the overall systems at the same time.

With a physical transfer, asset specificity is an issue. A company transfers equipment in order for their product to be produced by the other party. Is it therefore assumed that the equipment will only ever be used for this company's products? This may be acceptable if the equipment is fully funded by the customer company but if not, can priority access be guaranteed? Since capacity is so dependent on the patterns of demand actually experienced as opposed to that planned it might often be the case that supply is interrupted causing consequential costs not factored in at the make or buy decision. Conversely, dedicated but underutilized equipment could be increasing opportunity costs which are wastes in the system which someone pays for.

Here again we have a powerful argument to decide not on the basis of the latest guru speak or fashion but on the basis of a properly thought through strategic process where the longer term learning effects are weighed against any short-term savings.

SOURCES AND ENCOURAGEMENT OF IDEAS, INNOVATIONS AND IMPROVEMENTS

Setting the cost

The traditional ways of price setting in market transactions assume that the game is a zero sum one, i.e. that one party's gain is necessarily the other party's loss. In such bidding games the difficult decision is where to set the starting price to leave enough room for effective discounting during the protracted negotiations that follow. Sales negotiators in such companies make much of the market price they can obtain but in reality the price is only that which their immediate customer feels appropriate in the circumstances. Often there is little serious attempt to actually establish from the real final customers what price they would be prepared to pay. Note also that we have been talking here of price which is a market mechanism, not cost which is the internal measure of the resources used and margins achieved to enable a price to be agreed. All too often the price takers in the organization are not in communication and do not understand the point of view of the cost makers.

One way round this (an approach much in vogue in defence contracting until relatively recently) was the cost plus contract. In effect this simply logged any resource used in producing the items and added on an agreed profit margin before billing for the work. In reality such arrangements were open to abuse and were certainly not conducive to continuous improvement activities which would only reduce the amount on which to charge profit. They did however recognize that in such contracts there can be a lot of development work continuing during the production cycle and therefore this payment system recompensed the supplier for this degree of flexibility. We have already discussed the problem in the new situation of different bids for development and production contracts in these industries where the development effort cannot be spread over the production run and has to be recovered quickly. In the fixed cost form of these contracts there can be as much effort devoted to the contractual disputes after the fact about whose liability it is for changes in design requirements.

In each of these approaches there is a real disincentive to make improvements. In the first case it would actually reduce profitability and in the second would create additional costs through the need to renegotiate the specifications and design approvals. In each approach the value adders in manufacturing are far removed from the decision takers at the interface between the organizations.

The modern and successful approach is to work from the market place backwards. Firstly an acceptable product price is established utilizing the full range of market research methods. From this the target transfer cost of each item is established. This is set such that the price minus an acceptable profit margin sets the cost for the supplier to meet. This becomes the target cost for the supplier but note that it will not be static over the life of the product and will certainly not increase for reasons of inflation or material price variance as a rule. Rather the argument is that with repetition of production over the production run the learning effect comes in and the supplier will therefore be able to reduce the production costs from this effect alone. Thus the supply agreement will have a built in cost reduction year on year.

In addition, new target costs will be agreed to take more cost out of the item than could be achieved by experience alone. These improvement targets will then form the justification for improvement activities between the parties to work to reduce these costs. Up front however there will be agreement of how the benefit from these improvements will be shared. Within the target band the share is likely to be approximately even.

Anything above that band is likely to benefit the supplier directly. In this way customers gain the benefit immediately rather than having to wait until the next annual price negotiation when some recognition of a process or product improvement will have to be prized out of the supplier as part of the complex bidding and dealing process.

This process recognizes that the expertise to contribute to real improvement is likely to reside in the other party and that unless this is tapped then a competitive opportunity will be lost. However unless this is planned from the beginning the likelihood is that those same opportunities will be lost as some exercise in retrospective gain sharing is debated.

Believing in the shared future

For a supplier to be sufficiently trusting in the above scenario they will have to believe that by so doing, not merely the immediate requirements of a demanding customer will be met but that their own longer term interest will also be catered for. It is hard to envisage why they should freely offer improvement suggestions to customers if the customer is likely to take their business elsewhere.

One customer company told of a shared design approach where their six best suppliers for a particular range of items were invited to make presentations about how they would produce a new product variety. In effect they had to expose to their competitors elements of their competitive capability without any guarantee that there would be business for them in the end. It seemed to come as a surprise when a few of the suppliers refused to participate and when we criticized the thinking that set up the event.

There is a further danger that companies run with customers or suppliers who talk a good game but cannot or will not put it into practice. In any situation of supply and demand the balance of power can swing from one to the other. With any short-term swing it is possible to make a quick killing at the other's expense. This is the nature of the zero sum game and those who play it in the market place assume that for every supplier or customer wiped out by the sneak attack another will appear to take their place. This cannot be true in the longer run and companies so weakened cannot be part of the pool of victims next time around.

Unfortunately if the managers making the short-term opportunistic decision are not going to be in their job role for long then they will not have to live with the consequences. Organizations therefore have to put in place systems which will overlay and constrain such opportunism for their own longer term benefit.

Single, dual and multi-sourcing

Why multi-source?

In an uncertain environment where the likelihood is that things go wrong and that even the best intentioned of our business partners is subject to events totally outwith their control, then the old adage of not having all of your eggs in one basket has caused us to believe that multi-sourcing is a risk-avoiding way of ensuring continuity of supply. Thus if one of our suppliers fails to deliver, then attention can be shifted to another to recover the situation.

This argument is every bit as powerfully put from the other point of view in that Western suppliers do not as a rule feel comfortable being overly dependent on one customer's orders.

For customers the typical figure is around 25 per cent of business capacity while suppliers tend to the range 6–10 major customers. Customers with such institutional limits argue that one of the reasons is to protect the supplier company from going bust if they withdraw their business! We of course are arguing here that withdrawal of business from a trusted partner is not something to be done quickly or which would come as a surprise. Rather it should be the final act of an extensive effort by both parties to effect improvements and if it has to happen would be regarded as a failure by the company cancelling the orders as much as by the one unable to adapt as required.

If we then add to the multi-sourcing scenario the tendency to play off one company against the other in the zero sum game we see the further attractions of multi-sourcing in the power play negotiations which many still find great satisfaction in winning.

In circumstances like this it is not unusual for a company to have more supplier companies than it has employees and even if it were wished it would not be possible to partner with all of them.

In the other direction it can be more difficult depending on where the company is located in terms of the supply chain. The final retailer or wholesaler may well have to deal with very many customers and the relationship is unlikely to be of an explicitly partnering nature although the underlying attitudes certainly could be.

Multi-sourcing is also inherently expensive in administration costs as all of the numerous transactions have to be organized and monitored.

Single sourcing

The opposite extreme is where a single supplier has all of the business for a particular commodity or more likely a given part number within a commodity group. Single sourcing is vertical integration without ownership but unless the relationship is sound the benefits of vertical integration will not be achieved. Total single sourcing is less likely for the same reasons of protection against unforeseen catastrophes. When it does happen it can be for reasons of no other choice of vendor for a particular part. In this case however this is usually referred to as sole sourcing and certainly increases the potential severity should supply be interrupted.

One of the great benefits from single sourcing is quality consistency. With multiple suppliers working to the same specification tolerance there is going to be a range of dispersions of sizes around the acceptable size and the danger of an unacceptable build-up of tolerances between different versions of matching parts becomes more of a possibility.

A further point relates to Taguchi's view that any variation around the nominal size is inherently wasteful and should be reduced.[12] The task of so doing is easier if there is only one organization involved. Consistency of supply simplifies the job inside the customer unit allowing a free flow of materials which of itself will reduce the firefighting costs.

Guaranteeing future work to a chosen supplier partner avoids the overhead cost involved in re-tendering for annual contracts and the engineering effort devoted to producing the tender document can be directed instead at improvement projects.

There are however dangers in single sourcing of which the possibility of discontinuities in supply is the most serious. However the factor which seems to exercise Western companies at least as much, is that of dependency which has already been discussed. There seems to be a myopia in some customer companies that a supplier is only capable of supplying that which they have always supplied. Even if the customer has changed the product technology many times there seems little support for the view that the customer should not relinquish their investment in the supplier and instead help them migrate to the new technology as well. After all, technologies can come and go but people and relationships can last much longer. High levels of dependence can bring such solutions to the fore and the customer sees it as legitimate to look for new business opportunities for a faithful supplier. It is reported for example that when a supplier to the US operations of Honda went bankrupt the local Honda board members were called to Japan to explain what they had done to try and avoid it and why in the end it had happened.

Recognizing that high levels of dependence actually mean interdependence and that both are equally vulnerable, helps reinforce the need to continually work at the relationship so that the possibility of failure is reduced. It is in this mode that innovations are seen to benefit both parties and help demonstrate the belief in and the reality of the shared destiny. Supporting one's partner and the collective future provides a focus and motivation for improvement actions which will not be subject to any secrecy or use as bargaining chips since the real opposition is not in the other party but in the other supply chain.

There is one drawback in a single sourcing set-up in that the market mechanism created during a tender and contract bidding process is not present and therefore it can be more difficult to establish what the 'going rate' for a job might be. This should not be used as a justification for not trying partnering, rather it simply becomes an issue for which the relationship has to find solutions. As we will see shortly Benchmarking is one way forward.

Dual Sourcing

The Toyota example discussed earlier is instructive from a number of points of view. Part of the reason for dual sourcing is to recognize the real danger of interrupted supply and so dual sourcing within the same commodity group makes sense. Toyota however do not have a token second source on warm standby ready to take over the load if the main supplier fails. They deliberately split the volume demands between the two suppliers since in this way it is possible to modify the quantity demanded more easily by varying the short-term production schedules requested of each supplier. The suppliers themselves are not directly in competition, certainly not on quality or price. Rather the degree of innovativeness over the year might change the average call off of parts for the next year. Each supplier is however the lead supplier for a particular model type and each is expected to share with the other any improvement they have developed. In a sense the suppliers are also collaborating partners and collectively the supply chain is strengthened.

Of course if levels of dependency on the common customer are not high then it may well be that the lessons learned during the relationship with this customer will be re-applied to the benefit of their other customers, potentially weakening the customer who first initiated the improvement process. This last concern leads nicely into our next section.

Confidentiality and market intelligence

Chinese walls in new product development

If one of the purposes of getting closer to suppliers is because they have expertise which we do not have then one area where they will have much to contribute is in new product development. Early supplier involvement or simultaneous engineering brings such expertise into a common effort to design product correctly from the very beginning. New product ideas are however the very essence of competitive advantage for customer companies and now the partner is sharing in both the creation of that idea and the responsibility for the protection of that idea from unwelcome imitation. They may also be sharing in the legal liability for the safety of the design. In the supplier design studio, in the absence of a single customer, we have the problem of keeping secrets from other members of the design team whose inputs we might normally call upon. This was described by one company having such arrangements with a number of global customer company clients as a series of Chinese Walls in the design office. Chinese paper walls are of course very thin and not effective barriers or soundproof screens at all. Thus social convention and not physical structure makes it possible to live in close community with others of the same family without invading their social space. In much the same way the members of different customer groupings in the design teams were assumed not to release or discuss sensitive issues with others in the same company but working for another potentially interested party. This burden of confidentiality is a great one but very difficult to police effectively and in fact is largely dependent on the attitude and behaviour of individuals. Nevertheless its importance needs to be regularly reaffirmed and education and training provided, particularly for new team members.

Keeping up to speed with new developments

At least part of the reason that a particular supplier has expertise not available to a customer company is the fact that they are interacting with multiple customers and therefore are benefiting from a variety of ideas and approaches. If a supplier has too few customers this learning potential is reduced and yet we have just been arguing that transfer of knowledge from one customer's business to another is against the principles of the con-fidentiality of the design process. A careful balance must therefore be struck between limiting transfer of sensitive information across the customer boun-daries inside the organization and a full open system boundary to outside knowledge and development making learning available to all inside the company and also to the partners. There needs to be concerted action to scan the environment for new developments, particularly on the technical front, to identify generic processes which all customer groupings can make use of. The supplier expertise changes so that they are not simply learning from other customers' technologies but are interpreting the signals from the wider environment and adding value to them as this knowledge is applied in the individual customer projects. From the customer point of view we have already identified the danger of moving out of the learning loop through outsourcing previously internal technology. Thus a partnering agreement should make explicit how each party will perform the technological scanning process to mutual advantage. Customer companies can often help smaller suppliers greatly in this regard for the simple reason that they will tend to have more widely spread networks which can be set to this task with a regular commitment to share the future scenarios with their partners.

There are of course a whole raft of market research and technological forecasting techniques which might be employed as well as building up data bases of patent activity, research in universities, etc., along with monitoring trends in various business sectors. Here again the larger customer companies will probably already be doing some of this for their own internal strategic management processes. All that is required now is the belief that it is in their own interest to share this knowledge with those whose perspective may be different but well informed in their areas of activity.

Benchmarking

This is a process which has received much conference time in recent years and is credited with aiding the Xerox turnaround success as they fought back to competitiveness with their Japanese rivals.

The essence of the argument is that by defining processes in such a way that similar ones can be identified in other business areas then a new learning opportunity arises not bound by the original recipes in that company. By a conscious effort to gather data on such similar processes wherever they might occur the 'best practice' can be observed and individual performance against this benchmark can be calibrated.[13] Note that it is firstly about increased process understanding and only secondly about target setting in quantitative terms. Thus an exercise in customer order processing originating in the computer manufacturing business could find best practice in retail mail order operations. By careful analysis of what they are doing differently and some trials as to implementation it might be possible to emulate that best practice and perhaps improve on it. The idea is a simple one but the skill is in defining the processes, finding good exemplars, analyzing the differences and above all, making the changes happen in the target company.

Here is a great opportunity to start to build effective inter-company improvement teams through setting them a benchmark project in an area of common interest. The benefit of having your partner on the team is the increased spread of possible exemplar sites to study along with the understanding created through the definition of the process under investigation.

SUMMARY

- **Value is added in many different ways which will impact the nature of the supply chain.**

- **Wastes fall into clear categories and by re-examining the operating principles much of this can be reduced or eliminated.**

- **Mapping of the supply chain pipeline by activity, time and value can help prioritize improvement efforts.**

- **Information transfer is important and can be along the chain or across different chains, and can be aided by technology – but only after everything else is satisfactory.**

- **Encouraging innovations requires a fresh look at costing, information about future developments and the interaction between organizations within a network.**

In Chapter Four we will examine Partnership Sourcing from a number of theoretical points of view to demonstrate that what is being discussed here lies at the heart of strategic debate and that rather than 'doing Partnering' as a 'flavour of the month', there are strong intellectual reasons for developing the organization in this direction. Practical managers may be less interested in this academic discussion but we hope that by including it here, some greater understandings will be gained of the great managerial movement that is represented by these words: Partnership Sourcing and Supply Chain Management.

4

PARTNERING AS A STRATEGIC OPTION: THE THEORETICAL ARGUMENTS

In this chapter we will examine

- the ways in which academic thought is converging to create a strategic theory in which the role of Partnering is one of the key issues

- the different organizational options available in 'positioning' the organization within its business context

- how structures are chosen to fit current requirements but also to facilitate organizational learning.

Some academics and many managers believe that strategic thinking is not about planning for the future in the sense that strategies are more obviously observable in hindsight and such emergent strategies could not have been planned in a wholly predictable fashion. The strategists' counter-argument would be that by considering the patterns of decisions and actions that (even in retrospect) constitute a strategy, an insight into the decision-making process can be obtained. From this it is posited that at the next decision point a more informed choice can be made.

The issues involved in Partnering bring together views from a number of different parts of the academic world and demonstrate the centrality of the issues for the business future. In the opinion of Dan Jones (one of the authors of *The Machine That Changed The World*), there will be three key management tasks in the future: the management of change or transformation, the management of processes and the management of relationships. In our view Partnering brings all three of these into sharp focus.

We will see later some of the reasons for the Japanese evolution to their particular organizational partnering situations. Earlier industrial countries faced similar choices but usually branched down a different route.

In trying to understand managerial practice we have the beginnings of a convergence from parts of microeconomics (transaction costs and agency theory), industrial marketing and purchasing, business strategy at an industry level, contract law, the organization theory of networking, and a sociological interest in the nature of the new work environment in partnering firms. This latter[1] we will not develop here. This realization of wider interest and potential input allows us to expand our view from the relatively simpler procurement function's choice of 'make or buy' and its resulting forms of vertical integration or market transaction. Of course in that dichotomy Partnering is in fact intermediate in form.

Alternative business structures

One of the early attempts to produce a theoretical framework of understanding was called Transactional Economics, or more recently 'the new Institutionalists'.[2] Here the transactions at each of the customer–supplier linkages in the overall value chain are regarded as key and potentially difficult (and therefore costly) because of the following factors:

- *Bounded rationality* – the participants or actors in the transaction attempt to act rationally but are naturally bounded to some extent, by imperfect perceptions and understanding. These boundaries produce a result in some ways less than it might have been. (This is also a factor limiting detailed planning for future actions.)
- *Opportunism* – one participant looks for a short-term advantage over the other in an aggressive, adversarial way.
- *Small numbers bargaining* – the actors form a small subset of all possible actors and therefore the scope for informed decision is more limited.
- *Information impactedness* – where information is not freely available it might be used in an opportunistic way by one of the parties.

Both the degree of difficulty and the resultant cost is increased when the following features are associated with the transaction:

- *Asset specificity* – this is where particular assets are uniquely associated to one transaction. These can be natural or technical resources; physical assets (buildings and equipment); knowledge bases and operating procedures. Some are visible while many are intangible but possibly more important.

- *Uncertainty* – as to what the transaction is all about and what performance is required.
- *Infrequency* – if seldom undertaken, no party has an opportunity to learn how to transact more effectively and might spend time coming back to base level capability.

Note in passing, that Partnership Sourcing has impact on many of these costs.

The essence of transactional cost economics is that when these costs are high, organizations will tend to internalize them in the belief that bringing the transactions into the one, now vertically integrated, organization will reduce or eliminate and certainly control these costs. In manufacturing terms they decide to 'make'.

Where these costs are not perceived to be high then the efficiency of the market is assumed to be more suitable and the choice will be to 'buy'.

Vertical integration (or bureaucracy in Williamson's terms) has, since Henry Ford's River Rouge car plant, been seen as a model for total control.[3] In terms of our classifications in Chapter Three it was a true 'I' plant – 'any colour as long as it's black'. (Incidentally it was black because that colour dried fastest.) It was however totally inflexible and when General Motors changed the market-winning criteria to one supporting more variety Ford nearly went out of business while building a replacement production system.

Vertical integration is supposed to have the advantages listed in Table 4.1 and the disadvantages shown in Table 4.2.[4]

Let us look at the items in Table 4.1 in more detail.

Control is a major driver in the belief that information about transformation process costs are visible and not in anyone's interests to manipulate. This would be fine if it were not for political game-playing, turf wars and fast-track careerists.

Control of quality is also assumed to be easier since each party will have had similar training and use standard procedures but we now know that systems are not the complete answer. The parties must still want to satisfy their customers.

Quantity of supply is a powerful argument in any capacity constrained situation. Where supply might be limited, vertical integration ensures that any discrimination is not against the parent organization, and might be used aggressively against any competitor dependent on a common supply

- **Control**

  Uncertainty reduction
  Costs
  Quality of supply
  Quantity of supply

  Convergent expectations

  Reduced probability of opportunism

  Reduced probability of externalities
  Dependence on monopoly suppliers
  Protect important proprietary/competitive knowledge

  Ease of conflict resolution
  Easier to enforce/monitor internal compliance
  More readily available rewards internally

- **Communication**

  Improved co-ordination of processes

  Greater goal congruence

- **Cost**

  Economies of scale through avoidance of intermediaries
  Procurement
  Sales promotion
  Distribution

  Process integration
  Technical or physical integration
  Improved asset utilisation

  Avoid switching/transaction costs

Table 4.1   Advantages of Vertical Integration
Source: Ellram L, 'Supply Chain Management: The Industrial Organization Perspective',
IJPD & LM, 21.1

process. There is a suspicion that the microchip shortages which frequently appear are used in this way. Quantity should also be ensured with no excess through better communication as noted lower in Table 4.1.

Convergent expectations. As part of the one organization it is to be hoped that conflicts of interest do not occur but the politics still appear, especially in multinationals where the local interest is great when bidding for the product mandate against other locations.

Reduced probability of opportunism. Vertical integration forces supply chain partners to see the objective in the longer term since they are bound together and cannot go for the game-player's pre-emptive strike – not in pricing matters at any rate.

Dependence on monopoly suppliers. Integration in this sense eliminates any possible aggressive actions.

Protect important proprietary/competitive knowledge. This is a fundamental advantage which not only aids the parent organization but denies access to others, so the benefit is doubled. This relates not just to product but to processes as well and is often a better protection of intellectual monopoly than patents or copyright statements.

Easier to enforce/monitor internal compliance. At the end of the day in vertical integration all doors and records can be opened and the authority/ responsibility structures are clear and understood. This needs to be created in partnering structures.

More readily available rewards internally. Control of measurement and rewards systems can link performance to reward directly. In partnership this can be true but needs more creative thought to define the criteria.

Greater Goal Congruence. As one organization all should be headed in the same direction but supply partners to different customer partners might suffer some conflicts of objectives.

Economics of Scale through avoidance of intermediates. In each of the linked areas the transaction contact people at each location can be reduced in vertical integration if roles overlap. Scale factors in volume can allow different price/cost structures, e.g. quantity discounts.

Technical or physical integration. Multiple resources can be rationalized in the supply chain while in the product range overlaps can be eliminated and standardization spread through a coherent product range. Physical flows can be optimized.

Improved asset utilization. Coordination and scale effects can have positive benefits and joint effort can fill capacity.

Avoid switching/transaction costs. A major justification for vertical integration.

In Table 4.2 we see the potential disadvantages of vertical integration. These disadvantages are actually being viewed from a number of perspectives. At times the problems are for the vertically integrated

- **Limiting competition**

  More difficult for non-integrated firms to enter business

  Weaken non-integrated competitors

  Inability of vertical integration to replicate market incentives
  Less awareness of market issues
  Size preserving tendency

  Internal information distortion

- **Diseconomies**

  Balancing scale economies
  Volume requirements vary by process
  Firm has insufficient volume to achieve scale

  Inability of management to control large organisation effectively

  Limits on span of control
  Increased inefficiency

  Increased difficulty in communication
  Large size of firm
  All communication cost borne internally

- **Risk**

  Asset concentration
  Exit barriers

  Perpetuate obsolete processes

  Exaggerate synergies

Table 4.2   Disadvantages of Vertical Integration
Source: Ellram L, 'Supply Chain Management: The Industrial Organization Perspective',
IJPD & LM, 21.1

organization itself. Sometimes the disadvantage is to the wider community because in some way the societal benefits are limited.

More difficult for non-integrated firms to enter business. This is actually great news for the vertically integrated organization, but if we believe in competition in markets as a spur to improvement, such barriers to entry for newcomers limit that process.

Weaken non-integrated competitors. Similar argument to the above. These two factors suggest that being excluded from the vertically integrated organization or its supply chain cousin is a severe and perhaps fatal disadvantage.

Less awareness of market issues. Self-satisfaction and self-limiting objectives can seep into the organization to its ultimate detriment. Many large organizations benchmark against other parts of themselves rather than against the best of breed wherever that is to be found.

Size-preserving tendency. Like any bureaucracy the internally focused and empire-building managers can allow units to continue at too high a resource base for their value-adding contribution.

Internal information distortion. We alluded to this before where careers depend on looking good at the corporate review sessions irrespective of the reality hidden somewhere in the vast dinosaur of the organization.

Volume requirements vary by process. We want materials to flow at high speed through all the processes but if capacity and flow values are incapable of balance we introduce inventory buffers and control system wastes to manage the disrupted flow.

Firm has insufficient volume to achieve scale. The technological benefits of scale exist but the market-required volume keeps the requirement below the next scale threshold.

Inability to control large organization. If control is only exercised by the few over the many, the combinatorial complexity makes the task impossible. Smaller units and devolved responsibility can help anywhere.

Limits on span of control. In pure control terms one superior cannot manage large numbers of subordinates. This is similar to the above category and the practice of empowerment can make the current de-layering of management structures possible.

Communication costs through sheer size. More people and more locations means much more communication linkage and potentially more errors and misunderstandings. All of these are internal costs.

Asset concentration. The scale effects might suggest concentration for efficiency reasons when dispersion closer to actual need may be more effective.

Exit barriers. Unless past investment is truly seen as a sunk cost the danger is that the commitment to the status quo means that abandoning that investment is often delayed until too late.

Perpetuate obsolete processes. For a number of the above reasons new technologies might be slow to infiltrate an organization. It can often be seen that a former technology leader fails to react quickly to new innovations and a new start-up company captures the early market opportunity.

Exaggerate synergies. The justification for the vertical integration decision might have used this argument but synergy is a difficult concept to operationalize. Vertical integration can progress backwards up the supply chain or forwards through distribution to customers – Ford went all the way from raw materials to final customer.

> **Note that Partnering has the potential to deliver the benefits of vertical integration but avoids the need to own each of the transacting parties.**

However there remains the issue of how you influence such parties. That is to say, what incentives can be used to shape these parties in ways beneficial to your business? These are bound into the agency contracts put in place by the parties.

The Ford example provides another criteria which we will use in addition to the transaction cost ones to categorize types of structures. This is the degree of flexibility in both organizational and resource terms. We can therefore see, in Table 4.3, that high asset specificity, high transaction uncertainty, occurring relatively frequently, tends to suggest that vertical integration is appropriate, but the result is less flexibility in organizational and resource terms as Table 4.2 also demonstrates. Low asset specificity with low uncertainty at any frequency suggests minimal interaction and a market solution. Partnering is our name for the intermediate form but is not one of the fourteen names found by Mari Sako when she reviewed the literature.[5] Partnering has medium asset specificity (i.e. some things are unique and related only to the partner); low transaction uncertainty (both parties must work to remove any misunderstandings); high frequency of

	Asset Specificity	Transaction Uncertainty	Frequency of Interaction	Flexibility
Market	Low	Low	High/Low	High
Partnering	Medium	Low	High	Medium
Vertical Integration	High	High	High	Low

Table 4.3 Organizational Structures and Transaction Costs

transactions (otherwise why bother?) but still retains some flexibility on both sides.

Of course, not every set of transactions in an organization will fit into one or other of these classifications so we end up with a mixture of some transactions deliberately kept in-house, some left to be dealt with by market processes and, (the thesis of this book) many more increasingly being seen as more effective if done in the Partnering mode.

A major consideration now revolves around the decision about those transactions which we always internalize. Torger Reve[6] describes these as internal contracts and argues that from the viewpoint of the boundary between what is in-house and what is not, the efficient decision is to limit the internal transactions to those core skills having high asset specificity which significantly contribute to competitive advantage in the market. (Note that as already indicated these assets can be both tangible and intangible and the more they relate to human skills the less easy they are to quantify – a point we return to in Chapter Seven.)

This concern also reflects part of the 'Excellence' message,[7] which suggests that companies re-focus on their core competences ('get back to the knitting') and out-source everything else.

If however the core skills are less than the total necessary to be a player in a particular market, they have to be associated with complementary skills offered by other parties to whom they may well be core. But once part of a partnering relationship, such skills are medium asset specificity to both parties. (There is some blurring of distinctions here since we will argue that in a partnering relationship some of the interpersonal bonding of understanding and communication between parties is in fact a highly specific asset without which the rest will founder, but for the moment let us continue on this path.)

As in all business situations the strategic decisions, about what is core and should be retained and what is peripheral and can be purchased in the market or subject to a partnering agreement, are only ever 'correct' at a given point in time and it may well be that the boundaries ebb and flow. This has always been seen from the customer's point of view as legitimate so that in times of economic downturn what was previously outsourced in the market is brought back in-house to make some contribution to overhead recovery. This will not be so easy to do when these goods or services are subject to a partnership sourcing agreement with an extended life cycle. All the more reason, then, for care and clarity in the formulation of these strategies. We also highlighted earlier the dangers of not defining core competences clearly enough such that a skill is externalized with no monitoring or recovery potential of that skill's evolution in the outside world.

Role of trust

Trust between business parties takes three forms which Sako uses to investigate the market transaction (called Arms Length Contractual Relation) and the partnering approach (called Obligational Contract Relation). Contractual trust is the process which limits the lawyer's income. In effect, contractual trust is the belief that the other party will keep its promises and perform according to the agreement. Failure to do so might instigate litigation but by that time the damage is done and the additional cost involved in trying to obtain restitution can be hard to justify – nevertheless the wrong-doing is deeply felt by the aggrieved party. The second type is competence trust which is the belief that what the other party promised, they are actually able to deliver. In quality terms high competence trust would allow for the elimination or reduction of goods inwards inspection activities. The third type of trust is extremely important to Partnership Sourcing and that is goodwill trust. In this there is a belief on both sides that the other party is sufficiently committed to the relationship that they are prepared to do more than is contractually expected and will not expect prior or even immediate recompense for doing so. This aspect was often measured (albeit in one direction as we might expect) in Vendor Rating Schemes when the rather intangible 'service' category was evaluated. The key phrase above was 'both sides' and vendor rating is in one direction only.

High levels of developed trust (i.e. not blindly given without patterns of evidential behaviour) affect the transaction costs in any relationship, potentially reducing the number of them (understanding and definition is clearer), the need to monitor (as in the quality inspection example) and in the supply chain wastes of Chapter Three, especially those involved in second-guessing and building inventory buffers at the transaction points.

Interestingly, Sako's investigation of UK business found amounts decreasing from contractual through competence to goodwill. Given a consistent under-investment in people skills and capital investment, competence trust requires significant effort to improve. Goodwill trust can support mutual efforts on the competence front and in the meantime is itself enhanced. Sako therefore believes, as we do, that trust can be deliberately improved between carefully chosen and managed partners.

Strategic management

Torger Reve argues that the Porter positioning model[8] shown in Figure 4.1 is an incomplete definition of strategy, focusing not on enhanced consumer welfare but on how to restrict competition by raising barriers to market entry and thus increase the firm's profits.

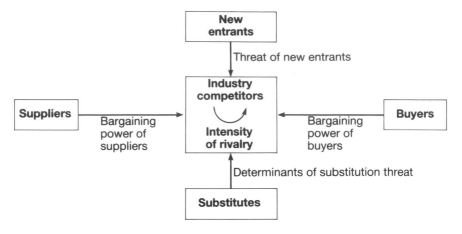

Figure 4.1   Competitive Positioning Model

Source: Porter ME, *Competitive Strategy: Techniques for Analyzing Industries and Competitors*, The Free Press, 1980.

What is missing from this view is any detailed discussion at the level of the firm. It is therefore not a sufficient definition of strategy. Much of what we have discussed so far constitutes a contract theory of the firm which is defined as being a function of the nexus of internal contracts around the core skills, along with the interorganizational contracts which define and manage the external complementary skills. In more common terms strategy consists of a merging of Porter's positioning within an industry with the contract theory of the firm which defines how far the firm's contractual arrangements extend. The range along the internal (vertical integration) and external (market) continuum is shown in Figure 4.2.

A decision to move to a more vertically integrated structure can be implemented by significant investment in new equipment and people skills to

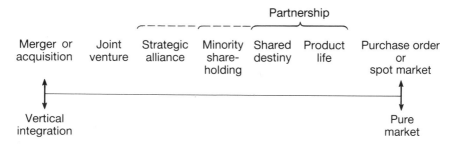

Figure 4.2   The Inter-Organizational Relationship Continuum

create the capability inside, which was once outside. Conversely, and usually faster, it is possible to invest in another organization's existing capability through merger with them or by arranged or hostile acquisition. A less all-encompassing approach is to collaborate in a third formal organizational structure as a Joint Venture. These can exhibit many features of our intermediate partnering model especially in the complementary skills criteria, but joint ventures can also be entered into between more equal partners for other reasons indicated in Table 4.4. Note that in Contractor's terms vertical quasi-integration is our partnering model.[9]

Joint ventures and alliances (JV&A)

Let us examine the contents of Table 4.4 in more detail. Here again there are contributions from a pure joint venture viewpoint that might be obtainable in the partnering relationship. Note that alliances are essentially the same vehicle as joint ventures but without the formal creation of a discrete offspring organization by the parent organizations. They are created for many of the same reasons as joint ventures but with perhaps a more deliberately open exit door. The categories listed in Table 4.4 intertwine with the following generic process drivers.

Technology development in many complex products means that the truly innovative system comes from the integration of state-of-the-art improvements in a wide range of core technologies. In any one organization the effort needed to remain state-of-the-art across a number of technologies is likely to be impossible. This is true in the aerospace, automotive and information technology industries, and in civil engineering, raw materials exploration and development, and process plant construction.

Another consideration in this is that if the technological development trajectory is not clear it may well be wise to keep involved with some of the strategic degrees of freedom by being part of different sets of development ventures until it becomes clearer which of the available new technologies stands a real chance of market success. In this way participatory organizations take 'options' on new technologies. (The success of the Japanese Ministry of Trade and Industry (MITI) is thought to be more based on organizing precompetitive collaborative technological research among clubs of industrial companies than the perception that they dictate to industry what they should do next.)

Market manipulation. JV&A can be used to gain entry into a strange or restricted market and to create higher barriers to entry to those markets for direct competitors.

- **Risk Reduction**
  Product portfolio diversification
  Dispersion and/or reduction of fixed cost
  Lower total capital investment
  Faster entry and payback

- **Economies of Scale and/or Rationalization**
  Lower average cost from larger volume
  Lower cost by using comparative advantage of each partner

- **Complementary Technology and Patents**
  Technological synergy
  Exchange of patents and territories

- **Co-opting or Blocking Competition**
  Defensive joint ventures to reduce competition
  Offensive joint ventures to increase costs and/or lower market share for a third company

- **Overcoming Government-mandated Investment or Trade Barrier**
  Receiving permit to operate as a 'local' entity because of local partner
  Satisfying local content requirements

- **Initial International Expansion**
  Benefit from local partner's know-how

- **Vertical Quasi Integration**
  Access to materials
  Access to technology
  Access to labour
  Access to capital
  Regulatory permits
  Access to distribution channels
  Benefits from brand recognition
  Establishing links with major buyers
  Drawing on existing fixed marketing establishment

Table 4.4 Strategic Contributions of Joint Ventures
Source: Contractor F J and Lorange P, *Cooperative Strategies in International Business: Joint Ventures and New Technology Partnerships Between Firms*, Lexington Books 1988

One wave of Japanese inward investment to the UK followed anti-dumping concerns in Europe. A number of Nissan's Japanese suppliers have formed joint venture companies with EC companies and set up supply plants on Nissan's factory-side supplier park. The strategic alliance in the computer industry to promote open systems was seen as an attempt to break the strength of proprietary systems and therefore the stranglehold on the market held by some of the major companies.

Operational cost reductions. In addition to those listed in Table 4.4 there can also be rationalization of production geographically or by specialist groups. What can result is a form of global sourcing where the different manufacturing tasks are concentrated in one region to supply a variety of collaborating

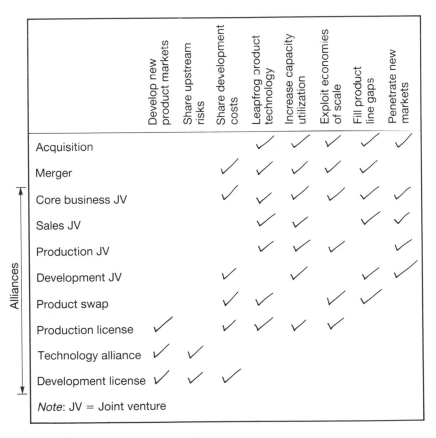

Figure 4.3 Strategic Options in Joint Ventures and Alliances
Source: *Technology Strategies*, MCB, July/August 1993.

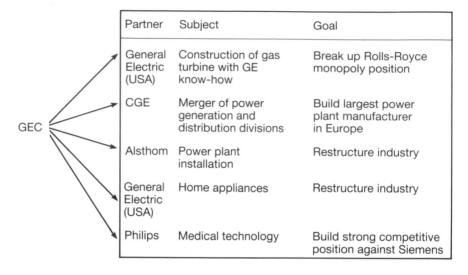

Partner	Subject	Goal
General Electric (USA)	Construction of gas turbine with GE know-how	Break up Rolls-Royce monopoly position
CGE	Merger of power generation and distribution divisions	Build largest power plant manufacturer in Europe
Alsthom	Power plant installation	Restructure industry
General Electric (USA)	Home appliances	Restructure industry
Philips	Medical technology	Build strong competitive position against Siemens

Figure 4.4 Alliance Marketing Goals for GEC
Source: *Technology Strategies*, MCB, July/August 1993.

organizations in other regions. The total supply chain costs of such global sourcing can be difficult to quantify however.

Each of these aspects is captured in Figure 4.3 and Figure 4.4

The different alliance options shown in Figure 4.3 expand out our simple joint venture and alliance to demonstrate that more strategic considerations are possible. In Figure 4.4 we see how GEC has set strategic marketing goals for their alliances.

The production sharing benefits are well captured by IBM's John Gillett.[10]

> To react effectively to demand, we are having to team up with niche technology leaders, companies who have reached a higher degree of specialization in particular areas than us.
>
> These partners include suppliers with whom we participate in joint ventures and also, more and more frequently, partners with whom we will share production facilities and alternate generations of technology to optimize our production runs.
>
> An example of this new type of relationship is IBM's agreement with Siemens and Toshiba on the manufacture of semiconductor memories. While one partner is making 64MB chips, another partner invests in production facilities for the next generation 256MB chips and the third is laying the foundations for the next generation after that.

By pooling both development and manufacturing resources, all three partners are maximizing their investment in expensive production facilities and maintaining their competitive edge by reducing development leadtimes and costs.

As a wide-ranging example, Mr Fumio Sato, President and CEO of Toshiba Corporation said:

> Toshiba is actively involved in international alliances.
>
> For example, in electronic components we have a very successful joint venture with Motorola to produce DRAMs and microprocessors in Japan. More recently, Toshiba and IBM Japan began producing 10.4 inch TFT-LCDs for use in PCs.
>
> Moreover, Toshiba produces 1-megabit DRAM wafers from Motorola's facility in Scotland, which are then assembled at our semiconductor facility in Germany for sale in the European market. With Siemens and IBM, we have entered an agreement to jointly develop the process technology for 256 megabit DRAMs, which will have the capacity to store the entire works of Shakespeare and Goethe, together with Japanese literary masterpieces such as *The tale of Genji*, the *Manyoshu* and the *Kokinshu* – with enough space left over for a typical edition of the Financial Times.
>
> We have also joined with Apple Computer to develop a CD-ROM-based multimedia player, and have a limited partnership with Time Warner for films, cable TV and software.
>
> In alliances with European companies, Toshiba has established a joint venture company with Ericsson for digital mobile telecommunication systems in Japan. We also have a joint venture with Thomson in Singapore for the production of VCRs.
>
> (*Financial Times* October, 30 1992)

The final driver is associated with **organizational learning**. This can be in each of the contribution and driver areas and can be significant enough such that they are justified even if defined operations' activities are not able to break even. Here again the definition of core skills becomes important especially if a collaborator is able and willing to learn from you and then set up as a competitor to you. Obviously the different forms of trust discussed above are relevant here too.

From the above discussion and from Table 4.4 it is clear that many of the contributions are equally possible in a Partnership Sourcing relationship and even highly technical design and development issues can be regarded as suitable candidates for classification as peripheral (in this sense) and better handled by the external experts. Of particular interest is the development of system integrators who take on much more responsibility from their customer companies and this is described in more detail in Chapter Five.

Let us now complete our discussion of Figure 4.2. As we move further into the intermediate forms between vertical integration and markets we move into the main area of concern in this book. Here the minimal involvement may be for the life of a particular product, perhaps evolving to the situation where the partner will remain so for as long as economic success continues and almost regardless of where technological change leads. The dotted links indicate that such partnerships might also have some exchange of equity and in terms of new product development has much similarity with strategic alliances.

We can now return to Torger Reve's new strategic management since by putting the possibility of collaborative forms of interorganizational structures together with Porter's positioning model we have a new definition. 'Strategy consists of critical skills and relationships held together by appropriate incentives. Skills and relationships need to be created, maintained and developed, and efficient boundaries have to be established to economize on transaction costs.'[11] From this definition a modified form of the Porter 5 force model is created with the replacement of the central competition box of the Porter model with the concept of the strategic core as discussed above. This is shown in Figure 4.5.

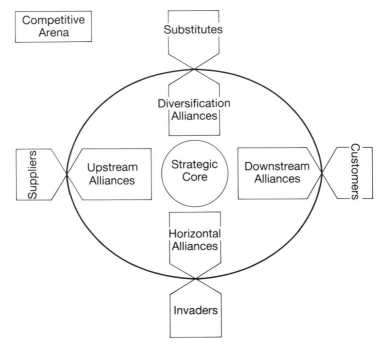

Figure 4.5 Strategic Contract Positioning Model

Source: Reve T, 'The Firm as a Nexus of Internal and External Contracts', in Aoki M, Gustafsson B and Williamson OE (eds), *The Firm as a Nexus of Treaties*, Sage, 1990, 155.

Here the horizontal alliances are more likely to be of the joint venture or alliance type and might relate to market manipulation as discussed above. Diversification alliances can allow an organization to move into new competitive arenas perhaps as the outcome of a technology development alliance. In similar fashion new product development within a partnership can open up further opportunities to market the newly developed capabilities of a supplier. In the terms used here Reve's upstream and downstream alliances would relate to Partnering along the supply chain.

The strategic process developed above is contiguous with a network concept of business strategy which argues that rather than discuss a business environment as an abstract concept we should focus on the relationships an organization forms with other entities in the wider environment. In this sense, it is these relationships which provide the business 'context'. This context is enacted or created by these interorganizational relationships and in a way define the organization. The continuous interactions with immediate counterparts are also conditioned by the counterpart's own unique sets of relationships with other entities and thus 'an organization's performance is conditioned by the totality of the network as a context, i.e. even by interdependencies among third parties'.[12]

Thinking about 'context' as a key ingredient of strategy forces organizations to engage in an active process of learning from relationship experiences and using this to inform organizational procedures, norms and behaviours which allow individual actors in the organization to react in desirable and consistent ways when, for example, an unprogrammed demand is made requiring the exercise of initiative and goodwill.

The role of the relationship in defining the organization is also used by the International Marketing and Purchasing group (IMP) whose concentration on the interaction between buyers and sellers follows a network model but called by them an interaction model. In a sense we have gone rapidly from a very large picture of networks of interconnected organizations interacting to create their strategic context, to a focus on what, in Partnering terms, is the customer–supplier link in the chain.[13] That being said, the model shown in Figure 4.6 does capture some features which are both consistent with our partnering model and with the strategic network approach. Note however that the exchange episodes in the figure do not include the technical, equipment or personnel transfers which can be seen in the partnering model and were discussed in Chapter Three.

The role of learning

At a number of points in the discussion so far the importance of learning has

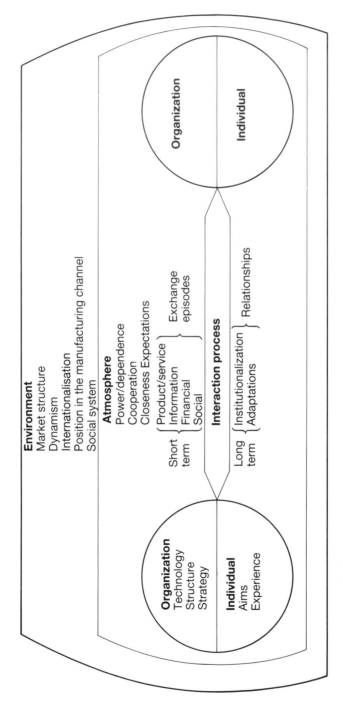

Figure 4.6 The IMP Interaction Model

Source: Ford ID (ed), *Understanding Business Markets: Interaction, Relationships, Networks*, Academic Press, 1990.

been touched upon. It is the basis of competence trust, it is a reason for joint ventures and alliances as well as the way in which relationship transactions can grow to support goodwill trust and the strategic value of the network. Learning permits knowledge transfer and development and creates new opportunities especially associated with the continuous improvement concepts we discussed earlier.

Others see learning as even more fundamental and Ronnie Lessem describes the 'next business frontier' of a series of transformations to business as a learning community.[14]

Lessem's approach brings together pragmatism (experiments), rationalism (abstractions), humanism (collaboration) and holism (systems) approaches by using action learning inside the learning company, rationalism inside the learning (core) organization, collaboration as the characteristic of the networks we have been describing and all utilizing the principles of Peter Senge[15] as the holistic approach to a learning system which combines knowledge disciplines. One other input to Lessem's model comes from Shosana Zuboff's work concerning the sentient knowledge base for the learning community.[16] This argues for learning focused by the needs of strategy and information systems developments based on what is referred to as 'informating' where new information technologies are used to re-skill people. In such processes, organizational class systems tend to decline in favour of a more unified 'professional career' for all the organizational members while the need for more active communication and interactive learning calls for active social system development.

A number of these issues are relevant to us later as we discuss the challenges of creating the effective partnerships that we believe will be so important to business success. For the moment, let us return to Peter Senge whose approach is less 'global' than Lessem's but carries within it key messages for the ways in which relationship change processes can be carried through.

Lessem provides a concise snapshot of Senge's five disciplines.

- Personal mastery is the discipline of continually clarifying and deepening vision, of focusing energies, of developing patience, and of seeing reality objectively. As such it is the learning system's spiritual foundation.
- Mental modelling is the discipline with mental models – of people and institutions – starting with 'turning the mirror inwards', that is, learning to unearth mental pictures of the world and bringing them to the surface and hold them to rigorous scrutiny. It also includes the ability to carry on 'learning-based' conversations that balance inquiry and advocacy.
- Shared vision involves unearthing shared 'pictures of the future' that foster genuine commitment and enrollment rather than compliance. In mastering this

discipline, leaders in certain organizations and in whole societies learn the counterproductiveness of trying to dictate a vision.

- Team learning, as a discipline, starts with 'dialogue', whereby members of a team, within and across organizations, suspend assumptions and enter into a genuine 'thinking together'. To the ancient Greeks, dia-logos meant a free flowing of meaning through a group, allowing the group to discover insights not attainable individually.
- Systems thinking is the fifth discipline. It is the discipline that integrates the four others, turning them into a coherent body of theory and practice. For example, a visionary leader without systems thinking ends up painting lovely pictures of the future with no deep understanding of the forces that must be mastered to move from here to there. Systems thinking also needs the disciplines of building shared vision, mental models, team learning and personal mastery to realize its potential.

Put in the language of partnering and the experiences of SCMG in reporting their Relationship Improvement Process in Chapter Seven, we can see that:

- personal mastery is related to the concepts of continuous improvement and self-development
- mental modelling will encompass the change in world view from adversarial relationships to collaborative ones
- shared vision captures such concepts as co-destiny, supplier for life, partnership
- team learning is fundamental to building collaborating relationships and in Chapter Seven is key to the relationship improvement planning process
- systems thinking is really what this book, and this chapter in particular, is all about.

We have been arguing that moving away from the discrete market transaction towards a supply chain of repeated transactions, as part of a network of supply chain organizations in which the relationships define context and strategy, is all part of no longer seeing 'us and them' but of seeing the whole complex interaction. It is rather as if we have moved progressively from microbiology to astronomy as our system boundaries have been drawn increasingly wider. Perhaps the analogy continues to have utility, for as individual atoms, cells or people we can have limited impact if the scale is too large. Undoubtedly however, through directed effort and organization a collaborative group of smaller units can most certainly impact their immediate surroundings.

We therefore argue that moving towards partnership sourcing along an appropriate supply chain can produce the kinds of ripples through the business world that will have great impact – positively for the collaborators and negatively for competitors in the other chains. The issues raised by the subject lie at the heart of strategic management theory and practice and as such represent an opportunity for significant strategic advantage for those successfully deploying them.

SUMMARY

- Transactional economics helps frame an understanding of the strategic choices which lie on the continuum from vertical integration through Partnership to pure market transactions.

- Partnering reduces transaction costs and provides the benefits of integration without ownership.

- Joint ventures and alliances share some features of partnership sourcing but can be entered into for different reasons, associated with technology development; production sharing and size effects; and market manipulation.

- By adding a new contract theory of the firm to Porter's positioning model, a new strategic contract positioning model is created which sets Partnership Sourcing, core competence and organizational boundary management in a business context.

- In much of this the importance of organizational learning comes to the fore and Senge's five disciplines provide a framework for later developments.

In the next chapter we will look in more detail at the two opposing viewpoints of adversarial and collaborative approaches before further development of the collaborative paradigm.

5

OLD AND NEW ORGANIZATIONAL FORMS

In this chapter we will examine

- the different operating paradigms associated with adversarial and collaborative relationships

- the nature of a win-win relationship and the structure of the Japanese Keiretsu supply infrastructure

- the barriers to change to this approach.

At this stage in the book we should perhaps retrace some steps to bring into a clearer focus the different paradigmatic approaches being considered here.

We have been arguing that traditional Western practice in managing the players in a supply chain is not suited to new market requirements. In addition it is wasteful of resources and effort and even more fundamentally, drags overall performance backwards instead of promoting continuous improvement. When we examine the detailed features which have been associated with the traditional approaches we also see the impact that a change to collaboration can have across many different areas of the business activity.

In order to better compare and contrast the two approaches we will use the same framework of categories. The first is time-span of interaction. The second two relate to personal attitudes and behaviour exhibited by the players in each organization. The final two relate to the organizational processes and measurements employed.

Time span of interaction – adversarial

- The interaction is regarded as taking place in one discrete event, isolated from other actual transactions or even memories of transactions. Of course the truth is that the parties do have memories and use these to inform their tactics in negotiations.

- Contracts or purchase orders extend only for a few months at a time (at most). Without any longer term guarantees of business, suppliers have to recover all of their costs in the one transaction. For similar reasons suppliers cannot justify any additional expenditure which would only be repaid using future cash flows, i.e. beyond the current contract period.
- Buyers incur low costs if they choose to change suppliers.
- Supply sources are frequently changed, often after open tender quotation exercises which are used to force unit prices down by playing one supplier off against another. Without any guarantees, suppliers must bid for more work than they have capacity to supply and expect only to win a given proportion to fit their capacity.

Time-span of interaction – collaboration

- Interactions form a continuous transaction history over an extended time-scale. Without the need to end an individual transaction absolutely evenly on each side, each party can afford to carry the obligation into the next transaction in the expectation of fair treatment to restore the balance
- Contracts or supply agreements are for an extended life and are guaranteed as much as they sensibly can be. Suppliers are suppliers at least 'for the life of the part'. The longer anticipated cash flow can be used to justify additional investment for cost reduction purposes or product development.
- Expense of switching suppliers is very high and will take considerable amounts of time. Very much a last-resort option when all else has failed. Re-sourcing decisions are infrequent.
- Single sourcing on part (but not often on whole commodities) provides benefits of consistency to both sides.

Personal attitudes – adversarial

- Expertise valued as individual property to be protected and only offered as part of a financial transaction.
- Centralized authority in customer with control exerted by negotiators fearful that someone else will give too much away in the deal.
- Purchasing power used explicitly and often in threatening manner by customers while supplier uses threat of disrupted supply as bargaining ploy.

- Buyer completely specifies their requirement down to the last detail with no interest in or acceptance of alternative suggestions. Supplier has given up making suggestions since no-one has listened or blamed head office design team rigidity or qualifying process for failure to act.
- Suppliers of similar products are regarded as homogeneous, distinguished only by the price that can be negotiated from them. Active searching for new suppliers who could undercut existing prices is a major role for procurement function.
- Suppliers are passive, doing only what they are directly asked to do. They will respond if prodded hard enough but do not volunteer.
- Interaction between organizations at the beginning of supply (bidding process) and then only when problems occur later on.
- Stress imposed by customer and high levels of uncertainty about the future and the outcome of bids and negotiations.

Personal attitudes – collaboration

- People involvement as wide as possible with a willingness to share, train and develop others for their own sakes, not explicitly tied to an immediate quid pro quo.
- Authority devolved to those most directly relevant. Production line workers empowered to contact their supplier's opposite numbers to order parts or discuss quality issues.
- Power is recognized as two-edged and in both sets of hands, so is kept in the background and not used or even threatened – not seen as a solution to most problems.
- Suppliers are highly differentiated and recognized as such. Individuals identify with counterparts and organizations are seen to offer services not provided by many or any others.
- Both sides actively working for improvements to help themselves and each other with agreed shares of benefits.
- Interactions frequent and not just problem-driven. Some are information-sharing and aimed at preventing difficulties. Some are explicitly for reasons of relationship-building.
- Stress self-imposed to avoid letting the partner down and to continue to develop and improve as fast as possible to keep the link to the partner strong and healthy.

Behaviours – adversarial

- Individual focus is on personal gain even if at the expense of internal as well as external contacts. Leads internally to political manoeuvring and turf wars.

- Transitory perception – that everything will change so do not try to build for the future – grab the moment and move on – to the next supplier, the next challenge, the next job position.
- Defensive of own turf or empire against all comers. Looking good is more important than doing good.
- Best form of defence often seen as attack – get the retaliation in first. Abrasive interpersonal relations not seen as a problem.

Behaviours – collaborative

- Atmosphere of mutual respect and recognition of others' situation – looks for benefits all round.
- Committed to building strength into the future, welcomes chance to be judged on pattern over time not instant snapshot response.
- Open/sharing approach welcoming input from all relevant parties wherever they come from.
- Tendency to look for and offer trust and backs this up in actions. Will fight against attempts to take advantage of others' trust.
- Focus on group's gains not simply on selfish benefits.

Organizational processes – adversarial

- Customer issues drawings, specifications, invitations to tender as finished documents unable to accept any alterations. These delivered impersonally and little discussion or interaction encouraged.
- Interactions depersonalized, cold and distant, limited only to the issues addressed by the financial need to transact for supply. Happy if all would happen as if by remote control – untouched by human hands.
- Very few people in possibly only one or two functional areas ever in contact about anything. Gatekeepers in purchasing and sales try to control, limit and filter all interorganizational communications.
- Systems unchanging and unchallenged. General feeling of stability, (over?)control and stasis.

Organizational processes – collaborative

- Shared involvement in design, capturing expertise and waste reduction potentials.
- Open information exchange about wide range of products, process,

market, technology and development issues.

- Organizations may be physically close to each other but even if not the process emphasizes building close, hands-on relationships.
- Many points of mutual contact in many functional areas. Organization structures and controls the decision-making mandate at each contact point but encourages the contact to build understanding and mutual commitment and support.
- Team based approach through cross-functional internal and cross-boundary projects. Sourcing decisions need team involvement and sign-off and re-sourcing cannot be done purely because of single criteria evaluations.
- Conscious customer strategy of investment in supplier capability through finance, people or process knowledge provision or physical transfer.

Measurements – adversarial

- Unidirectional with customer performing a vendor rating exercise which is a variation on a weighted average of price, quality, delivery and service. Such a view suggests that customer takes no responsibility for influencing the supplier's ability to perform. Suppliers do little formal evaluation of customer other than in financial terms or contract bid acceptance ratios.
- Unidimensional in reality. Since suppliers are regarded as homogeneous with only price being variable the final discussions come to be price-focused.
- Internally focused on efficiency and cost reduction – which is narrowly defined.
- Focus is on inspecting outcomes of processes and reporting (internally) on them. Multiple inspections are common, e.g. quality of incoming goods. No serious attempts to get to root causes of poor performance.
- Feedback on performance very limited if at all and often restricted to providing ammunition for the next round of price negotiations. Used for punishment not improvement – a blaming approach.
- Any successes are kept as local benefits or saved up for the negotiations. Learning not disseminated.

Measurements – collaborative

- Multidimensional trying to capture the total cost of doing business to include such things as unit price, costs of current quality and delivery performance, logistics costs and stock holding. This total acquisition cost gathers data from all relevant departments over a longer time scale.

- Use of measurement tools that look critically at both sides of a relationship to recognize the mutual responsibility for success or failure and to position the relationship on an improvement path with directions and actions indicated and agreed.
- Relationship focused on effectiveness and improvement – widely defined.
- Aim is to measure processes and inputs to processes so that an understanding of why outputs are as they are, is obtained. This understanding is tested and reapplied to aid improvement planning.
- Suppliers are regarded as self-regulating – once capability has been demonstrated. Thus multiple inspections are eliminated.
- Evaluation of improvement progress is frequent, wide ranging and used constructively in organized and frequent feedback sessions which are not blaming or excuse sessions. The evaluations set agendas for discussion and action planning not punishment.
- Successes are shared throughout the network and rewarded on an equitable basis.

As you read through these descriptions we are sure that you will have recognized some features that fitted your own organization for some of the time for certain situations. This is to be expected as most classification systems like this are unlikely to produce a perfect fit. Nevertheless as you worked your way through the lists you might well have begun to realize how far your own organization has come or how far it still has to go.

We have yet to see an organization which exhibits all the features of the collaborative approach. Not all the Japanese companies would be able to meet all the requirements. In fact, Mari Sako's findings in the UK electronics sector indicates a tendency towards what she calls the Obligational Contract Relationship (i.e. collaboration) in Japanese transplant companies but her sample also found some closer to the other extreme.[1]

At this stage in the Western development of this approach it is not surprising that the take-up has been limited. There are precipitating factors needed to provide the stimulus. We have already highlighted the market requirements whose details might vary across sectors so that some organizations may not yet have felt such pressures to change. In addition, the possibilities of the collaborative approach may not be fully realized or understood. Even if the possibilities are visible, the will or the means to change might not be in place. Finally, a collaborative approach needs a partner and all of this discussion applies to them as well.

The major features of the two approaches are gathered together into two Ishikawa (cause and effect) diagrams. Note however that in certain respects the logical link is not strictly causal since the features on the ribs of the

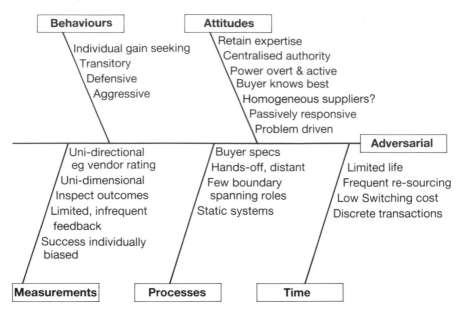

Figure 5.1 Principles of Adversarial Relationships

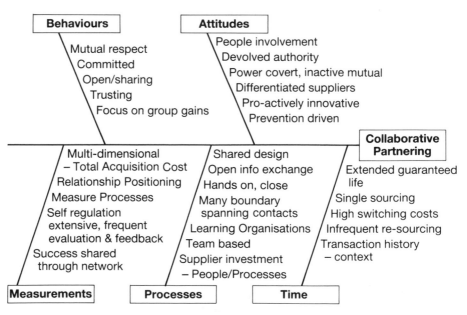

Figure 5.2 Principles of Collaborative Relationships

diagram really explain rather than cause the effect of adversarial or collaborative approaches.

In the next section we will examine how the collaborative or partnership relationship can be formed and also explore the nature of the processes which support conflict or collaboration between business partners.

THE COLLABORATIVE FORM OF CUSTOMER–SUPPLIER RELATIONSHIP

In Chapter Four we discussed the particular arguments in favour of the supply chain approach as opposed to vertical integration. Here we will think more about the actual form that a customer–supplier relationship can take. The areas of strategic alliances and joint ventures, while sharing some similarities with this sub-set of the network phenomenon, do not always carry with them the baggage of pure market transactions and often adversarial relationships at the operational level which typifies old style customer–supplier relationships. In fact, the explicitly strategic, expensive and often high risk aspects of alliances and joint ventures requires senior level investigation, decision and commitment. Too often the apparently more operational customer–supplier relationship is not regarded in the same light and is not managed properly as a result.

It is our contention that an effective, collaborative partnering relationship is every bit as strategic an issue as any other and should be as carefully nurtured.

The adjectives used above, i.e. distant, market transaction, adversarial, captures one extreme in the relationship continuum. This is the distant, hands off approach where multiple, undifferentiated suppliers offer commodity products in a competitive market place. Unless significant advantage can be gained from differentiation in terms of service or support aspects in the product/service package the likelihood is that a closer, more collaborative approach is not justified and that minimizing the transaction costs of doing business with such suppliers makes more sense. In fact it may make even more sense to let another of your more strategic suppliers handle these items for you as we shall discuss shortly.

At the other extreme, and the basis for our best practice model, is a fully functioning collaborative partnership in which both parties have their immediate needs as well as their future aspirations met as fully as it is possible (both economically and morally), to do.

The reasons an organization moves in these directions are partly to reduce the supply chain wastes that we have discussed already but it can also be for reasons similar to the strategic alliances arguments. These include concerns about: technology; market access and/or protection and size effects.

The technology dimension covers the availability of materials and specialized knowledge and support to new product development. As we have discussed before, gaining supplier expertise (especially for complex and integrated technologies where keeping up with the state of the art is a significant problem), is a major aspect of the drive for supplier design involvement at an early stage in the new product development and introduction cycle. We have also indicated that such interactions provide real learning opportunities for the partners. There needs to be a clear understanding that the intention is not to learn of others' core capabilities in order to supplant them later, for if such doubts exist then the likelihood is that information sharing will not be complete.

The market dimensions cover those situations where local sourcing requirements 'force' a presence in a market place or where customer expectations require immediately local support for Just-in-Time delivery and occupation of the provided supplier parks. Many Japanese transplants to the UK have followed this form and their suppliers have formed alliances or joint ventures with locally based companies. Thus the Japanese suppliers gain a toe hold in the new market along with insider status to appease the political concerns, while the local company gains access to new customers and very significant learning opportunities from their new partners.

A further very important consideration is the effect that a successful partnership sourcing agreement will create a major barrier to market entry for other suppliers and one which can be demonstrated to be economically justifiable in terms of reducing real costs, through the collaborative reduction in the supply chain wastes and innovative approaches. (Whether pure-market politicians will accept a route to economic benefit not dependent on an annual bidding contest in the market place, is still a moot point in both America and the European Community however.)

The final consideration is associated with size. In certain circumstances there will be advantages through size which suggest that collective presence will counteract any concerns about capability. This could well be a feature of service based groupings for example in the distribution sectors where physical presence in all the targeted locations could be a key success factor, or at least a qualifier. However relative size between the customer and the supplier is also an issue.

Relative size effects

In theory, since the customer is always right it should not matter how big that customer is in relation to its supplier but we all know (if only as individual consumers) that the world is not yet like that. A customer who takes a significant proportion of a supplier's total business will always be more equal than another one out of hundreds on their list. Thus a large difference in size in the customer's favour will be regarded by them as no bad thing and will tend to reinforce existing power perceptions.

Many companies have a policy of not taking more than say 25 per cent of any supplier's capacity to avoid the supplier becoming too dependent on the business. Such limits reinforce the belief in the supplier that the customer is likely to remove the business with little concern about its effect since the 'damage' has been contained. The damage to potential relationships is unconstrained however.

A small customer dealing with a large supplier presents different problems and opportunities. Such situations are common in supply chains as we get back towards the raw material suppliers, e.g. resins for plastic moulders or steel or aluminium for product fabrication. The situation can be further complicated by possible engineering benefits of scale in the raw material producer such that small quantity orders are simply not acceptable unless as part of a larger batch run at some future date. An associated problem is that of quantity price discounts which the small demand of the customer cannot attract.

One approach is to enlist the power of the final customer in support of the intermediate customer. In this approach the final customer moves down two levels in its supply chain to negotiate supply and price agreements for the intermediate company based on an aggregate buying pattern from the final customer spread over a number of similar supplier companies to itself who as customers of the large supplier can now call off requirements as required. This is a demonstration of a supply chain approach benefiting the whole chain – even the inflexible large supplier who can retain business which would otherwise be sourced elsewhere.

This is one answer to the question of why should a supplier listen when a customer asks for service which the supplier is not normally able to provide. In this case the super-ordinate power of the final customer was significant. In more equally based arrangements the supplier is only likely to listen if the message is sensible and believable. If the history of transactions between the two parties has been adversarial, the customer company will be obliged to demonstrate that there is a genuinely new approach being operated. Here again care is needed since many suppliers talk of other 'new' approaches in the past which went the way of all flavours of the month as company personnel or fashions changed. Why should they believe that this change will stick any more than any other has?

Learning from the best of the Japanese

The approach in Japan after the war was largely to 'get round' the American forced break-up of the major trading houses (the Zeibatsu) which were regarded as instrumental in supporting the rise of the war effort. These powerful groupings created (or reinforced) the clan or feudal approach which was the base for society. What was created to replace them was the *Keiretsu* described by Womack et al as follows.

> The Japanese companies initially were financed almost entirely by loans supplied by the big Tokyo banks and guaranteed by the American government. Since companies only had these loans and their physical assets their capital was very modest. As the economy took off and many companies became profitable, they began to worry about being bought up by foreigners. They also distrusted the arm's length stock market as the primary means of generating equity, because *they couldn't imagine a system in which there was no reciprocal obligation.* (emphasis added)
>
> To address these concerns, the growing companies of the 1950s and 1960s hit upon the idea of selling equity to each other, often with no cash changing hands. So each member of the pre-war groups, and some newcomers as well, joined the new Keiretsu in which the equity went round in a circle. . . Their stocks traded in small volumes on the highly volatile Tokyo stock market, but the stock that really counted was not for sale.[2]

The Keiretsu are also instrumental in the pyramidal structure of the supply base where it is deliberately tiered such that the major producer or Original Equipment Manufacturer (OEM) only works with a reduced set of first-level suppliers. These in turn take responsibility for managing the next level down (or back up the chain) and so on. In this way the task of the OEM is much reduced and the benefit of the Keiretsu is that the common interest in the lead customer's success is transmitted through the chain. In similar fashion the reciprocal obligation from the larger customers to the smaller suppliers means that when market conditions change the customer will 'stay with' the supplier as they adjust to the new challenges.

Within the supply chain network the relative positions of the lower level suppliers are subject to some movement relative to others' positions mainly as a result of success in innovation for the benefit of the customers. At the bottom of the pyramid, suppliers will perhaps be supplying more than one OEM so some technology and knowledge transfer can be expected. As Japanese business conditions change this effect is moving up the pyramid as organizations try to build scale effects for traditional efficiency reasons.

Within one level, supplier clubs are encouraged where there is sharing of best practices and knowledge. As an example of how these can operate consider again the case of Toyota who deliberately dual source major assemblies, e.g. brakes. The supplier clubs (called Kyoryoku Kai) work in similar ways in terms of knowledge sharing if not production scheduling. Figure 5.3 shows these complex interactions as seen by Hines which also

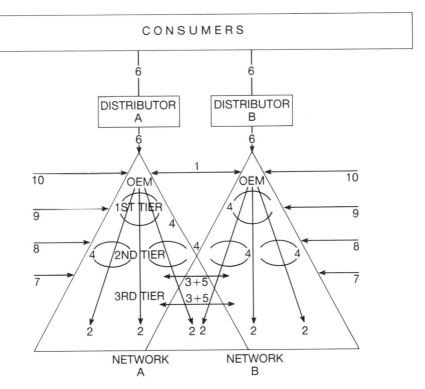

1. Creative tension between cooperation and competition, perhaps between different industrial sectors.
2. Supply chain development and OEM development by equitable profit feedback benefits.
3. Cross network benefit spread effect.
4. Kyoryoku Kai internal subcontractor development.
5. Inter-supplier rivalry to find a favoured network position.
6. The consumers changing needs and tastes.
7. New entrants.
8. Substitutes.
9. Stable long term cheap finance.
10. Government Agencies creating a developmental environment.

Figure 5.3 Japanese Supply Structures: The 10 Forces Model

Source: Hines P, 'Integrated Materials Management: a post-Porterian Paradigm?' *2nd Int Conf PSERG*, Bath, 1993.

highlights the role taken by government agencies in facilitating the inter-actions and industry structures.[3]

The importance of the first tier supplier has also been recognized in the West where the concept of system integrators has gained ground. Figures 5.4 and 5.5 show the changing nature of roles and responsibilities of the integrators. In effect they act as the Japanese first-tier suppliers to remove from consideration some of the component complexity and assembly problems from the OEM. It is in this way that sensible supplier reduction programmes are possible. The numbers can be dramatic. Womack et al indicate that a Japanese best practice car project will deal with 300 suppliers while their more traditional Western competitors deal with all of the logistical problems of 1000 to 2500!

There are large strategic opportunities to be thought about in this.

In the development of anti-skid braking (ABS), what were formerly roughly equivalent suppliers in Lucas Braking Systems and Bosch Electronics changed their relative position and market presence through Bosch becoming the systems integrator for ABS and buying from Lucas what they once supplied directly to the car companies. Yet either company could have been the integrator since neither had all of the technology and had to outsource it somewhere. For the OEM, they now have a much reduced effort and timespan of simply bolting the complete assembly, quality assured, onto their product.

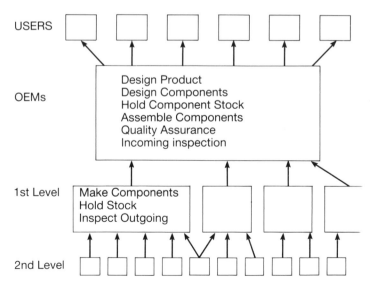

Figure 5.4 Traditional Supply Chain Structure

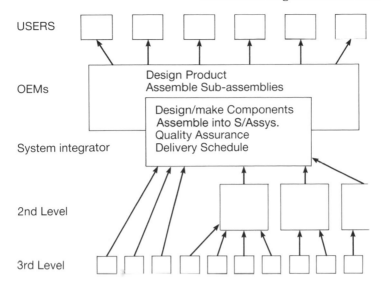

USERS

OEMs

System integrator

2nd Level

3rd Level

Figure 5.5 The Systems Integrator Chain

TYPIFICATION OF WIN/LOSE

The essence of the zero sum game is that one party's loss is the other party's gain, i.e. a win/lose outcome. Many games are like this at least on a single play of the game. Our concept of the 'free' market is very similar and we even believe that evolution supports this approach of survival of the fittest. The point however is that in many cases the game is not an isolated incident, it is rather only one in a history of transactions between the game's players so that the probability patterns should change to recognize the chances of recovery from incidences of relative disadvantage. Repeated rounds of the game also allow the parties to understand better the motivations of the other party and allow for agreements which permit more mutually acceptable outcomes.

The problem with the Western industrial market model is that what is acceptable behaviour in the real market place for the final cash customer is assumed to be best practice for the members of the supply chain who should actually be on the same team and not subject to the opportunistic behaviour of a raw competitive struggle.

In order for this to happen we are back to the consideration of potential sub-optimization in the supply chain. If the actors at particular points in the chain are only aware of their immediate surroundings and its business pressures then there is a tendency to go for the local optimum. Often this attitude is reinforced by measurement and reward systems which encourage localized self-seeking. Thus buyers who are rewarded for incremental reductions in the unit cost of items purchased, without an understanding of the total cost of supply or the interaction with quality and delivery requirements, can 'play the market' and switch suppliers frequently.

Treated in this way suppliers have no option but to play the mirror image and go for a quick hit since there may not be another opportunity to benefit. Such suppliers will not invest to improve performance or if they do will not share the improvements with their customers. Rather they will have to hold such opportunities in reserve for the next round of aggressive negotiations over prices.

Without reasonable prospects of continuing business from existing customers such suppliers are obliged to devote significant effort to the search for replacement customers and given the uncertainties inherent in the resultant 'beauty contests', the resources have to be over-allocated to allow for the low success rates.

Each of these behaviours is wasteful but are 'caused' by the economic logic of the free market which is being seen by some as not logical at all and particularly in the context of Japanese practice actually counterproductive. In fact Nissan's presentations to suppliers point out that they would rather the effort normally devoted to creating next year's business bid is devoted to continuous improvement in the expectation that next year's business will come because of such improvement activities.

TYPIFICATION OF WIN/WIN

Our colleague John Carlisle introduced us to his version of the Prisoners' Dilemma which he calls the Red/Blue game which we use in a very interesting and stimulating way to explore how competition and collaboration feels in practice.[4] This demonstrates that the risk averse, apparently rational decision mode means that ultimately no-one can win. Conversely, collaboration can pay off in the game but the issues of information, mandate and trust, along with wider considerations about what the real game is about, are difficult to come to terms with and manage. In his terms playing a Red (i.e. offering collaboration) is both risky and necessary. We have also seen this demonstrated in our dealings with suppliers and their customers and have gathered examples of playing both reds and blues on both sides. Nevertheless the important point is that in any relationship which has been typified by adversarially playing blues the customer has a major role to play in sending a different message. They have to be the ones playing red and seriously demonstrating that the rules of engagement are now changed.

That this is in fact less counter to the received wisdom in evolutionary terms as well, is demonstrated both in Axelrod's work on *The Evolution of Cooperation* and Richard Dawkins' *The Selfish Gene*. In effect survival over generations (or repeated plays of the game, or business transactions) is less about a macho quick hit, survival of the fittest mode of behaviour and more about ensuring that the other transactional partners also have a chance to survive in order that, through their survival, the first party is allowed the opportunity also to prosper. Thus Axelrod determined that the most successful strategy was the 'nice' one of 'Tit for Tat' (TFT).[5] This starts by playing red (in our terms) and then simply follows the pattern of the other players previous choice but without carrying a grudge. As Dawkins describes it '. . . it (TFT) doesn't try to beat the other player. The other player is not treated as an opponent, but as an accomplice. It is remarkable, though obvious when you think about it, that neither TFT, nor any other nice strategy can actually win a game against an opponent. It often loses, and it can never score better than a draw, because it is never the first to defect. The reason nice strategies can still end with more winnings is that their drawn games are high-scoring games, their lost games are low-scoring. While nasty guys win low-scoring games, nice guys quietly get on with accumulating their winnings in unspoken collaboration.'[6]

In partnership sourcing the collaboration should however certainly be spoken about.

By re-focusing on the medium to longer term benefits we can also begin to understand how learning curve effects will begin to flow through which will of themselves reduce the costs of operating the relationship. Until partnering is fully embedded there are certainly going to be activities which will look more like costs in the short term. These activities will revolve around the building of understanding and communications channels between the parties and while there will continue to be a need to maintain such channels the high investment up front can be expected to diminish. On a continuing basis however the monitoring of mutual satisfaction in the relationship and the incorporation of new approaches and technologies into the operating practices must be institutionalized. Joint benchmarking and market assessment studies should also avoid any tendency towards 'coziness' creeping into the situation.

In this way intelligent and considerate partners look for opportunities to assist each other to grow both in business terms and in competence. In this the suppliers have a new role since they can act as their customers' eyes and ears in a wider environment and bring to their customers' attention new developments in a pro-active way.

Suppliers will however only do this with customers who they regard as 'preferred' in the same way as customers talk of 'preferred suppliers'. Perhaps the critical strategic task for major customers is to so organize themselves that they will appeal as 'preferred customers' to the very best of the supplier companies. This is no idle threat since it is already evident that the very best supplier companies know clearly who they would choose to work with if market conditions allowed them the freedom so to do.

IF IT IS SO GOOD WHY DO MORE NOT DO IT?

Hopefully this book is demonstrating both the logic and practical applicability of the partnership sourcing approach. In business, many have also examined these factors but as yet the degree of take up of the approaches has been limited to relatively few and even there, in some cases, close questioning of their partners often indicates the rhetoric being more impressive than the practice. Why should this be?

Perhaps we should not be too surprised. What we have been describing is certainly not a quick fix and is certainly not a unifunctional solution. The number of changes necessary to gain full benefit are large and few organizations are sufficiently proficient at change management to do it without assistance.

In Kurt Lewin's work on field analysis[7] he identified a set of restraining forces which acted against any changes. From individuals they included: fear of failure, loss of status, inertia (habit), fear of the unknown and loss of friends. From a wide organizational viewpoint they are: strength of culture, rigidity of structure, sunk costs, lack of resources, contractual agreements, and strongly held beliefs and recipes for evaluating corporate actions.

These are all likely to apply to some degree in most changes but in our experience we can identify five main groups of factors which make it difficult to move in these directions. The factors are social; attitudinal; structural; organisational/managerial and procedural.

Social

Like any change there are inherent barriers associated with the perceived pain of change. Undoubtedly, if the process is complete, then much of what was once taken for granted and well understood, practised and often manipulated has had to be modified or discarded. Such a process calls into question the very being of participants, the relevance of their experience and their ability to learn and adapt.

There is an inherent comfort in existing work patterns and contact with established opposite numbers. In fact this is often true even in apparently highly adversarial situations where we have experience of people talking about suppliers consistently 'being our worst supplier for years'.

In the purchasing department, and especially in the buyer role, we also identify an enjoyment with and manipulation of power, often built and developed over many years of training and experience and it is still clear that some professionally supported workshops still fill places on traditional 'how to screw your supplier' events. Some of these are reinforced by basic attitudinal traits of the reciprocal contact personnel in the intercompany relationship.

Attitudinal

By definition most of the employed population is to some degree risk averse and at least to some degree operate their respective systems to avoid criticism or blame. There is much in the partnering approach which is potentially risky. Indeed to be a partner requires a recognition that one is to some extent dependent on the other partner and that a failure of the one adversely affects the other. In fact Glaxo describe their approach to partnership sourcing as to some extent managing failure since they could no longer walk away from a failure, they now had to be part of the solution.[8]

Closely associated with this is the tendency to be non-trusting. Often this is for very good historical reasons but all too often the mutual responsibility for problems is not appreciated.

One of our supplier companies plotted the schedule changes imposed on them by their customer and then tried to establish why the change had been imposed. In around 30% of occasions no traceable reason could be found and in another 25–30% of occasions it was simply to counteract internal problems the customer was having. The suppliers' failure to deliver against the new requirement was however carefully monitored and scored in the vendor rating scheme! Remember however that vendors of excellence need customers of excellence too! If as a customer you were to deal with your own organization as a supplier, would you buy from them?

The Western social focus on the individual rather than the group is another barrier which may well be one of the more significant ones. Then again, perhaps not, since a number of new wave American and European companies have managed to realize the development potential of their people power when encouraged and supported in teams. The training effort and supporting organizational systems to make this a reality are not trivial however and take time to be effective.

The final category in this group is the use of information as power. In non-trusting, risk-averse situations this is perhaps understandable and many careers have progressed on the basis of gathering, rationing and manipulating information but in the new situation information is both a lubricant of the relationship process and a cement for the structure of the relationship. As such its real power is as an enabler of improvements and as feedstock to the trust building process.

Organizational/managerial

Suppliers have historically been seen as a procurement issue based on the Tayloristic or Adam Smith position of division of labour. Certainly this has been true but most companies actually have a multifunctional team involved in the basic sourcing decision and purchasing can no longer simply re-source on the basis of a lower unit price without sign-off by technical, quality, commercial and logistics personnel. Partnership sourcing is not just supplier management and supplier management is not simply buying. The team also has to have some form of continued involvement if only to avoid the tendency for suppliers to treat the new approach as yet another fad to be tolerated – become fluent in – minimize its influence and get on with the 'real job of the business'.

Lack of awareness and understanding of the nature of the required changes is another issue. The pressures on current activity and the continuing general under-investment in education mean that many in organizations simply know of no other way to operate. Even if they have heard the language of the new approach they will not comprehend what it is all about. This is further complicated by a tendency to assume that because a word description sounds familiar then it follows that a previous understanding of that word in a different context can be transferred over without modification. Put this way it is so obvious and one would wonder why we see it is a barrier. However any trainer knows that the difficulty is often unlearning old practices before learning the new.

Skill bases and job roles will be modified under the new approach. While many will welcome the principles of the new approach nevertheless the change has to be staffed and once embedded in place must be maintained less the old ways creep back in. Some may not be able to make the transition and will have to be relocated in some way. External change agents may be necessary for a variety of reasons to support in-house developments.

Current operational stress is a major concern especially at times of severe recession and concern about survival. If partnering is seen as nice to have but not just yet, this misses the real competitive advantages achievable. Companies are subject to continual changes in their environment and if these changes are sufficiently severe then their natural tendency to think short term and in survival mode makes it difficult for them to do other than look after number one. This came home with a vengeance with one company who in the middle of a partnership development process came with a dictat from their corporate masters to 'get a 10 per cent cut in prices across the board'. You can imagine the reaction from their supplier company! Companies have to understand that while there will be short-term waste reduction possibilities the real benefits are more intertwined with others and more medium term. They have to see relationship building as an investment and not a cost!

Some of these organisational/managerial barriers overlap into the Structural category but there are others here as well.

Structural

Purchasing is often perceived as merely operational. This was certainly true when purchasing was little more than order placing but not when procurement spend is 60–80 per cent of total turnover and strategic partnerships are one of the differentiating characteristics of best practice companies. Purchasing's role could evolve into more of a relationship/management one with strategic partner selection and mutual performance monitoring being needed. Much of the routine purchasing can be devolved to the shop floor operational people. With continuously high quality and reliable delivery and no supplier switching investigation needed, there is reduced clerical effort needed but a greatly enhanced influence on competitiveness. One new role for the function might be to coordinate joint benchmarking exercises with partners to ensure that the continuous improvement targets are properly focused.

As organizations become leaner and cut away layers of staff in the name of employee involvement and devolution of responsibility and cost saving, we are left with fewer people to handle the day-to-day work. Lean in this context can sometimes mean under-capacity staffing. This is a classic catch-22 situation and leaves even fewer people capable of finding time to do the strategic stuff up front when the investment looks more like a cost.

Simultaneous engineering has demonstrated the importance of breaking out of serial modes of activity and forming more parallel tracks but there is comfort in clearing up one task before moving to the next. Systems to cope with multiple concurrent work tasks are clearly more complex and the mind patterns of the individuals prone to confusion but in order to achieve the time compression needed in many business areas this new approach will be needed. Of itself this factor helps explain the moves to reducing partner numbers. Many supplier-base reduction programmes are in evidence but it is not always clear if companies know why they are doing it.

By definition, partnering crosses company boundaries but the internal boundaries between functions and organizational groupings are no less real. In this, the perceived status of the purchasing function and the internal evaluation of relative worth and professionalism are more subtle boundaries to be bridged. Narrowly functional organizations need to reconsider their structural organization to fully develop and implement new approaches. A greater emphasis on the major business and process flows can guide such structural reorganization thoughts either as a review of the Deming flow of Chapter Three or as part of Business Process Re-engineering.[9]

Western companies, unless they are already committed to Total Quality and continuous improvement, are unlikely to have sufficient information to actually make informed judgements about partnering potential and realized capability. Where data is available it will be one sided (e.g. vendor rating schemes), inadequate in coverage (e.g. quality performance measures in place but delivery not monitored) and certainly not integrative across the boundaries or communicated properly as an aid to improvement. There is also a tendency to look only at the industry in which one is currently operating. Thus we find electronics buyers only looking for metal component suppliers within the group of organizations supplying other electronics companies and yet similar process skills will be supplied to companies in aerospace and automotive and such supplier companies may well be better placed in terms of having the inherent capability to be good partners. This experience-based myopia is a major reason for the reluctance to local source under the excuse that no capable source has been located. We would contend that the search has not been well enough undertaken. (This was a major finding of a research grant looking at increasing the potential for local sourcing.[10])

Procedural

For many of the above reasons a lack of commitment to the full scale of effort needed to make the many changes necessary is a well-recognized problem of this as any change process. Moving to a partnering relationship is definitely not a quick fix and a full change might last longer than some of the management team will be in their particular post. Maintaining involvement and commitment in these circumstances requires further systems support in re-sensitizing and re-orienting the new incumbents and giving them time to build the interpersonal bridges which are so important.

If this process is seen as simply a different way to operate procurement then it comes as no surprise that an overall plan to manage the change process is not put in place.

Partnering is a further manifestation of total quality but this time the effort is spread across boundaries. A coherent structure to manage the overall process is essential and leaving the process to be handled in an ad hoc fashion is to guarantee failure.

It is well demonstrated that individuals cannot change organizations on their own – they must work through a team. That team has to be properly constituted and effectively managed and must agree their mandate before entering into the overall change process. The mandate must empower the team to agree appropriate boundary spanning linkages and flows of information, technology, and people to support the legitimate needs and aspirations of the other party. The mandate team has to have responsibility to set directions and monitor achievements but they must also facilitate the change processes for the action teams set up as part of the process.

In the partnering relationship the processes of assessing each other's contribution and effectiveness has to be in place with appropriate feedback mechanisms and also social meetings. Partners should not simply meet together because there is a problem to be resolved. Rather they need to meet to build the bonds of mutual commitment and responsibility. Underlying this is the nature of the internal measurement and reward system, for most people will perform according to how they are measured. This requires careful consideration, for the relationship enhancing activities may appear to be less than optimal for individuals and unless they have a belief that those doing the measuring are properly focused it is to be expected that they will revert to the old ways.

This can happen very rapidly and inadvertently and the systems have to be robust to recover or better still avoid such results.

This section has laid out the problems to be overcome in a management of change process and in Chapter Seven we will address ways to do so and describe a structured approach to implementation of partnering relationships in the supply chain.

TRANSITIONS TO WIN/WIN

From our earlier discussions it comes as no surprise that many initiators of a

Partnership Sourcing approach are from the customer company. Often this has come from moves towards Just-in-Time manufacturing or Total Quality Management Programmes. Both of these show relatively quickly that while it is nice to put your own house in order before attacking the external challenges you simply cannot afford to work serially any more. Apart from anything else the opportunities are more numerous than any one group can sensibly address and besides that, getting your suppliers up to speed creates its own pressures to improve internally to handle the new, improved supplier's operation.

Who actually acts as the change champion inside the company is however another issue which will be discussed in Chapter Seven. For the time being let us simply understand that unless the whole organization understands and is committed to the changes in business practice required by partnership sourcing then it will go the way of previous (non) change programmes.

SUMMARY

- **Adversarial and collaborative relationships need different approaches to time, personal attitudes, behaviours, organizational processes and measurements.**

- **Working in a collaborative way mirrors the Japanese Keiretsu in some respects.**

- **WIN-WIN is the objective but there are significant barriers to change associated with social, attitudinal, organizational/managerial issues as well as structural impediments and the lack of a coherent procedure.**

In the next chapter we will look at the issues of managing change and propose our own model or project guide as an aid to implementation planning.

Part Three

MAKING THE CHANGE

6

A MODEL FOR CHANGE

> In this chapter we will examine
>
> - the nature of change and the effect the predominant style of management can have
>
> - the SCMG change model as a generic approach.

PLANNED OR EMERGENT CHANGE

There is some debate amongst management thinkers as to whether the management of change is 'valid' in the sense that perhaps it depends rather too much on prescription according to the latest 'guru' speak rather than being founded on a base of theoretical understandings of management and change itself. As David Wilson puts it:

> Change is a phenomenon which cannot be restricted solely to the 'behavioural' aspects of management learning. It needs a perspective which can blend the behavioural with the economic, the historical with the future-oriented decision making, and the political with the social and economic factors of change. Unfortunately, current thinking in the analysis of change has developed along the either/or path of skills versus context.[1]

There is an apparent dichotomy between the skills of managers in their immediate environment (of leading, directing, involving etc.) according to some new panacea skill toolbox, and the context argument which says that it is the rich tapestry of the complete system-in-interaction that creates, permits and can limit the amount of change that is feasible at that time. This is non-productive in our view.

There can surely be little doubt to practitioners, if not to the academic interpreters of their actions, that all of the features of a complex issue need to be managed with skill.

We have argued in this book, especially in Chapter Four, that a wide system view is required but the dichotomy described above exists perhaps because of a tendency to separate ends and means, and to create information and career structures which make it difficult for inhabitants of the two domains to communicate properly. This is most visible in the traditional Anglo-American split between strategic considerations of finance, business futures, markets and macro-structures (often expressed in financially oriented indicators) and the operational supply chain issues described in Chapter Three. This split is perceived to be a problem also in relations between the financial institutions of the 'City' and the operational managers inside their organizations. The failure (on both sides) is to construct a meaningful dialogue (in Senge's terms) to demonstrate the causal relationships between operational actions and financial/strategic results. Worse still, the reverse flow of desired strategic results and the supporting or restraining effects of current operational practices are not fully worked through, thus leaving the strategic vision unfulfilled while the operational people struggle with another impossible set of tasks. Terry Hill's manufacturing strategy process[2] can help bridge the gap for the organization but the evidence from the field is that few in the UK at least understand the need for it and its power to focus energy where it will be most useful.

At this point it is worth using some of the material from the Customer–Supplier Relationship Audit to highlight some of the features of the possible split between strategy and operations.[3]

Strategic and operating objectives

What kind of benefits can we realize from managing the Customer–Supplier Relationship in an improved way?

The precise benefits you aim for will be specific to your own business. But above the detail there is an important choice about the overall thrust or emphasis of an innovation. You need to know what that choice is, and which route your own organization is likely to take. You can decide if that is the route you prefer.

Before reading further, note below the main benefits which your current project is expected to achieve. Rank them, placing the benefit which *you* feel is most important to the organization at 1, the second most important at 2, and so on.

1 _____

2 _____

3 ───────────────────────────────────────

4 ───────────────────────────────────────

You will be able to compare your list with some other examples later.

From many discussions we have had within organizations about the specific benefits they expected to obtain from new approaches to management of the Customer–Supplier Relationship, we have grouped these benefits into five types:

To control quality by:

- tightening acceptance standards
- expecting suppliers to use Statistical Process Control
- developing part and/or company certifications.

EXAMPLES:

'Quality has to be perfect and is not negotiable.'

The use of Supplier of the Year Awards.

To improve delivery performance by:

- tightening time specifications
- demanding smaller, more frequent deliveries
- specifying material transportation and packaging methods.

EXAMPLES:

Delivery date minus 2 plus 0 days specification.

Unit of use containers.

To control cost by:

- charging full cost of quality problems to suppliers
- increasing stock turnover
- reducing obsolescence costs.

EXAMPLES:

Jaguar's suppliers being responsible for *all* of the warranty costs incurred when their part fails.

Pressures on inventory pipeline and the impacts of order cancellations.

To improve decision-making by:

- providing more accurate and timely information
- carrying out fuller analyses of data
- Allowing alternative actions to be assessed more fully.

EXAMPLES:

Communications from one Production Planning system to another to match capacity allocations against changing customer demands.

Electronic Data Interchange permitting short-term readjustments in supply schedules in a 'what-if' mode.

To improve market position by:

- increasing the rate at which new products are introduced
- reducing the wastes and providing opportunities for price reductions
- enhancing quality and product design.

EXAMPLES;

The company which reduced its own costs and passed these on as price reductions to its customer at a time when their competitors were seeking price increases.

'Black Box' component design where functional and location requirements – not detailed specifications – are given to suppliers whose output goes straight into the customers' products.

We group these five types of objectives as follows:

Quality/delivery/cost: an operating approach.

Here emphasis is on existing products/services; immediate problems; techniques like SPC; suppliers/customers as the enemy; reducing overall costs; clear benefits, quickly obtained.

Decision making/market position: a strategic approach.

Here emphasis is on new/modified products/service offerings; medium/long-term opportunities; focus on collaborative involvement; customer is king – but everyone has a customer; control the value add – cost reduction will follow; benefits less immediately quantifiable.

Many organizations have improved their performance dramatically by concentrating on the Operating approach and essentially gaining control where they did not fully have it before.

The *danger* is that focus on the short term ignores the opportunities and threats of global competition in many markets. It also fails to target, and therefore can never achieve, significant improvements above the current base level.

Some organizations see the development of the Customer–Supplier relationship as one which can provide just those significant improvements which are required to develop a competitive advantage and then mobilize their supply chain against the competition.

So the danger in an operating emphasis is that of lost opportunity compared with

- what your organization could be doing
- what your competitor companies may be doing.

The following example shows how one company looked not only for operational improvements in a new situation.

Local design for global markets

The company was one which had been largely an assembly, test and distribution operation for its US parent since it opened its UK plant. Local expertise had developed, however, through limited customization of the US design to cope with EC market situations.

The local engineers wanted to do their own thing, since they believed they understood their EC customers better than any US designer could.

The local group therefore designed the new product, but they wanted to source materials locally and build locally to avoid the problems they had had getting materials from the US. They therefore worked along with local supplier companies on the new product design and ensured its design for manufacture was good and that suppliers were capable from day one of supplying high quality with reliable delivery.

The thrust of this approach was **strategic**. *The relationships they built with suppliers were not just to control quality, delivery and cost, but were intended* *to mobilize the whole supply chain to grasp and satisfy the new market opportunity presented by the new product design.*

This example illustrates the strategic possibilities that new relationships can create. Managers in the buyer company realized that concentrating only on the operational aspects would have failed to motivate their suppliers to the same extent as being part of the new market opportunity.

To relate this example to your own situation you can

- complete the questionnaire and analysis below
- read the note on 'Strategist and Operationalists'
- review the questions following the note.

Management decision-making style questionnaire

This questionnaire is designed to help you analyze the dominant management decision-making style in your organization.

The twenty-four questions are divided into pairs and you have to allocate a total of ten points to each pair. Ask yourself in each case which of the two statements best describes the decision-making style of the managers in your organization *at your level and above*.

If one statement seems to describe that style give it the full ten points and give the other one zero. If on the other hand both statements could be correct in some ways, allocate the ten points accordingly. But try in each case to identify the *predominant* style and avoid giving '5 and 5' for each answer.

This is not a test with right or wrong answers. The aim is to describe the management decision-making style in your organization as accurately as possible. You may find, however, that some of these statements are worded in a way that does not quite match the way you would describe your organization. That does not matter too much. We are looking for dominant trends.

Do not spend a lot of time working out the perfect response for each pair of statements. Go through them as quickly as possible. This should take you only around five minutes. This exercise is especially useful when done by a group of people in the same organization or department. Complete the scoring individually, and then compare your results. Prepare a flip chart with two columns, one headed 'S' and the other 'O'. Group members call out their scores, compare them and discuss what that indicates about the prevailing style in the organization.

1 Objectives are on the whole expressed in general and loose terms.

2 Objectives are on the whole expressed in clear and specific terms.

3 The main emphasis is placed on the achievement of short-term goals.

4 The main emphasis is placed on the achievement of long-term goals.

5 Corporate strategy and major investments plans are kept secret until implemented because they are sensitive in industrial relations and commercial terms.

6 Corporate strategy and major investment plans are explained fully in advance to all employees because management believe they need to be kept fully informed.

7 Managers on the whole have a clear understanding of what constitutes good performance.

8 Managers on the whole have no clear understanding of what constitutes good performance.

9 Managers are always challenging the traditional ways of doing things.

10 Managers prefer proven traditional ways of doing things.

11 Changes in the Customer–Supplier Relationship are primarily designed to remove the problems associated with failures of various kinds.

12 Changes in the Customer–Supplier Relationship are primarily designed to contribute to organization strategy by improving the product or service in line with customer's needs.

13 Alterations to organization structure are common.

14 Established organization structures are rarely altered.

15 Individual managers promote changes primarily to improve the performance of the section or department for which they are responsible, on the assumption that this will ultimately benefit the organization as a whole.

16 Individual managers promote changes primarily to improve the performance of the organization as a whole, on the assumption that this will ultimately benefit the section or department for which they are responsible.

17 Supplier improvement projects typically concentrate on improving quality, delivery and cost performance.

18 Supplier improvement projects typically take human and organizational matters into account, along with performance considerations.

19 New ideas, technologies and systems are introduced slowly and cautiously to avoid disruption.

20 New ideas, technologies and systems are introduced rapidly so they can contribute as quickly as possible.

21 Managers on the whole tend to emphasize the opportunities and possibilities of change.

22 Managers on the whole tend to emphasize the doubts and uncertainties of change.

23 Investment in supplier development would only be undertaken when clear, short-term financial returns can be shown.

24 Investment in supplier development would be undertaken if the long-term benefits were thought to be worthwhile, even if short-term returns were uncertain.

Scoring:

First add up the points that you gave to statements: 2, 4, 6, 7, 9, 12, 13, 16, 18, 20, 21, 24. Your 'S' score is this sum.

Then add up the points that you gave to statements: 1, 3, 5, 8, 10, 11, 14, 15, 17, 19, 22, 23. Your 'O' score is this sum.

Then read the descriptions below. If your 'S' score is higher than your 'O' score, read 'Strategists' first, and vice versa.

Operationalists

Operationalists prefer to specify organizational objectives in tight, specific terms. Any aims and plans for future development may be communicated within their own organizations, but they will certainly not tell suppliers anything about them. They prefer to pursue short-term performance measures without seeing the 'big picture'. They will tend to focus on their own departments, sections or functions and will not seriously challenge the purpose or appropriateness of their performance measures.

In summary, Operationalists are concerned with managing current problems and are aiming to be better at doing essentially the same thing. By nature they tend to be incrementalists and small team players trying to look good in their own areas.

Strategists

Strategists have a vision of where the market is leading them and what must be done to establish and achieve long-term objectives. The visions and the plans are widely communicated both within their own organizations and to customer and supplier companies. While interested in good short-term performance, they will be likely to question the performance measures themselves and modify them if appropriate to improve their competitive position. Strategists recognize the multidimensional nature of managing customers and suppliers and look for the business performance before narrow departmental or functional interests in the expectation that these interests will be better realized by success on the larger scale. Strategists looking for benefits are prepared to experiment and allow people to contribute to improvements.

In summary, Strategists are concerned with creating and managing future opportunities as well as satisfying immediate requirements. They recognize the need for and rate of change, but welcome the opportunities thus provided, rather than baulking at the difficulties. They are more comfortable with qualitative, uncertain or potential benefits of closer relationships and give as much weight to these considerations as to the more obviously quantifiable and immediate ones.

Analysis

When you have completed the scoring, you should be able to identify whether managers in your organization adopt a predominantly strategic or a predominantly operational emphasis. You, and your colleagues, could then consider these questions:

1 Are the results of this short exercise consistent with your understanding of the way in which you and your colleagues take decisions about the customer–supplier relationship?

2 How has the emphasis that you have identified as dominant in your organization affected the way in which suppliers/customers are treated?

3 Can you identify factors (such as tradition, top management values, management appraisal and reward systems) that encourage a particular decision-making style in your organization?

4 What does this suggest to you about the difficulties of relationship development projects your organization is likely to invest in?

CHANGE MODEL

We must recognize that no external party can know what is best for any one organization. It will however always be possible for experienced, external people to ask the kind of simple questions that set the insiders back on their heels as they come to realize that long established and unchallenged behaviours do not fit with current realities or needs. To assume however that any outsider (regardless of how charismatic the persona or message) has the 'key to the future' as a guaranteed prescription, does not accord with rational consideration by intelligent managers. The reality is that even the normative suggestion of 'do the following things and you will be excellent' school of managerial advice cannot be true unless the things suggested are more to do with the organizational learning discussed in Chapter Four – that is to do with increasing understanding of the issues involved and competence in resolving difficulties – not as a one time application of the toolkit but as part of an ongoing learning process, the results of which are more due to the efforts of the participants than with the outside stimulus or facilitation.

For these reasons we offer the basis of a change model, not because we believe that it is the answer to everyone's decision choices but rather that it has proved its utility with practising managers particularly if they use it as a guide to examining the issues and their implications and working out their own unique solutions. It is also context sensitive, best used in interactive, group-based action learning programmes where some at least of that organizational context is surfaced and considered.

The framework to be presented forms the core of *The Customer–Supplier Relationship Audit* which itself drew from earlier work by our colleagues David Boddy and David Buchanan. Their formulation of the framework was used with practising managers implementing technical change and we adapted it for the interorganizational change of improving relationships.

With the passage of time and with input from different groups of managers working together in SCMG workshops, what is presented here differs in some ways from the earlier one but the underlying principles are consistent.

The framework has also influenced our work in capturing the nature of relationships in the Relationship Positioning Tool and in the Relationship Improvement Process described in the next chapter.

Results through action on purpose, people and process

As the earlier exercise on Strategists and Operationalists hopefully showed, we all exhibit features of both in some measure. Often our job roles force the balance one way or another but we must also realize that the requirement is not simply to be one or the other but that each must be properly represented and in dialogue with the other.

Purpose

There are three subsets to this section. The first recognizes that true partnership sourcing really has innovative potential and that this cannot properly be forecast or forced. The supply chain situation must be such as to encourage and reward innovations as they occur. Thus this section has the aim of engaging and enhancing potential from wherever possible and in support of a *strategic balance*. As we will indicate in the next chapter, gaining short-term operational benefits will be important, both for their own sakes and as an indicator of early success to reinforce interest and commitment. Focusing only on operational aspects does not do enough and without the medium to long-term goals to drive for, the danger of slipping back to a short-term, limited-scope programme will be very real.

This also suggests the importance of the mandate teams on both sides and the composition of these must have a proportion of senior level strategists as well as the interorganizational contact people.

To support innovation, sharing of information and the development of individual and joint capability, there have to be *positive policies* in place to assist these activities. Particular areas are in employment policies where recruitment specifications might change as buyers need less aggressive negotiating skills and more interorganizational coordination ones. Likewise payment systems and training might change to emphasize a wider range of skills being employed, especially in teams, so that narrow job descriptions and individual reward structures and demarcations are no longer appropriate.

In any rapidly changing environment innovation and productivity improvement can be perceived as a route to reducing employee numbers. Senior managers need to be clear what policy for continued employment they have for their own people and realize how strong their commitment to the business partner must be.

Total quality policies of employment and quality at source must clearly be in place as well.

Investment appraisal policies may be one of the more difficult areas but moves to activity-based costing and a recognition that the real strategic benefits might appear after the calculated payback period, would be helpful in justifying the upfront investment in the relationship improvement process. Activity-based costing should provide believable numbers for potential cost savings through the reductions in transaction costs already discussed. In this way the real cost-benefits are more apparent than if we are being asked to quantify or justify some 'expected' reduction in general overhead.

The final sub-set of this section is *compatible structures* and covers both hard technology and more organizational aspects on either side of the relationship. Given the range of issues that we have been discussing it is important that both parties share common understandings and compatible systems of management and decision-making approaches. Thus partnering with the local branch of an international organization which had little devolved authority might make the shared development of responsibility for design involvement (for example) very difficult. This is a real problem when the design authority resides overseas and any change (especially one suggested by a supplier) has to go through very many organizational levels and takes longer than anyone has patience for.

Another example would be decision-making authority processes in terms of cost and pricing information. The matching of mandates on each side so that the joint development teams are fully empowered to commit their respective organizations is also crucial.

At the technology level the issue of Electronic Data Interchange will be an early entry on many agendas. While we would argue that establishing effective person to person communication is the first step, nevertheless EDI, properly installed, can reinforce the partnership's supply chain effectiveness. However unless 100 per cent dependency is acceptable a supplier is probably going to need multiple sets of EDI equipment to link to different customers. The customers incidentally do not usually see this as a problem that they should share in. The customers could support a speedier move to standardization and thereby reduce these supply chain wastes. After all, where is the justification for imposing a unique solution on a supplier when you force them to work with other customers because you have an upper limit of 25 per cent capacity dependence?

People

As we discussed in Chapter One the new requirements include people *involvement* for which the strategic purpose sets the broad parameters. At a more operational level, enabling involvement will affect the management style in both organizations such that collegiate discussion and agreement will feature much more than traditional direction. Middle management's role (for the reduced numbers remaining) is certainly less that of a policeman and decision maker and more coordinator, facilitator and link person to other organizational groupings, both internal and external to the focused organization. This will be a major challenge for all concerned as the middle manager group have largely been the source of much information manipulation and political power playing in the past. Like any other group of people in the new situation they will have to demonstrate that their contribution is a value and not cost-adding activity. With universal responsibility being allocated to the doers and direct value-adders below them in the traditional structure then they have to reorientate. This is also likely to mean that career structures for many people will be less narrowly and vertically directed within one specialist area and more horizontally based as breadth of experience and interpersonal and interorganizational network management skills come to the fore.

Major new opportunities within the Purchasing/ Procurement function will revolve around the relationship management role where setting up and maintaining relationships with a number of business partners will significantly change the job description. This becomes immediately more strategic (in recognition of the arguments here and the sheer financial importance of the spend on outside sourced materials and services) and less operationally involved with order placing, expediting and firefighting.

Hopefully in our new integrated supply chain approach, expediting and firefighting will have reduced but all three operational aspects can be and are being done (in progressive companies) by the direct people in the operations area.

As this book has been discussing, the major difficulty in the change process is the need to develop *understanding* about the need for change, the alternative principles of operation and the basic attitude change that cooperation with business partners is more effective than competing with them. In order to do this a 'hearts and minds' campaign is needed to change any adversarial mindsets over to that of collaboration. This is one process which certainly should involve workshop type activities where people can experience different operating principles and think through how their situation will change. Sometimes this change will not appear to be in the participant's short-term interest and so there is an organizational issue of how to convert these 'losers' in the change programme into 'winners' ideally but at least avoid the real possibility of them turning into saboteurs.

Attitudes will not change however unless associated changes are made in work organization and *support systems*.

In many cases work organization has been modified. The sourcing decision is one example where multifunctional teams for Finance, Procurement, Engineering, Quality and Manufacture or Operations work through a comprehensive supplier audit and qualification process before the sourcing choice is made. This team must also agree on any supply resourcing decisions so buyers can no longer switch sources for a few percentage points reduction in the unit cost.

Simultaneous engineering, value analysis and early supply involvement as well as continuous quality improvement projects all suggest a more team based approach. Business process re-engineering and reorganizing around process flows also suggest new forms of work organization.

Information system support and performance visibility are also likely to be at higher levels once the partnership is working well but here the support systems which are allied to internal performance measurement also must change. People perform against the units of measure used regardless of how illogical or counterproductive they are seen to be at the local level. This can be a big problem if the systems are based on overhead recovery, price minimization and output quantity and quality. The challenge is to redesign the support systems actually to support the new definitions of performance requirement. These support systems are paralleled in the partner organization while the interface produces new measurement and support system requirements. For example, we argue that people from many different functions and capabilities should exchange visits to build contacts and network influence and intelligence gathering. If such activities are perceived as time-wasting 'vacation trips' the real opportunity cost incurred during the visit (on both sides each time) will be regarded as a negative and not a positive investment.

Process

This forms the application phase of our change model and is the subject of the next chapter. At this point it is worth noting some key features.

The *mandate team* is crucial. Without their understanding and commitment (neither will do on its own), and their ability to act as gatekeepers to the other stakeholders involved, then progress will be intermittent at best.

Setting up and managing the mandate team is one of the skills of the change agent or champion of the new approach and here the work of Boddy and Buchanan is again relevant.[4]

Part of the quality understanding is that there can be no real improvement without *measurement*. This is true also of relationships which might seem to be somewhat ephemeral in nature. The Relationship Positioning Tool process developed by SCMG in association with very many managers from different organizations and business sectors has proved its utility. It compares existing practice with externally observed best practice and theoretical ideals to produce indicator numbers of relative performance. These numbers form a basis for the agenda at joint improvement meetings and provide input to action oriented improvement programmes.

The final part of the jigsaw is the *Relationship Improvement Process* (RIP) which is the backbone of the next chapter. This is a structured approach to capturing all of the previous considerations in a coherent framework or

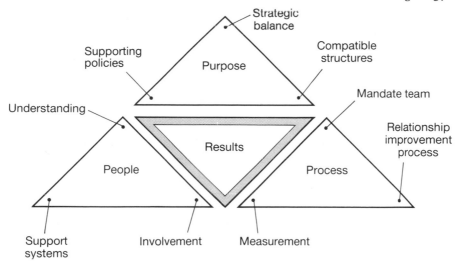

Figure 6.1 The RAP-3 Framework: Results Through Action on Purpose, People and Process

change management project plan.

Results can be obtained by considering the interactions between each of the elements of the change model and working through their implications in cross-functional and cross-organizational working teams guided by a joint steering committee of the partner's senior managers who act internally as the mandate team. The RAP-3 framework captures the range of issues through the three Ps of Purpose, People and Process and Figure 6.1 shows this graphically, but the beginning of the phrase is important and up to you – *Results* through *Action*.

SUMMARY

- **Change needs to be viewed from both a strategic and an operational perspective.**

- **While contexts will be unique to some extent, a change model provides utility if it helps formulate issues for detailed discussion and development.**

- **The RAP-3 framework suggests that Results will come if consistent and considerate action is taken on the Purpose of the change, the People involved in the change and in the Process of managing the change itself.**

- Within each major section, three more interrelated issues must be just as carefully managed.

- Purpose includes: strategic balance, positive policies and compatible structures.

- People includes: involvement, understanding and support systems.

- Process includes: mandate team, measurement (the Relationship Positioning Tool) and the phased programme itself (the Relationship Improvement Process.)

In the next chapter we will go into detail about the change process and how SCMG have learned how to assist teams of managers in working through the issues. There is also a case study report based on recent work with industrial companies.

7

MAKING IT HAPPEN

In this chapter we will examine SCMG's approach to helping organizations move towards Partnership Sourcing.

We will examine:

- why a structured approach is useful

- the nature of a phased change process model

- the underlying factors which need to be measured against best-practice as a diagnostic aid

- a case study of companies working through this approach

- the threats which can grow after a partnership has lost its freshness.

As with any new theory or innovative idea, the challenge lies not just with understanding the concept but also the process by which it can be successfully implemented. This is especially true of Supply Chain Management (SCM) and Partnership Sourcing. In its work with many hundreds of firms we have come across a common theme: companies that have grasped the essential message of Partnership Sourcing and its relevance to their need to take cost out of their operations, have then wanted to make it happen in their organization. They will often have had some experience in implementing TQM practices in their environment and hence expect that 'doing Partnership Sourcing' will not present too many problems However, few have been totally successful in converting the theory into effective practice.

In this chapter we will develop from the general treatment of Chapter Five particular aspects of the barriers to change which are particular to the implementation of Partnership Sourcing, and outline some practical techniques which have been used to tackle these barriers and facilitate the process.

It should be said here that in almost all cases the initiation for change comes from the customer, i.e. where the power normally lies in a traditional, adversarial relationship.

As we have seen, the barriers to implementation lie in a number of areas but two key issues are a) commitment, and b) understanding.

Dealing firstly with commitment, (or more importantly, the lack of it); this can manifest itself in a number of ways

1. Most management practices are to some degree risk averse, i.e. there is a tendency to go for the most conservative solution to avoid any potential criticism or blame. Partnership Sourcing requires a commitment from both sides for some quite often radical change. This risk aversity can manifest itself at the beginning of the change programme with individuals regarding the development of new relationships as being 'new-fangled' and alien to the existing culture. Commitment therefore is never fully established and reversion to the old ways is always at hand. More commonly is that many companies embark on a Partnership Sourcing programme and discover half way along that there is a need for some radical decisions. One of two things can then happen; either the middle manager will seek guidance from senior management only to find that they don't appreciate the problem and take a negative viewpoint or the middle manager decides to put the particular issue to one side. In any case the implementation process becomes ineffective.

2. Lack of trust with respect to suppliers is endemic in most firms who are about to tackle Partnership Sourcing. In fact, it could easily be argued that without Partnership Sourcing being in place, there can be no 'corporate' trust. The lack of trust is an obvious barrier to gaining commitment to the relationship change process, on both sides. The scepticism which greets the suggestion of forming a collaborative relationship with an organization which has normally been adversarial usually means that there is going to be little impetus to the implementation process. However, the realization that there is mutual responsibility for problems can sometimes avert the feeling of non-trust and open the door to more objective discussions.

3. A very salient comment was made on Partnership Sourcing by a MD in a small machining company that had a 'partnership' with a major OEM; 'It sounds good, but will it last when things get tough?' The application of external stress to the relationship can seriously dilute commitment to building true partnerships. Very often it's a case of 'everyone for themselves' when the recession comes along or the competition gets tougher. However there are many examples which have emerged of customers who are prepared to support their supplier partners when times are hard in the belief that this is a lower cost option for the medium-to-longer term than the

risk of losing the supplier and having to re-source. This perhaps illustrates best of all the depth of commitment that is required.

4. A lack of mandate for the individual(s) who are trying to progress the relationship improvement programme usually results in a serious under-commitment to the change. Without the proper backing from senior management to pursue the relationship change programme the champion will find it hard to build commitment in the rest of the organization. A common situation which occurs is that Partnership Sourcing is seen as a rather alien concept to the company but allowed a 'trial run' anyway and senior management then delegate the task to an enthusiastic individual, without keeping it on their agendas. Other managers in the champion's peer group will tend to take the attitude that their method of dealing with suppliers is fundamentally sound and that there isn't much that they can be taught about the subject. This endemic arrogance means that any champion of the relationship change, without the express backing of senior manage-ment, faces an uphill struggle in gaining true commitment from these managers. They will go along with the idea to a certain extent, talk the right language, etc., but when it comes to the crunch they will revert back to the established attitudes and systems. The individual pushing for change must be empowered to set directions and build appropriate structures to realize the change in relationship style.

Real commitment, throughout the organization, tends to come from com-panies who are either enlightened enough to cast off their dogged attitudes and make the relationship successful or are in the position of having no other choice to stay in business. The latter is rare, but there are examples in the UK Oil and Gas sector where operating companies have realized that their core competence does not lie in drilling and production and have seen a need to encourage contractors to take the responsibility for these activities. The only way they have been able to achieve this is through developing rela-tionships with contractors which enable a transfer of expertise and a sharing of risk and benefit through collaboration.

More typical is the company which realizes that its chances of success (or survival) in the market place are increased significantly by adopting a strategy which will realize benefits through collaboration with suppliers. The commitment in this company comes from the top and is sustained in the company through regular reinforcement by senior management.

Turning to barriers to understanding, some typical problems are:

1. Lack of understanding about the range of issues involved. This is very

common. Many companies like the concept of Partnership Sourcing as a means to save them money but very few have a total grasp of all the areas which have to be tackled in putting it into practice. In particular, there is a tendency to tinker with what already exists in the belief that cranking up contracts, for example, will cement the relationship. There often isn't the realization that Partnership Sourcing is a rather revolutionary concept which requires the discarding of many traditional attitudes and practices and the establishment of new goals and systems.

2. Allied to the above, power manipulation by the customer can be a serious impediment to the development of collaborative relationship. There needs to be an understanding that the master–servant situation has to be relaxed throughout the change process to allow the best opportunity for the relationship issues to be explored in a frank and honest manner. Without this realization there is little possibility of the relationship becoming a true partnership.

3. A major problem is to do with a lack of company-wide understanding of what Partnership Sourcing is all about. This is a feature of companies which are heavily compartmentalized. The theory of Partnership Sourcing and the building of collaborative relationships will be regarded as an issue for the Purchasing department only and hence the topic is never fully pursued with functions other than Purchasing. The resultant lack of awareness and understanding can lead to conflict within the company and the eventual breakdown of the implementation process.

4. Further to the above, there has to be an understanding that there is often a need for cross-functional solutions to problems with relationships. Hence there is a requirement for more functions to become involved with and understand the company's suppliers. The lack of this basic understanding is most prevalent in the relatively 'unsophisticated' company which works in an essentially traditional manner. This type of company will not have had any background in Total Quality Management or any other practice which involves a holistic approach to managing the business.

5. Finally, there is a lack of understanding about the most appropriate programme of change to ensure that the adoption of Partnership Sourcing is effectively managed. In essence this lack of understanding can give rise to all of the problems listed above and all too often managers prefer to 'play things by ear' rather than attempt to manage what is quite often a difficult and complex problem. Even when an efficient manager sits down and tries to think through what action is required and when, the manager is overwhelmed with the potential barriers to the implementation and finds it hard

to identify precisely what is required. There is still a prevalent viewpoint that the implementation of Partnership Sourcing involves a bit of 'black magic' and, worse still, is solely dependent upon interpersonal relationships, rather than being a managed and controlled business process.

So, these are some of the barriers to successful implementation to Partnership Sourcing principles. In the next section we will look at how these barriers can be overcome and real improvements in supply chain performance realized.

In the course of our work with many companies in a variety of sectors it has become apparent that the most successful implementations of Partnership Sourcing have been characterized by the following:

- top down approach, with ongoing support from senior management
- formal commitment by both parties and definition of benefits sought on both sides
- use of internal cross-functional teams and joint teams with the supplier
- clear process for changing the relationship
- mechanisms to identify key issues and put corrective actions in place
- regular reinforcement of principles and reporting of benefits as part of continuous improvement.

An interesting observation is that no two companies seem to adopt precisely the same approach. Very often there are similar techniques employed, particularly the building of inter- and intra-company teams, but the sequence of actions is often unique to each company. To a degree this reflects the newness of the Partnership Sourcing concept on the industrial scene. Without any documented, standard approach available via literature, companies have tended to go their own way and rely on their own learning experience to gain the best results.

It is clear that there is a need for a practical model of the change process for implementing Partnership Sourcing to help companies avoid going down the same blind alleys as others before them. With this in mind we have collated all of our understandings from extensive research and commercial work carried out with UK companies to determine the most effective sequence of actions which companies could take to implement Partnership Sourcing. The model produced a framework for change called the Relationship Improvement Process, shown graphically in Figure 7.1.

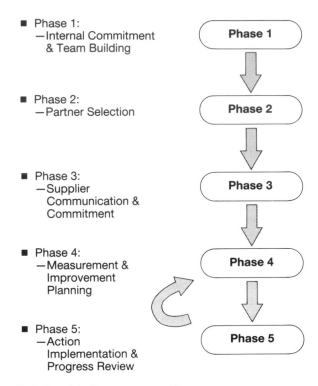

- Phase 1:
  —Internal Commitment
  & Team Building

- Phase 2:
  —Partner Selection

- Phase 3:
  —Supplier
  Communication &
  Commitment

- Phase 4:
  —Measurement &
  Improvement
  Planning

- Phase 5:
  —Action
  Implementation &
  Progress Review

Figure 7.1 Relationship Improvement Process

The Relationship Improvement Process is described in five phases;

PHASE 1: INTERNAL COMMITMENT AND TEAM BUILDING

As discussed previously, lack of understanding and/or commitment within the customer company can be a serious impediment to taking the important decisions and actions crucial to the development of the relationship. Hence, the development of management understanding and commitment is an essential prerequisite to this relationship change process. Moreover, the change process requires coordinated effort and hence the establishment of a cross-functional implementation team is an essential mechanism in this effort.

PHASE 2: PARTNER SELECTION

Very often one of the first tasks for the implementation team is to select those suppliers with whom the company wishes to form collaborative relationships. Due care and consideration is required here because if this phase is hurried then the customer company could end up trying to partner with wholly unsuitable suppliers.

PHASE 3: SUPPLIER COMMITMENT AND JOINT TEAM BUILDING

The first two stages are concerned with internal perspectives. The spotlight now shifts to encompass each supplier with whom the customer wishes to form a collaborative relationship. The main aim of this phase is to encourage the supplier to buy into the relationship improvement process and having gained that whole-hearted commitment then to set up a *joint team* with each supplier to carry forward the rest of the programme. This phase should also mark the formal commitment of both parties to building a collaborative relationship.

PHASE 4: MEASUREMENT AND IMPROVEMENT PLANNING

The main action of the joint customer–supplier team is to analyze the relationship, identify its shortcomings and put actions in place which can counter the weaknesses and build on the strengths and hence improve the effectiveness of the relationship.

PHASE 5: ACTION IMPLEMENTATION AND PROGRESS REVIEW

Once the joint team has identified the actions which should be pursued then the responsibility for the actual implementation is allocated. Very often the actions require joint effort and hence sub-teams are formed to tackle specific issues.

An important feature of this phase is the establishment of progress review procedures and feedback loops to the rest of both companies, especially their senior management. Success has to be demonstrated to ensure that commitment is sustained by senior management and also to encourage new initiatives to be set up. It becomes much easier to convince the next batch of suppliers to enter into a Partnership Sourcing relationship if benefits are being realized and reported by the 'pioneers'.

These five phases describe the type of effort and action required to build collaborative relationships. The following text describes in more detail the activities which have to be undertaken in each phase.

PHASE 1: INTERNAL COMMITMENT AND TEAM BUILDING

Very often the task of managing the relationship change programme is delegated to one individual within the customer company. The most common mechanism used by this *champion* to increase understanding and commitment, and to build an *implementation team,* is some form of training session or workshop to explore the issues involved in collaborative relationships and promote the change process itself. This workshop normally covers the following issues:

- Supply Chain Management strategy
- why collaborative relationships are important for competitiveness
- what is a collaborative relationship?
- the type of management attitude shift required
- the process of change required
- skills and range of interest required for the implementation team.

The implementation team will normally consist of the champion and like-minded people who have the mandate (from senior management) and expertise to expedite the sequence of events required and also carry the collaborative relationship message throughout the organization. More specifically, the team should have the following profile:

Stakeholders As well as managers from Purchasing, the team should include representatives from functions which are likely to be affected in some way by the change in relationships with suppliers, for example, managers from Production, Engineering, Sales and Quality. It is important that there is a broad representation of views on the team to ensure that the correct decisions for the whole company are made and also to sustain a whole-company commitment to the collaborative concept. In the consideration of which groups or individuals are stakeholders there should also be some thought given to whether or not these parties will see themselves as being positively or adversely affected by the change in relationships. This then raises the question of just how the potential 'doubters' should be incorporated in the change process. Certainly it is important to keep the balance of the team on the side of positive thought about the proposed change and perhaps the real sceptics need to be kept more remote from the initial activity until positive benefit is realized.

Technical expertise Obviously, the team has to have members with a deep knowledge of products and processes.

Organizational expertise Managers with a strong understanding of the various interactions between functions and suppliers can provide useful input for the team. We need someone who knows how to pull the organization's levers.

High level Junior managers are not suitable for the team. The type of decisions to be taken are very often of a strategic or fundamental nature and hence require input from the more senior members of company management.

Strong leadership The team requires a leader who has a good understanding of the whole company and the supply base and strong interpersonal and chairing skills. The latter quality is very important because the issues being tackled are often highly contentious. It is also important that the leader of the team has a direct link with senior management, if not already a member of the senior management team.

Right size The above points to the need to have a comprehensive team membership but it has to be borne in mind that the team could become too cumbersome if the numbers are too large. Eight to ten members is a manageable size. If the initial selection of team members points to an over-large grouping then perhaps it is necessary to consider which of the stakeholders have a truly significant influence on the change process, and definitely have to be on the team, and those stakeholders which simply have to be kept fully informed and involved only occasionally.

Implicit in all of the above description of this phase is the commitment of senior management to the development of collaborative relationships with suppliers. Without the backing of the most senior company representatives the change process is doomed to failure. As has been described in previous chapters, the development of collaborative relationships often requires a fundamental shift in attitude and behaviour and the drive for this change must come from the top down.

PHASE 2: PARTNER SELECTION

We now understand that suppliers who can provide the lowest prices are not necessarily the most suitable candidates for developing long-term, collaborative relationships with. The identification of suitable partners requires a much broader examination of supplier capabilities and the careful weighing of qualities and future opportunities. Remember that we should be looking at total acquisition costs not unit price alone.

Obviously existing levels of business, technical capability and component 'criticality' are crucial factors, however other criteria for selection need to reflect the supplier's capability to develop as a partner. For example design capability, research and development effort, personnel capability and supplier management are all areas which can indicate a supplier's suitability as a long-term partner. Hence there is a need for companies to take a lot of care in understanding just what makes certain suppliers more effective than others as well as their own role in helping or hindering them.

Some companies have already rationalized their supply base to the extent that they have a very small number of major suppliers who are predominantly single sources and hence there is little need for a selection exercise. However most companies have choices to make, and the best have used the following process.

Initial selection ('rough cut') of suppliers

For each of the suppliers, the following criteria are considered:

	'Ideal' Partner
● Amount of spend	High spend
● Criticality of parts	Critical parts
● Availability of parts	Sole source
● Location of supplier	Local
● Performance	Good*

(**Alternatively, many companies choose to concentrate on the suppliers who give them the most pain and hence are the biggest potential source for cost savings.*)

This process usually produces a short list of suppliers consisting of around 10 per cent of the original number examined.

Final selection ('fine cut')

Having reduced the number of potential partners, the implementation team then needs to examine the short-listed suppliers in greater depth to identify those with the most capability to develop as effective partners. This involves examining a wide range of issues associated with the supplier's business, including strategies, systems, organization and behaviours. For example

- Does the supplier have a strategy which is compatible with forming collaborative, long-term relationships with customers?
- Does the supplier have an organizational structure compatible with a TQM environment? Who meets customers/suppliers? What is the turn-over and experience of staff?
- Does the supplier have a clearly defined and appropriate business strategy which includes formal plans for pursuing improvements?
- Experience of the supplier with respect to the industry. Are the turnover, profit, asset and investment levels healthy?
- Is the supplier recognized as being capable by the industry?
- Does the supplier have access to other markets/technologies which might provide a basis for increased levels of service?
- How well does the supplier organize, train and use its people resource?
- Does the supplier have a capability for design and is it experienced in working with customers in design?
- Does the supplier have processes which are fully capable now and plans in place to ensure that they will be effective in the future?
- Does the supplier have established systems which can guarantee a high level of performance now and continuous improvement in the future?
- Does the supplier have appropriate procedures which ensure that the company has access to state-of-the art level of technology?
- Does the supplier have too many suppliers for effective control? What plans does the supplier have for developing its supply base?
- Does the supplier pass on the right information at the right time?
- Does the supplier openly disclose information to the customer about business performance and internal performance measurements?

More often than not, the answers to these types of questions involve a visit to each supplier's premises and interviews with key personnel. This effectively begins the process of closer working and examination of the relationship.

This type of analysis enables the identification of the suppliers who are going to be suitable for working with through the remainder of the relationship improvement process. Moreover, the increased understanding within the customer company of just what makes an effective partner is a useful exercise in itself and contributes to the overall process of changing attitudes and behaviours.

PHASE 3: SUPPLIER COMMITMENT AND JOINT TEAM BUILDING

By the time that this phase is started the selected suppliers will already have had some understanding that the customer is intent on making some important changes to the relationship. What is important in this phase is that the customer takes time to clarify what its intentions are and goes through a process to develop full understanding amongst supplier management of the partnership concept and a deep-rooted commitment to make significant changes and improvements.

As for Phase 1, the basic requirement here is the provision of information and education from the customer to each supplier. The actual sequence of events, however, is important. In the first instance, the customer should approach the most senior managers in the supplier to discuss the overall thrust of the collaborative relationship strategy and seek to gain these individuals' commitment to the process of change. This then makes it easier to sell the concept to the rest of the supplier management. Workshops similar to those held during Phase 1 can then be conducted within each supplier to make sure that there is widespread understanding of the principles of collaboration and to start the process of identifying members of the joint team which will drive the rest of the relationship improvement process. Again, the prime factors for consideration of team membership are as before.

- Stakeholder representation, including the key operational people
- Technical expertise
- Organizational expertise
- Management grade
- Leadership
- Size

The culmination of this phase should be a formal commitment from both parties to building a long-term collaborative relationship. Companies which have gone down this road have cemented their relationship by arranging for senior management on both sides signing a *Partnering Agreement* which sets the future tone for the relationship. This doesn't mean that the traditional contract is torn up and thrown away but it has to be realized that contracts are often simply preparations for failure. The Partnering Agreement should be a statement of positive intent from both parties covering items such as length of commitment, mutual goals and responsibilities. An example of a Partnering Agreement is given below:

Statement of principle
This should be a short statement setting the tone for the future collaborative relationship. There should be a commitment to create an open and trusting relationship which delivers tangible benefits to both sides and allows the sharing of ideas and information.

Commitment
Length of time that the agreement will be in force. Ideally this should be greater than five years.

Targets
These should be jointly agreed for the reduction of costs associated with the supply of goods and a commitment from both sides to work towards these targets.

Sharing of Benefits
There should be an agreement that any cost reductions achieved by meeting the targets will be shared with respect to an easily understood formula.

Expectations
There should be a clear statement on what each partner expects of the other. For example, the customer might expect certain levels of service from the supplier and the supplier would look for accurate order information from the customer.

Confidentiality
The nature of the partnership will involve the passage of sensitive information between both partners so there needs to be a joint commitment to complete confidentiality.

Review Procedures
There should be a commitment to hold regular review meetings to assess the overall progress of the relationship.

Joint Team Members
A list of the joint team members at the onset of the relationship improvement programme.

Mutual Termination
Agreement on the terms by which the relationship will come to an end.

Partnership Sourcing Ltd. have also produced guidelines for agreements which are worth considering.

This phase has often turned out to be a crucial step for companies in their attempts to implement a Partnership Sourcing strategy. Without the whole-hearted commitment from the supplier the chances of producing real benefits from the new relationship are limited. The tone of approach by the customer is all-important. The customer must show that it is ready to give up some of its 'power' in return for a more effective relationship and express a willingness to share any benefits emanating from improvements to product or process.

PHASE 4: MEASUREMENT AND IMPROVEMENT PLANNING

This is the phase which often generates the most enthusiasm in both com-panies but is tricky to get right. Many managers are keen on getting to grips with some of the more obvious operational problems but are less decisive when fundamental changes are required. The focus tends to be rather narrow and on day-to-day issues rather than the strategic viewpoint which is required to re-build the relationship and provide the basis for far-reaching improvements. So, measuring the relationship essentially requires a systematic process of rating key elements of the way in which both sides do business with each other, ideally against demonstrated or perceived best practice. This points to the need for some sort of benchmarking exercise covering a broad range of issues connected with the relationship and which contribute towards excellent supply performance.

Obviously, determining just what to measure is a difficult exercise. To capture all of the factors that determine a good relationship requires con-sideration of a wide range of management issues, many of which would be regarded as rather qualitative in nature and hence not easily measured. SCMG carried out an extensive research project in 1987 to find out what these factors were. The results of this research were captured in a manage-ment aid known as the Relationship Positioning Tool (RPT), which is described below.

The Relationship Positioning Tool is an attempt to capture all of the factors that determine the effectiveness of the relationship and is based on a model of the customer–supplier relationship shown in Figure 7.2.

As the leaves on a tree can indicate its overall health, the *Performance* elements of *Quality, Delivery, Cost* and *Innovation* provide historic evi-dence of the general health of the relationship. Adverse variations from targets for Quality, Delivery and Cost with respect to supplied goods are unwanted wastes and indicate weaknesses in the performance of the relationship. Similarly, the relationship has to be effective in a way which ensures that continuous improvement through Innovation of the supplied goods and services takes place.

However, the health of a tree's leaves, now and in the future, is dictated to a certain extent by the strength of its root system. Similarly, the RPT model shows that *Performance*, now and in the future, is influenced by four major contributory factors, divided between the customer and the supplier.

The potential of the relationship to meet present and future demands with

THE CUSTOMER-SUPPLIER RELATIONSHIP

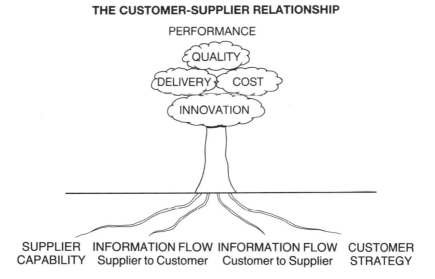

| SUPPLIER | INFORMATION FLOW | INFORMATION FLOW | CUSTOMER |
| CAPABILITY | Supplier to Customer | Customer to Supplier | STRATEGY |

Figure 7.2 Relationship Positioning Tool

respect to Quality, Delivery, Cost and Innovation is therefore dependent upon:

1 Customer strategy

How well the customer creates the right conditions for a successful, world-class relationship with the supplier; a contributory factor towards good *Performance*. This can be more fully described as follows:

1.1 Requirements The targets/drivers the customer sets for supply in terms of *Quality, Delivery, Cost* and *Innovation*. These targets should be set with the intention to move towards more efficient practices. Elements under *Requirements* are:

1.1.1 *Quality* Has the required quality of the product/service been clearly and reasonably defined, based on past performances and has the supplier been involved in the definition?

1.1.2 *Delivery* Has the required delivery pattern for the product/service been clearly and reasonably defined, based on past performances and has the supplier been involved in the definition of requirement?

1.1.3 *Cost* Is the total cost of supply being properly assessed? Is the supplier involved in the setting of targets for cost containments/ reductions?

1.1.4 *Innovation* Are targets for improvements in product, processes and operations clearly defined, reasonable, based on past performance and does the setting of the targets involve the supplier?

1.2 Attitude Does the strategy and attitude that the customer adopts towards the supplier provide the basis for a close and effective relationship? Elements under *Attitude* are:

1.2.1 *Business* Does the customer appreciate the need to look at more than just the unit price and work with the supplier in trying to reduce costs? Does the customer allow the supplier to share the benefits of a successful relationship?

1.2.2 *Commitment* Is there a long-term commitment to the supplier by the customer?

1.2.3 *Involvement* Does the customer involve the supplier in decision-making processes? Is there a real attempt to develop an open relationship?

1.2.4 *Dependency* Is the customer's desire for a closer, long-term relationship backed up by policies which mean that the supplier is a genuine stakeholder in the customer's business?

1.3 Systems Does the customer have the right procedures in place to aid the development of the relationship? Does the customer do all it can to smooth the supply process? Elements under *Systems* are:

1.3.1 *Cost* Does the customer have a method of accurately assessing the true cost of supply and does the customer use market cost information to establish costs and margins with the supplier?

1.3.2 *Evaluation* Is there a formalized supplier audit and performance measurement system in place?

1.3.3 *Approval* Does the customer have a formal procedure to qualify suppliers as reliable partners?

1.3.4 *Schedule* Does the customer have an effective and reliable supply scheduling system?

1.3.5 *Involvement* To what degree does the customer use their resources and influence to assist the supplier to solve day-to-day problems and pursue operational improvements?

1.4 People Is the way that the customer organizes and rewards employees the right one to support more effective relationships with the supplier? Factors under *People* are:

1.4.1 *Organization structure* Is the customer organized in a way which allows a broad awareness/involvement with respect to dealings with the supplier?

1.4.2 *Involvement* Does the customer have the right training and information systems to create a broad awareness of supplier operations within the organization? Is there an attempt to involve the supplier in the customer's activities through appropriate contact between the two companies?

1.4.3 *Reward systems* Are Procurement personnel rewarded by getting basic price reductions or do internal reward systems reflect a greater understanding of total operational cost?

2 Supplier capability

The supplier's raw capability to deliver products/services at a high level of quality, at the right time and the lowest overall cost. This also includes the supplier's ability to pursue improvements and provide a full service; a contributory factor towards good *Performance*. Again, Supplier Capability breaks down into the following factors and elements.

2.1 Profile/Strategy How well the supplier creates the right conditions for a successful, world-class relationship with customers. Factors under *Profile/Strategy* are:

2.1.1 *Customer base* Does the supplier have a strategy which is compatible with forming collaborative, long-term relationships with customers?

2.1.2 *Organization* Departmental structure; who meets customers/ suppliers. Turnover and experience of staff.

2.1.3 *Strategy* Does the supplier have a clearly defined and appropriate business strategy which includes formal plans for pursuing improvements?

2.1.4 *Financial Health* Experience of the supplier with respect to the industry. Are the turnover, profit, asset and investment levels healthy?

2.1.5 *Approval* Is the supplier recognized as being capable by the industry?

2.1.6 *Flexibility* Breadth of supplier's abilities. Does the supplier have access to other markets / technologies which might provide a basis for increased levels of service?

2.2 People How well the supplier organizes, trains and uses its people resource. Factors under *People* are:

2.2.1 *Skills* How competent are the workforce?

2.2.2 *Organization* Are the supplier's employees organized in a way that will allow them to meet new requirements and targets?

2.2.3 *Involvement* To what extent does the supplier fully utilize its people resource?

2.2.4 *Training* The supplier's commitment to enhancing the abilities and awareness of its employees and procedures to back this up.

2.2.5 *Flexibility* How task-flexible are the supplier's employees?

2.2.6 *Reward system* How effectively payment and appraisal systems motivate employees to contribute effectively to the achievement of excellent performance.

2.2.7 *Attitude* Willingness to be proactive in meeting the customer needs. Level of awareness of the customer needs and attitude to new demands.

2.2.8 *Competence:* Does the supplier have an effective competence assurance system?

2.3 Process Are the supplier's processes and techniques capable of meeting the customer's needs and is that capability effectively utilized? Factors under *Process* are:

2.3.1 *Design* Does the supplier have a capability for design and is it experienced in working with customers in design?

2.3.2 *Capability* Does the supplier have processes which are fully capable now and plans in place to ensure that they will be effective in the future?

2.3.3 *Capacity* Operational capacity and efficiency in utilization.

2.3.4 *Systems* Does the supplier have established systems which can guarantee a high level of performance now and continuous improvement in the future?

2.3.5 *Management of Safety* Does the supplier have appropriate procedures which ensure that all operations are carried out within an environment geared to Total Safety?

2.3.6 *Management of Quality* Does the supplier have appropriate procedures which ensure that all operations are carried out within a Total Quality Management environment?

2.3.7 *Process Range* Is the supplier capable of providing a full range of processes, now and in the future?

2.3.8 *Management of Technology* Does the supplier have appropriate procedures which ensure that the company has access to state-of-the art level of technology?

2.4 Supplier Management Does the supplier manage its supply base in the most effective way? Factors under *Supplier Management* are:

2.4.1 *Supply base* Does the supplier have too many suppliers for effective control? How big are suppliers when compared to the supplier, i.e. for mutual dependency and control? What plans does the supplier have for developing its supply base?

2.4.2 *Selection* Does the supplier have an effective supplier evaluation/selection procedure?

2.4.3 *Approval* Does the supplier have an effective supplier qualification procedure?

2.4.4 *Evaluation* How effectively are suppliers assessed, *and* are the results fed back?

2.4.5 *Communication* Who talks to suppliers, how often and about what?

2.4.6 *Involvement* The nature of the relationship with suppliers; dependency, contract basis and commitment.

2.4.7 *Delivery* Supplier delivery performance and method.

2.4.8 *Quality* Supplier quality performance.

2.4.9 *Cost* Is the total cost of supply properly assessed? Are there targets set for cost reductions?

A major feature of companies who are excellent partners to customers and/or suppliers is their ability to communicate effectively. Hence the remaining two major headings are:

3 Information flow; customer to supplier

The customer's effectiveness in creating a flow of information to the supplier which provides the basis for effective supply and the sharing of knowledge and ideas; a contributory factor towards good *Performance*. Factors under this section are:

3.1 Technical Does the customer pass on the right technical information at the right time? Elements under *Technical* are:

3.1.1 *Specifications* Efficiency of transmission of initial technical details, from the customer to supplier.

3.1.2 *Updates* How closely does the customer keep the supplier informed with regard to changes and developments?

3.1.3 *Problems* To what extent does the customer keep the supplier informed on operational problems?

3.1.4 *Innovations* Does the customer inform the supplier of general innovative techniques which emerge from its own investigations?

3.2 Involvement To what extent does the customer involve the supplier in its evaluation, measurement and action procedures through the disclosure of information, to enable a closer relationship. Elements under *Involvement* are:

3.2.1 *Evaluation feedback* Does the customer feed the results of efforts taken to familiarize themselves with the supplier's operation back to the supplier and how much is the supplier involved in the discussion of these results?

3.2.2 *Performance feedback* How efficiently does the customer feedback performance information to the supplier? Is it discussed formally?

3.2.3 *Approval* How valuable is the customer's approval program in terms of involving the supplier in the process?

3.2.4 *Teamwork* Does the customer involve the supplier in appropriate internal decision-making processes or developments?

3.3 Business Is the customer's desire for a more open relationship with the supplier reflected in the type of business information it communicates? Elements under *Business* are:

3.3.1 *Window* The customer's effectiveness in giving the supplier advanced warning of orders.

3.3.2 *Lead times* The customer's effectiveness in giving the supplier advanced warning of future trends in product and process developments.

3.3.3 *Cost* Degree by which the customer's desire for a longer term relationship translates into a relaxed attitude to disclosing internal cost information and results of market analyses.

3.4 People Does the customer effectively inform the supplier about its organization and personnel? Factors under *People* are:

3.4.1 *Organization* The customer's effectiveness in communicating details about its organization structure.

3.4.2 *Interpersonal* Degree of customer effort in establishing close interpersonal links with supplier personnel.

4 Information flow; supplier to customer

The supplier's effectiveness in creating a flow of information to the customer which provides the basis for effective supply and the sharing of knowledge and ideas; a contributory factor towards good *Performance*. The contributory factors are:

4.1 Technical Does the supplier pass on the right technical information at the right time? Factors under *Technical* are:

4.1.1 *Capability* Supplier's effectiveness in communicating details about process and equipment capability.

4.1.2 *Problems* Supplier's effectiveness in communicating information about operational problems.

4.1.3 *Improvements* Supplier's willingness to communicate details of possible improvements to operations which would benefit the customer.

4.1.4 *Quality* Supplier's effectiveness in communicating information about the control and management of Quality.

4.2 Involvement To what extent does the supplier involve the customer in its internal procedures and decision making to enable a closer relationship? Factors under *Involvement* are:

4.2.1 *Feedback* Does the supplier openly disclose information to the customer about business performance and internal performance measurements?

4.2.2 *Teamwork* Does the supplier involve the customer in appropriate internal decision-making processes?

4.3 Business Is the supplier's desire for a more open relationship with the customer reflected in the type of business information it communicates? Factors under *Business* are:

4.3.1 *Supply Source* Supplier's willingness/effectiveness in communicating information about *its* suppliers.

4.3.2 *Cost* Supplier's willingness/effectiveness in communicating cost information.

4.3.3 *Lead times* Supplier's willingness/effectiveness in communicating information about the availability of resources.

4.4 People Does the supplier effectively inform the customer about its organization and personnel? Elements under *People* are:

4.4.1 *Organization* Supplier's effectiveness in communicating details about its organization structure.

4.4.2 *Interpersonal* Degree of supplier effort in establishing close interpersonal links with the customer personnel.

This RPT framework provides the basis for measurement. As for any analysis procedure, data has to be gathered to provide a base of information on which the identification of strengths and weaknesses can take place. Two questionnaires, one for the customer and one for the supplier, gather over 300 pieces of data. Each response to a question is scored against 'best practice' as identified by SCMG's work with research and client companies. This comparison produces a mark out of 10 for each question. Scores for questions are then aggregated to produce a mark out of 10 for each of the elements of the RPT. (Each element can be fed by scores from supplier questions and/or customer questions.) The scores for the elements are then aggregated to produce marks out of 10 for the factors.

The results from the RPT analysis are usually presented as shown in Table 7.1.

It becomes clear from this type of analysis that poor practice on both sides of the relationship can lead to a shortfall in expected performance. It also shows the need for joint improvement actions to be developed through discussion at joint review meetings. Moreover, this type of measurement touches upon issues which are not normally discussed between the customer and supplier and hence in itself can initiate a change process.

A major benefit of using third parties to gather the scores is that there is no concern that the answers are being used in inappropriate ways. The process itself is self-regulating as regards honest responses. Since each side's responses are being scored and aggregated, the resultant answers are numerical indicators of problem or opportunity areas. Since both sides have contributed to the scores, 'blame' is not easily attached to any individual. The joint review process becomes positive and forward-focused instead of recriminating.

Use of the independent third party also allows responses to be more critical than in traditional evaluations where the real danger is obtaining the kind of responses that the other party thinks you want to hear. The need for the third party's involvement will diminish as both sides learn to be more open and trusting.

To give an example of how the Relationship Positioning Tool has operated in practice consider the following case study. (NB. The following case study is a real life example but for reasons of confidentiality the names of the companies involved have been changed)

PERFORMANCE	
Quality	5.1
Delivery	7.2
Cost	7.7
Innovation	8.3

CUSTOMER		SUPPLIER	
Strategy		*Capability*	
Requirements	4.1	Company Profile	5.6
Attitude	8.7	People	4.5
Systems	7.5	Process	6.2
People	4.5	Supplier Management	3.6
Information flow Customer to Supplier		*Information flow Supplier to Customer*	
Technical	5.8	Technical	6.6
Involvement	7.9	Involvement	3.1
Business	6.9	Business	6.2
People	8.7	People	5.0

Table 7.1 Sample RPT Results

Case Study: Hometool and PMC

BACKGROUND

Hometool are a multinational corporation involved in the production and marketing of a wide range of electrical consumer goods on a worldwide basis.

At their English plant they employ 1300 permanent, plus approximately 600 seasonal staff on the design and manufacture of a wide range of consumer power tools for DIY in the home and garden. In total they produce about 10.2 million units per year which are sold mainly throughout Europe and the United States.

PMC comprises a group of companies manufacturing technical plastic components and assemblies for a wide range of Original Equipment Manufacturers in the Business Machine and Telecommunication, Medical, Industrial, Aerospace, Defence, Consumer Electronic and Consumer Durable and Disposable market sectors. It is in turn part of a multinational company operating in the United Kingdom, the United States and Australasia. There has been considerable capital investment in new advanced machinery and equipment in the last five years and new techniques introduced include Statistical Process Control, Total Quality Management, Failure Mode Effect Analysis, Just in Time and Electronic Data Interchange.

The company is certified to BS5750 Part 2, ISO9002 and BS5295, meeting the needs of the Medical and Pharmaceutical industries, and offers a comprehensive design, manufacture, finishing, assembly and customer support service. As well as Hometool, other major customers include Northern Telecom, Guinness, Ford (the company has also achieved Q1 status), IBM, Royal Ordnance, Polaroid and Toshiba.

PMC had been a supplier to Hometool for a number of years up until the mid/late 1980s. However at that time, PMC were no longer considered by them to be price competitive, and the business was moved elsewhere. In 1989 the company was again selected as a supplier of plastic components to Hometool, this time on the basis of cost rather than price and currently supplies approximately 4.4 million tool body mouldings per annum spread over 39 part numbers.

At the beginning of 1991, the relationship between the two companies could best be described as compliant. Long-serving employees at PMC remembered quite clearly what they regarded as unacceptable behaviour on the part of Hometool in the past, and in industry in general, Hometool had acquired the reputation of being quick to move plastic moulding tools from one supplier to another for short-term price benefits. There was a very obvious reluctance to become too dependent on, or too closely involved with them again.

PMC clearly welcomed the opportunity to participate in the RPT project, seeing it as a valuable opportunity to voice their concerns over the nature of the relationship; Hometool welcomed the opportunity to demonstrate that things had changed and they were now the kind of customer that PMC would like to have.

The RPT questionnaires were applied to both companies and the results calculated. The major features of the results were as follows (remember the scores are out of 10):

Performance, Quality – 2.0
It was recognized that Hometool's continued use of percentage terms to measure quality was not best practice and a move to the use of Parts Per Million was agreed. It had also been agreed that this would be one of the key criteria used. In addition it was also agreed that knowing what PMC's Cost of Quality was would be a powerful motivator for improvement, and the establishment of a Cost of Quality project team was agreed as one of the key improvement actions.

Customer Strategy, Requirements, Delivery – 5.5
Hometool do not measure suppliers' delivery performances and it was agreed that a pilot measurement project should be set up to do so for PMC.

Customer Strategy, Requirements, Innovation – 1.7
Hometool had no track record with respect to setting targets for improvements to products. Whilst no specific action was agreed to improve this target setting, PMC were asked by Hometool to design from scratch, and on their own, the moulding for a new drill. They were somewhat taken aback by this and suggested to Hometool that on this first occasion it would be more appropriate to participate in Hometool's design team rather than work on their own.

Customer Strategy, Systems, Scheduling – 3.2
The almost daily changes that Hometool make to the delivery schedules that they give to their suppliers has been one of the most common causes of complaint voiced about Hometool by supplier company personnel. Whilst it was agreed that increased flexibility of response to changes in customer demand is one of the key elements of increased competitiveness, Hometool agreed to carry out an analysis of the changes made to their schedules.

Supplier Capability, Process, Flexibility – 5.1
Hometool were very keen that actions were taken to improve PMC's flexibility of response to the changes in their schedules, and because of this it was agreed to try and reduce the set-up times in the cells where Hometool product was manufactured.

Information Flow (Customer to Supplier), Technical, Innovations – 3.0
Information Flow (Supplier to Customer), People, Interpersonal – 5.4
Neither party was provided with information from the other that would help to increase the familiarity with each other's developments and techniques

and hence the scope for continuous improvement activities was limited. It was agreed to arrange visits by line operators to each other's factories given that this was one of the most valuable, yet simplest actions to set up.

Information Flow (Supplier to Customer), Involvement, Cost – 0.0
PMC were the only 'plastics' supplier who did not supply Hometool with information about their cost structure, and Hometool were very anxious to have access to this data. There were clear concerns on the part of PMC personnel about the accuracy of their standard costings, on which prices are based, and about whether senior management would be willing to pass on the information at all. However it was agreed that this would be considered by senior PMC management.

The joint team meeting to discuss the RPT results was held at PMC and proved to be a very constructive discussion. It soon became clear, however, that the respondent from PMC was not empowered to make decisions as to precisely which improvement activities would in fact be carried out. At the end of this meeting the under-noted list of desired improvement activities was created and the meeting closed with the PMC contact accepting responsibility for 'selling' these to the company's Managing Director.

- *Set-up time reductions* It was agreed that PMC would establish a set-up time reduction project team in one of the manufacturing cells that produced Hometool product. Hometool had developed their own set-up time reduction training course and video, and agreed to provide training for the team members.
- *Changes to Hometool schedules* It was agreed that PMC would carry out an analysis of the changes made to delivery schedules by Hometool. Hometool agreed that they would investigate the reasons for the high number of changes being made.
- *Sharing of cost information* It was agreed that PMC would carry out an investigation of their actual and standard manufacturing costings, and would share the results with Hometool.
- *Cost of Quality initiative* PMC agreed to set up a Cost of Quality project team with a view to establishing an objective measure of what poor quality was actually costing the company.
- *Inter-company visits* Both companies agreed to arrange visits to each other's factories for those direct and indirect employees who produced or used the relevant products.

Progress as detailed below was made in respect of each of the agreed action.

1 **Set-up time reductions** The project team was established and training received in October/November 1991. An initial study of each of the tool

changes in the particular cell was carried out, and the following target reductions were set. The level of capital investment required in each phase was also categorized.

Stage 1 – Better preparation: 35–40%: no capital investment.
Stage 2 – Actual change: 10%: low investment.
Stage 3 – Actual change: 40%: high investment.

By the end of May 1992, actual set-up time reductions of between 25 per cent and 50 per cent had been achieved, and the number of set-ups carried out in the cell had been doubled with batch sizes halved.

2 Changes to Hometool schedules An initial analysis of changes made to delivery schedules was carried out by PMC over the period January to March 1992. This analysis showed that of the 36 part numbers analyzed, changes of up to ± 100 per cent were made in each of the three months in 34 of the part numbers. This information was given to Hometool.

During the data gathering for this particular project it transpired that PMC accepted and ordered the raw materials for any quantity of product appearing on the schedule. In one particular instance, the quantity shown as required had in fact been overstated by mistake by a factor of 10. Yet PMC had not queried this massive change and had in fact ordered the raw materials. As a result of this discovery, PMC have been told to consider the possibility that dramatic changes in volume requirements may in fact be errors and they should raise them with Hometool, rather than simply accepting them.

3 Sharing of cost information The study of actual manufacturing costings was carried out, and despite massive reluctance on the part of the Managing Director of PMC, the information was shared with Hometool. This was done in a private meeting between the Managing Director and the Senior Buyer from Hometool. The contents of the meeting have not been disclosed to any other PMC employee, and the managing Director is unwilling to tell anyone within PMC who does not already know, or anyone outside the company that they have done this.

The significance of this meeting should not be underestimated. It was as a direct result of the personal relationship between the two individuals that the Managing Director of PMC felt that he could trust Hometool not to abuse the cost information which he was reluctantly, willing to give them. It was also as a direct result of this meeting that PMC decided to ask their Works Manager, who was about to take early retirement, if he would be willing to stay on in a role dedicated to Hometool. The Works Manager agreed and now spends between two and three days each week in

Hometool's factory working with Hometool's operators to identify improvements that can be made to product and process specifications. A significant number of modifications have already been made to individual product quality plans that have allowed PMC to raise dramatically the level of quality they deliver to Hometool.

One example related to the packaging and level of care with which PMC handled completed mouldings. These were individually inserted into clear plastic bags and placed by hand into the cages supplied by Hometool for their delivery. On Hometool's production lines, when mouldings were needed the cages were simply and roughly tipped out onto the work area with little concern for the careful handling that PMC had used. Indeed, the process of removing the mouldings from the plastic bags frequently generated static electricity and Hometool's operators were constantly receiving small shocks. This had never been mentioned to PMC whose only reason for putting the mouldings in the plastic bags was to protect them from the rain when they were being moved between the production and storage buildings.

In a second example the PMC Works Manager saw that Hometool operators frequently banged the assembled plastic moulding on the work bench. On inquiry it transpired that the operators always had slight difficulty in getting the two halves of a clam-shell moulding to fit together, and so they banged them on the workbench so that they fitted properly. Very occasionally this practice caused cosmetic damage to the mouldings which were then rejected by Quality Inspectors. It was a very simple matter of slightly adjusting the tolerance on the moulding tool, whilst keeping within the Hometool design specification, and the difficulty in assembling the clam-shell was eliminated.

4 Measurement of delivery performance No progress was made on this action. In the words of the PMC Manufacturing Services Manager the reason for this was that 'neither organization has been able to allocate resources, the constraint being time and cost'.

5 Cost of quality initiative No progress was made on this action either. Again the reason given by PMC Manufacturing Services Manager is that 'the volume of the task appeared daunting for the Quality Manager. The volume of the data and its collation into quantitative measures of cost is unknown territory, which may account for the non-completion. The Quality Manager subsequently left the company and this initiative was not set as one of the objectives of the new manager.'

(The above two sections have not been removed from the collective agendas but are considered to be more suited for medium-term actions and reports. This account was essentially of short-term impacts.)

6 Inter-company visits Despite a number of postponements the first visit took place in January 1992. Since that date a number of further visits have been made by personnel from both companies.

Benefits achieved
1 PMC's delivered quality performance measured in parts per million (ppm); this data was first reported to PMC in January 1992 but with figures going back to September 1991. The monthly figures to the end of May 1992 are shown below.

Month	PPM Score	6 Month Trend
September 91	17,669	17,669
October 91	15,982	16,825
November 91	20,285	17,978
December 91	8,340	15,569
January 92	580	10,619
February 92	5,715	11,286
March 92	2,377	9,523
April 92	8,605	5,524
May 92	136	4,190

Whilst this demonstrates that there was still a considerable level of inconsistency at the end of May 1992 the six-monthly trend has continued to show a reduction, and by the end of August 1992 was 2,390. This is compared with a 31st December 1992 target of 1,250.

2 From final discussions held with both companies it is our firm belief that the very significant change in attitude by the management of PMC was brought about to a large extent simply by their involvement in this project. The willingness of Hometool to submit themselves to the critical appraisal of a third party, the Supply Chain Management Group, combined with the trust developed between the Senior Buyer from Hometool and the Managing Director of PMC persuaded the Managing Director that Hometool meant what they now said about changing the relationships between the companies, and that Hometool were now the kind of customer that would help PMC meet its strategic objectives. The companies are now much more open about saying what they expect from each other, and about sharing information. There is a much more positive feeling in each company about their role in the future of their business partner.

Given that the measurement of the relationship is problematic, many companies have used third parties to facilitate their investigations, for the reasons discussed earlier.

The key requirement of this phase, and in fact of the whole process to improve the relationship, is that both parties step back from their day-to-day situations and take a methodical and reflective look at how effectively they work together on all fronts. Moreover, as has been stated before, the support and involvement of senior management during this phase is key. The individuals involved in identifying the actions must have a clear mandate from senior management to propose and implement changes which might often confront traditional company policy. There should be no ambiguity in the effort to find better ways for the companies to work together. Trust is all-important here, but it needs to be built.

PHASE 5: ACTION IMPLEMENTATION AND PROGRESS REVIEW

This phase covers the actual effort which has to be put in by both parties to realize the improvements identified by the joint team during Phase 4. In essence, this is the phase where the real donkey work is put in and where the whole concept of achieving mutual benefits and competitive advantage through collaboration is put to the test. If no reports of improvements are made during this phase then the belief and commitment from both sides can quickly disappear.

In light of this, in the early stages it is important that a mixture of fundamental and minor issues are tackled. The fundamental issues, such as the sharing of benefits, are important because unless the difficulties are ironed out early on, and the 'goal posts' firmly established, misunderstandings can arise later on which can jeopardize the whole relationship. Tackling minor problems often allows early success and helps to build enthusiasm and confidence into the relationship.

In any case it is important that there is the feeling of progress in this phase, not only amongst the members of the joint teams, but in the other parts of both companies. Some key points for this phase:

- Targets and time-scales for each identified action should be established at the beginning. Responsibility for each action should be allocated to relevant individuals of the joint team.
- Pro-formas should be devised which detail the action to be taken, subteam members (where appropriate), original targets and time-scales and subsequent progress for each action identified. These pro-formas should

form the basis of the agenda for the joint team progress review meetings. Most companies hold such joint meetings every quarter alternately at each other's premises.

- One of the main outputs from the joint team meetings should be a brief report detailing progress for the eyes of senior management on both sides. It is vital that senior management are kept up to date and in touch with developments to ensure their continuing commitment and enthusiasm.

- Another useful mechanism to keep the profile of the relationship improvement process high is the provision of a regular newsletter for other managers within the customer company and more generally amongst the rest of the supply base. The key thought here is that the more people that hear the good stories, the more enthusiasm and commitment there will be for the change process.

- Some customer companies have held conference-style events at which each joint customer–supplier team have made presentations detailing the progress which has been achieved in developing the relationship. This provides a useful mechanism for the cross-fertilization of ideas and promotes the suppliers' feeling of being part of a larger team or 'family'.

The message from the description of the Relationship Improvement Process above is that companies following such a process stand a better chance of developing effective Partnership Sourcing relationships with suppliers than those who rely on ad hoc, fragmented approaches. However, there also has to be an awareness that the change to collaborative relationships is not going to happen overnight and hence resource has to be allocated to give the best chance for success. We noted earlier how Nissan and ICL have a ten-year horizon for widespread adoption and benefit. Going through a systematic process certainly provides a new focus for building close, trusting relationships but even so, changing attitudes and behaviours developed over many years does take time. Any company with a strong desire to go down this road must be prepared to put extra effort in over at least six months to get relationships on a 'self developing' footing.

So far in this chapter we have looked at the barriers to implementation of Partnership Sourcing and a methodology to overcome these barriers. One major question still remains; how do you sustain the relationship over the longer term, i.e. how do you keep the mutual trust, confidence and commitment going through thick and thin?

There are considerable potential threats to any relationship between a customer and supplier. Moreover, a relationship characterized by mutual dependency and high levels of trust is especially vulnerable, i.e. the stakes are high. There is nothing more offensive than being 'wronged' by a party whom you had trusted implicitly. Once the trust is broken there is often no chance of going back to what had existed before.

An alternative viewpoint, of course, is that the collaborative relationship should be more robust than the traditional here-today-gone-tomorrow relationship. The fact that the stakes are so high should mean that both parties are highly motivated to find ways around problems which crop up and their experience of working in a collaborative fashion aids the quick settlement of disagreements.

Whatever the theory, there is no doubt that the healthiest situation is for both parties to have a finely tuned awareness about all the potential threats to the relationship and hence be in a position to work together in a way which will neutralize any of them.

First of all, consider some of the *external* threats:

- A new supplier approaches the customer with a substantially lower price. In the traditional relationship model it is more than likely that the customer would switch to the new source.
- A new supplier company appears on the scene with a product or process which demonstrates a significant technological advance on what the current supplier has to offer. Again, the customer's gut feel is to switch sources.
- Market trends demand that the customer has to change the basic specification of its products very quickly. For example, environmental concerns contributed towards car manufacturers switching from metal fuel tanks to plastic ones. The 'natural' reaction of the customer would be to find a new supplier with the appropriate technology.
- Recessionary pressures on the customer means that they have to reduce output and costs to survive. This in turn means reduced orders for the supplier and there is also a tendency for the customer to look for swingeing price cuts.

In all these cases the threat arises from reversion to old attitudes and practices on the part of the customer. Again, it could be argued that if the Partnership Sourcing philosophy is well ingrained into the customer company's culture then the immediate thought would not be of these alternatives. However, most companies still have a foot in both the old and the new and therefore in times of stress returning to the old comfort zone can seem to make a lot of sense. Most businesses are relatively conservative, after all.

However, there are sound reasons why customers should stick to their partner suppliers and precedents have emerged which show the way for relationships to survive through thick and thin. The common thread is that the particular threat has been tackled by the customer and supplier working in a joint manner, i.e. thinking as a relationship pair.

For example, in the case of the threat posed by a cheaper source, as described above, the most successful relationships have gathered detailed information to find out just why the price is so much lower and then used that information to feed a greater understanding of the processes and procedures being used at present and to identify opportunities for improvements and cost savings on a joint basis. Moreover, the best relationships will pro-actively use this type of cost benchmarking exercise in their continuous improvement efforts, either through the customer inviting tenders for the particular item or service or, involving less subterfuge, set up a system for information exchange with firms in a similar customer–supplier situation. The latter technique is easier to set up if the link is made with companies in different sectors. In this way the customer and supplier can keep themselves ahead of the game without jeopardizing the relationship and hence incurring the sizeable on-cost associated with finding an alternative source or user.

The scenario posed by a major technological innovation brought forward by a third party to the customer presents a similar type of dilemma to that above. The pressures on the customer to 'get into' the new technology by sourcing from, and working closely with, the new supplier instead of the existing one are strong. As much as anything this is a powerful argument for the customer and supplier to keep a careful eye on developments and be proactive in a way which ensures that they stay ahead of the game. For example some have consciously developed close links with industrial technology network groups, universities, etc. to allow them to anticipate forthcoming innovations. For the case where the new technology comes 'out of the blue', i.e. where there has been no anticipation by either party, some companies have invested in the new technology through acquisition or license, rather than switching sources. The acquisition route is particularly appropriate when the new supplier is small and companies such as IBM have been known to take this type of strategic action.

The potential threat, involving a fundamental change in supplied product specification, differs only from the second one with respect to time. The sudden announcement of a new technology can lead to panic in the customer, with decisions being made very quickly and without analysis. An essentially end-user-driven change in specification still needs prompt action but the change has usually been flagged from various sources, hence there is an opportunity for careful planning. Traditionally companies would have conducted extensive research to locate the right supplier without even considering their existing supplier but increasingly the best customers have recognized that the true qualities of the suppliers with whom they have developed collaborative relationships, lie in their ability to be good partners. The technology in most cases, therefore, is not necessarily a major issue and can be overcome by the customer and supplier investing their efforts in bringing in and developing the technology required. A recent example of this idea concerns one of the Japanese car manufacturers in the UK. They had a requirement to fit catalysts to all new cars sold in the UK and chose to ask their existing exhaust system supplier to take on the catalyst manufacturing technology. Although the supplier had absolutely no background in this specialized technology, careful investment of money and training by the customer ensured that the supplier was up to speed in a relatively short space of time.

Above all else, the most recent recession has posed a serious threat to Partnership Sourcing arrangements between customers and suppliers, as identified above. Many customer companies have gone to the wall and taken their suppliers with them. However, for those companies who believe they can survive through recesson, there are options other than saving costs by simply dropping suppliers and leaving them to fend for themselves. There are examples of customer companies who have recognized the major investment that has been made in a partner supplier and appreciated the high cost of picking up a new source from scratch when the dust settles. These companies have opted to support their key suppliers either financially or by finding new business when times are hard in the belief that the competitive edge achieved through having an effective supply chain will give them pole position when the markets improve. More than simply being customer benevolence, this feeling of shared destiny is a powerful factor for sustaining the commitment in a collaborative relationship. This concept of almost complete mutual dependency might perhaps be regarded by customers as being at odds with the fact that the supplier has relationships with other, and possibly competing, customers. The customer might see its commitment as being total but the supplier's commitment as being diluted by the fact that they have to service all the other customers. This is an entirely valid point of view which perhaps suggests that complete commitment can only be gained from complete mutual dependency. However, the customer has to balance the desire for reliable service from the supplier with the undoubted benefits that can arise as a result of developments initiated by the supplier's customers – any one of the relationships can benefit from the cross-fertilization of ideas.

These external threats can pose some significant problems for the relationship but in some respects there is a more significant threat from inappropriate actions taken by either party after the partnership has been sealed. The authors have seen numerous examples of relationships breaking down very quickly because of mistakes being made in the management of the relationship. Again, the catalyst for the breakdown is the removal of trust and confidence. With the external threat there is some time available for joint discussions and actions to counteract the problem but once trust breaks down things can slide very quickly.

Let us take a look at these *internal* threats.

1. *'Surprise' change in relationship interface personnel – a common problem.* The most extreme example of this is when the main contact point manager in the customer is suddenly moved to a new job within the company and a new person is drafted in who has little understanding of what has gone before. The main 'live wire' link between the companies has been severed and the supplier's trust and confidence in the customer can evaporate. This situation is exacerbated when the relationship has essentially been built around personal friendships, which is the tendency when goodwill trust is seen as a prerequisite. The counter to this particular threat is to build strong inter-company structures and systems through a joint team and to manage the transition of personnel very carefully. If the main contact point is to drop out then the replacement has to be well trained and eased into the new situation. Of course there have to be good interpersonal relationships present between the two parties but the business relationship should not be dependent on individual personalities.

2. *Misunderstandings about requirements/intentions leading to mistakes.* This is bound to happen from time to time and, unless corrective actions are taken, can lead to mistrust and resentment. The answer is essentially to maintain a high degree of mutual awareness through clear and frequent communication. There is the viewpoint that once the Partnership Sourcing relationship is established operations can more or less run themselves. Although the overall level of effort encountered during the change to collaborative relationships should drop there is still a need to maintain the channels of communication. One important feature of this communication is the regular affirmation of commitment from both parties to the relationship. It is important that the medium and long-term objectives of going down the road of collaboration are always at the forefront of everybody's mind when a crisis occurs. Moreover, regular information about the successes of the relationship keeps confidence high and strengthens senior management commitment.

3. *Problems arise and there is a desire for blame to be apportioned.* Again, this reflects the forces which drive management to revert back to old ideas. Quite possibly there is a need for somebody to pick up the 'bill' for mistakes made. However, the emphasis should be on seeing any problem as a joint issue and creating actions which can resolve the difficulties once and for all.

In quality terms we need the 'fixes' to be permanent.

These are some of the threats which can seriously damage the Partnership Sourcing relationship. As a general principle, with a fully effective collaborative relationship in place both parties should actually have more time to commit to positive developments as opposed to activities such as expediting, haggling over price and chasing invoices. Some of this 'free' time has to be committed to maintaining the relationship in the ways described above, in order to counter the threats to the relationship when they crop up. However the majority of the time can be channelled into value-adding activities such as pursuing innovations and improving performance.

In this chapter we have tried to capture all of the aspects of building then maintaining a collaborative relationship. Some of the above may seem rather alien to some readers but it is apparent that many companies are now reaping the benefits from Partnership Sourcing having planted the seeds and tended the crop in a similar manner to that described above. Without doubt, the transition from an adversarial relationship to the collaborative model will not be without its difficulties; mistakes will be made and blind alleys will be explored during the essential learning experience. However, if companies can learn from the mistakes made by others, not necessarily in their industrial sector, then the lead time for realizing the major savings in cost and time which can be gained from Partnership Sourcing will be dramatically reduced. The wheel need not be reinvented if new understandings can be adequately translated and understood by all those who are embarking on this quest for supply chain improvement.

SUMMARY

- **A change programme needs commitment and understanding by all involved, especially senior mangement.**

- **The Relationship Improvement Process covers the five phases of internal commitment and team building; partner selection; supplier commitment and joint team building; measurement and improvement planning; and action implementation and progress review.**

- **The Relationship Positioning Tool measures visible, current performance against the business deliverables of innovation, quality, delivery and cost but also looks below the surface to examine those factors creating tomorrow's performance. These include customer strategy, supplier capability and the two-way information flow.**

● Moving towards Partnership Sourcing needs time to be measured in months rather than weeks but threats to the relationship should be regarded as an opportunity to strengthen the customer–supplier unit by joint action to convert threats to opportunities.

Part Four

SUMMARY

8

SUMMARY AND
MATURITY GRID

In this book we have travelled along the road to Partnership Sourcing. The underlying factor which must never be pushed to one side is that this is not a panacea. It might not always fit in all its features and it will not be easy or quick, although some short-term operational benefits can come within weeks at little or no cost.

We argued that the nature of competition in global markets is driving organizations to satisfy customer demand in new and innovative ways, often through reorganizing both internal and external activities.

We examined the basic need to perform against the Business Deliverables and argued that done in the correct sequence, these need not be trade-offs but rather, by switching existing effort and ensuring that targeting and control are appropriate, then what results is the ability both to control but more importantly, to reduce costs in real terms.

The basic concepts of supply chains extend the world-class manufacturing models to cross the former organizational boundaries, but done in the recognition that an integrated supply chain of partners without common ownership must be managed in a way different from that of a single monolithic bureaucracy.

In all of the above we have focused on manufacturing industry, but the important task for any manager is to avoid the trap of thinking that one's current situation or organization is unique. Of course to an extent any organization's context is unique (otherwise the organization would easily be replaceable) but we all need to learn to dig below the surface of management techniques, fashions and guru speak to understand the real message or generic principle which might be adapted by us to fit into our unique situation. This approach can be developed in all of us. The Japanese are said to ask the question *why* five times, each questioning round stripping off another layer of the onion of preconceived, unchallenged, received wisdoms.

We firmly believe that the basic tenets of the approaches discussed here can be applied in most aspects of human endeavour, and without going too far into the metaphysical, what could our lives be like if instead of the first (and often only) path to be chosen being conflict, it was cooperation?

We need caution, however. It must be cooperation where possible and conflict where necessary. The market place for the final consumer is still a tough place where, all other things being equal, price will prevail. Of course, part of the strategic trick is to demonstrate that all other things are not equal and actually provide value in themselves, and consequently price becomes only a part of the package. What we have also discussed is organizing the supply chain so that real cost is actually reduced, thereby allowing the sales team the space to play war games on price if needed. This is a double-edged sword against the market enemy since the fighting of a price war might damage them in income terms while their already higher cost base squeezes their margins further. In such a war the lean supply chain will be victorious. However please remember that members of your own supply chain are not the enemy.

Another of the strategic issues for the supply chain is being inside or outside which chain. By definition a fully functioning supply chain provides real barriers to entry for new participants, but possibly also barriers to exit. A long-term continuing commitment should need something drastic to cause it to be seen as no longer meeting the organization's needs.

Choice of partner and supply chain is thus a very important issue and it must also be recognized that (particularly further back up the supply chain), some of the participants will be partners in other chains. This realization might be enough to encourage greater efforts from their customers to keep them supportive of the customer's own chain.

We also developed the academic aspects of this subject as we described how convergence in thinking was producing a theoretical justification for Partnership Sourcing. This is an important aspect because there are those who dismiss the 'best practice' approach as fundamentally flawed. After all, how many of yesterday's best companies are paragons today? Given our discussion of context, then at the level of simple replication of the rules of 'best practice', it must be true that this is not feasible. Reverting to our earlier point about understanding the underlying principles, we can see that there are principles here which are consistent with a number of theoretical academic approaches. This is good news for management scholars, while the practitioners (more important in our view) can perhaps take comfort from the fact that not only do good companies do these things, but adoption and adaptation has a greater logic than 'me-tooism'.

At a number of points in the book we argued that there is emerging (in the

West) a new operating principle. We also extended the discussion to examine the differences between the adversarial and collaborative approaches before moving into a series of further explications of our chosen path. This was supported by a management of change model and by the Relationship Positioning Tool and Relationship Improvement Process developed by SCMG.

We hope that Chapter Seven in particular provides encouragement to you to move along the Partnership Sourcing path. In our roles as academics and consultants there are limits to what we can do since ultimately the decision is yours, or more accurately yours and your mandate teams', on both sides. The action responsibilities are all yours. The evidence is growing that Partnership Sourcing can make a competitive difference, and we have provided some examples both as role models and as encouragement to at least try.However, the impact on the organization is major and should not be underestimated. We have tried here to provide support to those of you making these strategic moves. The high-level support provided to Partnership Sourcing Ltd. encourages us that 'UK plc.' recognizes the competitive leverage that is here to be exerted, but the will to try and to succeed will make the difference.

To bring our discussion to some conclusion, we have drawn up a Relationship Maturity Grid against which you can plot your organization's current position. This obviously does not capture the detail of the Relationship Positioning Tool and is only looking at one organization, not both partners. Nevertheless we hope it provides some insights into how far you might still have to go along this road.

If you manage a profile of all 7s with one partner, will it be true of all your strategic partners? Would they have scored the same? How do you know?

The grid makes use of the same key criteria as the Relationship Positioning Tool but adds rows to indicate the nature of the current relationship and the current business outcomes obtained. The scales go from pure Adversarial at a rating of 1, through a Transitional phase where some changes have happened, to Partnership with a rating of 7. The scoring cannot be exact but hopefully it is still meaningful, so position your organization against each criteria and join your dots to produce a profile.

If you plot a number of profiles for your Partner Relationships, perhaps it will help target some improvement actions and form a comparator for a review later.

At that later date we feel sure that significant changes in key business criteria can be obtained and overall that your organization and your partners' will be much more satisfying and interesting places to work. If this turns out to be true please tell someone about it and help all of us learn from

	Adversarial	Transitional	Partnership	1	2	3	4	5	6	7
Quality	Variable, high inspection/rejects	Some SPC, Taguchi, QFD begun	<100 parts per million, improving trend							
Delivery	Not measured but complained about	Some ship to stock 90% on time target	100% on time, lead time reducing							
Cost	Hidden, tough price negotiations	1-way open book, beginning Cost of Quality	Reducing in real terms. Joint action improvements							
Innovation	· Used as negotiation tactic · 'Forces' supply switch	Welcomed but not co-ordinated	Major differentiating factor among peers							
Customer Strategy	· 'Win' in the market · Power play negotiations	· Customer recognises responsibilities · Open to question	Co-destiny fully understood and operating, shared vision							
Supplier Capability	Limited, focused, protected	Moving towards increased service range	Contributes multiple skills, solves customer problems							
Information Flow	Need to know, filtered	Limited, unbalanced	2-way, multiple paths, interchanges of personnel							
Nature of Relationship	What relationships?	Tentative, experimental – are they serious?	Demanding but supportive, belief in one another							
Business Outcomes	Uncertain	Early performance pay-offs	Increased market share, reduced costs greater competitiveness							

Table 8.1 Relationship Maturity Grid

cach othcr and provide real added value to society. If you can do this then the future will truly be, (in Lessom's terms) based on a learning community and the power of collaborative working will be seen as exerting much greater leverage than any simple minded view about the 'efficiency of the market'.

This concludes the main part of this book. The next chapter is even more optional than the rest although if you have come this far we hope you will continue. The style is different, however, because what is presented is a case study format which can be used in your own organization, to surface and discuss the issues we have covered or perhaps only touched on in the book so far. As we say in the briefing note we had fun 'performing' this case and we hope you also have fun as well as significant learning opportunity when you use it.

9

CASE STUDY: JONES AND SONS LTD. (ENGINEERS)

BRIEFING NOTE

This case is reproduced for illustrative purposes here and to provide the opportunity to consider many of the aspects of this book as they might apply to this business, facing the opportunities and threats of the new contract.

What is provided is the basic background case material, including the attachment data sheets 1–4 'a' versions, and sheet 5. The 'b' versions of the data sheets are revised budget figures produced by the managing director as he reacted to the new opportunity presented to him by the letter from Nissoto Motors (UK) Limited. The letter from the bank highlights the seriousness of the forthcoming decisions for survival, let alone success.

When we ran this case for the final annual conference (1993) for the then Institute of Materials Management (now merged to form the Institute of Logistics), we had as actors David Farmer as David Jones, Tony Borlace as Technical Director, Mark Weber as Manufacturing Director and Douglas Macbeth as Materials Director. We played our roles with much enjoyment, prompted by the 'speech bubbles' of instant reactions. The participants were used as the internal management team developing 'answers' to the analytical frameworks attached as Strategic Evaluation sheets for Technical, Manufacturing and Materials.

One way to use the case is to introduce the issue areas and then allow general discussion to fill in the blanks on the grid for each function on its own.

The next exercise is to pull together the separate functional views into a coherent Board view for presentation to the managing director. This should bring out the real strategic as well as operational difficulties of accepting the challenge of Nissoto or slipping out of the market altogether. Of course, David Jones could simply sell the freehold of his factory site to the super-market chain for its expansion plans – the offer is a good one and he is getting older, and who really cares about the nation's manufacturing base?

(The case attachments leave blanks for your use. There are available 'solutions' as proposed by the team of authors, as well as key points for the board presentation to the MD. These are available free of charge from SCMG Ltd., Glasgow University Business School, 59 Southpark Avenue, Glasgow G12 8LF. Telephone: +44(0)41 330 5696, or Telefax +44(0)41 330 5669.)

JONES AND SONS LTD. (ENGINEERS)

Jones and Sons Ltd. is a mechanical engineering parts manufacturer which has been part of the component supply industry of the West Midlands since 1923 when the first Dai Jones moved his small company from Wales to be closer to the action in the automobile manufacturing business building up around Birmingham. Since that time Jones and Sons has remained a moderately successful privately owned company whose reputation was built around the total customer orientation that Dai first established. To the outside world this was captured in the motto 'Whatever the customer wants we will provide'. Insiders however knew the sub-title 'and we will make our margins later!'.

While still prepared to bid for almost any mechanical part Jones and Sons had gradually specialized in car seat components and sub-assemblies. They did most of the operations 'below the seat cover'. This included: tube forming, welding, painting, forming of mounting brackets and slides, actuation arms, linkages and mechanical controls for front seats. Rear seats were of course much simpler constructions, earning less than front seats.

The current requirement was to deliver these to their customers' goods inwards inspection areas for onward transport to a sub-assembly manu-facturing area where the electric motors, heaters, electronic controls and connectors would be fitted prior to final cladding in cloth or leather against a final assembly line call off.

As part of the process of learning from and keeping up with their cus-tomers Jones and Sons had invested in a new automated paint oven in 1990 and in an extensive Material Requirements Planning (MRPII) computer system linked into their embryo Computer Aided Design computer system.

Although initially specified by consultants working through the DTI scheme and approved by the Board, concerns were now being expressed that the paint shop only seemed able to progress large batches of similar parts. The MRP system had recently been audited and showed a data accuracy of 68 per cent in its inventory records while its Bill of Material accuracy had improved to 90 per cent.

Over the last two years the company had been coming under increasing pressure from one customer in particular about quality and had begun to work towards BS 5750 part 1 but David Jones, the current MD, was worried that the bureaucracy of it was going to stifle the company. In the meantime there had been a limited introduction of automated test equipment which was used on a 1 per cent audit basis for life-testing the safety critical aspects of the seat adjustment mechanisms.

While successive managers had tried to spread the customer base, the automotive sector was by far the most important part of Jones and Sons' business so the recent troubles of the local assemblers had proved painful for Jones and Sons as well. Thus when the opportunity arose to supply to Nissoto Motors (UK) Ltd., David Jones jumped at the opportunity. Being a careful man his jumping was in slow motion as he checked out what the new customers might expect of his company. David's contacts in the industry proved useful. They told him that Quality had to be even better than he was currently providing for his existing customers, that delivery, reliability and speed would come under pressure and that the pressure on cost effectiveness would be relentless.

So it proved, but Jones and Sons were up to the task. The initial small orders for a limited range of part numbers had led to more business although the whole process had taken much longer than expected and Nissoto's engineers had been everywhere in Jones' plant making suggestions galore. The company had even implemented some of them but change was difficult.

While David Jones was glad of the turnover Nissoto provided, the business had not made the same margins as Jones had been used to. In the past it had been normal to recoup some expenses after the beginning of the contract due to 'special circumstances'. This was a dance that Jones and the 'old' customers knew well but it seemed that Nissoto worked to a different tune. Nevertheless David Jones was glad to keep busy and having the name of being one of Nissoto's suppliers must be worth something in his dealings with other customers he thought.

All of this paled into insignificance against the prospects offered in the latest communication from Barry Greenwood, Supplies Manager at Nissoto who were accelerating the move to 100 per cent local sourcing. Jones and Sons were being asked to be involved in producing a complete assembly incorporating not only the mechanical componentry they were used to but also the electrically operated actuators and associated electronic controls and connectors to enable the complete assembly to be delivered, quality assured, direct to the assembly line. This was in addition to a welcome increase in orders for their normal work.

This raised big questions in David Jones' mind. For example how could they provide the new technology? Build up a resource in-house? Buy-in finished parts or form some sort of arrangement or merger with an electronics company? The whole question of sourcing and manufacturing planning became much more complicated and danger prone. The pressures to provide an increased product mix on reduced lead time for direct feed to the assembly line, synchronized with the assembly flow, frightened David Jones more than he was prepared to admit in public.

The volumes being talked about were dramatic while the expected price looked good – at least it might if David could understand how to cost the new technology element to his satisfaction!

This was certainly a big opportunity. Could Jones and Sons afford not to go for it? Could they manage it if they got the work? Could they actually make money in the new situation?

These were going to be crucial decisions for the Board. Here was a real test for his three main directors. They were always going on at him to develop the company in ways they thought best. It would be interesting to see how they would propose solving this 'opportunity'.

David was willing to be convinced but it had better be good! Particularly since this morning he had received a rather firm 'invitation' to meet with Cyril Montague who wished to introduce his young successor as manager of the same high street bank that had handled Jones and Sons accounts from the very beginning for old Dai Jones himself.

(See the attached data sheets for more background. The figures relate only to the automotive side of the business which accounted for around 85 per cent of the total).

This case was prepared with input from the following:
Jonathan Anscombe, A T Kearney; Tony Borlace, Schlegel (UK); Douglas Briggs, Glasgow University Business School; Brian McKibbin, IMM; Simon Tomlinson, The Logistics Business; Mark Webber, Tinsley Bridge and David Farmer. It was produced by Douglas Macbeth of Supply Chain Management Group.

The case represents no known real company and is intended for use as a management development exercise. The presented 'solutions' are for illustration of possible outcomes but each user is encouraged to think through the issues for themselves. Many of the issues are real enough.

List of Attachments

Data Sheet 1(a)   Sales units per Model and Customer

Data Sheet 2(a)   Sales and Inventory

Data Sheet 3(a)   Financial Results Year Ending 31 December

Data Sheet 4(a)   Composition of Labour Force

Data Sheet 5   Cost Breakdown of a Car Front Seat

Data Sheet 1(b)   Sales Units per Model and Customer (revised)

Data Sheet 2(b)   Sales and Inventory (revised)

Data Sheet 3(b)   Financial Results Year Ending 31 December (revised)

Data Sheet 4(b)   Composition of Labour Force (revised)

Nissoto Motors (UK) Limited, Letter

Welsh Linen Bank Limited, Letter

Speech Bubbles for the main actors

Strategic Evaluation (a) Technical

Strategic Evaluation (a) Manufacturing

Strategic Evaluation (a) Materials

Data Sheet 1 (a) Jones & Sons Limited

SALES UNITS PER MODEL & CUSTOMER
1989–1993

Model Type	Customer	1989	1990	1991	1992	1993 (Budget)	1993 (Revised)
LB60	FGM	165000	176340	171590	163380	150000	
HB60	FGM	81102	97670	89965	94167	90000	
Customer %		67	63	61	59	57	
HB605	UKM	100953	144255	136590	141250	140000	
FR90	UKM	10695	12020	14700	15276	15000	
Customer %		31	35	35	36	37	
HFR 100	Nissoto	7250	8015	15000	16000	17000	
HFR 150	Nissoto			455	5927	6300	
Customer %		2	2	4	5	6	
TOTAL		365000	438300	428300	435000	418300	100
Customer %		100	100	100	100	100	

Notes
1. Figures for 1993 have been estimated
2. Each model type consists of a number of front and rear seat variations each at a different stage in its own life cycle
3. New Integrated Seat Assembly

Data Sheet 2 (a)   **SALES AND INVENTORY**   **Jones & Sons Limited**

| Year | Sales £m | Inventory (£000s) | | | | Stock Turns |
		Raw Materials	Work in Progress	Finished Goods	TOTAL	
1989	21.9	555	4855	2715	8125	2.7
1990	26.3	616	6507	2109	9232	2.9
1991	25.7	600	6831	2192	9623	2.7
1992	26.1	646	6471	1863	9000	2.9
1993 (Budget)	25.1	660	6600	2013	9273	2.7
1993 (Revised)						

Data Sheet 3 (a)

FINANCIAL RESULTS YEAR ENDED 31 DECEMBER

Jones & Sons Limited

All figures in £000s

	1989	1990	1991	1992	1993 (Budget)*	1993 (Revised)†
TOTAL FIXED ASSETS	7562	11520	13000	12500	12700	
CURRENT ASSETS						
Inventory (See sheets 1 and 3)	8125	9232	9623	9000	9273	
Debtors and Prepayments	2865	2910	2860	2903	3417	
Cash	9	10	15	13	14	
	10999	12152	12498	11916	12704	
LESS CURRENT LIABILITIES						
Creditors and Accrual	2635	2928	2120	2737	3330	
Bank Loans & Overdraft	5673	5529	7529	8210	8372	
	8308	8457	9649	10947	11702	
WORKING CAPITAL	2691	3695	2749	969	1002	
NET ASSETS EMPLOYED	10253	15215	15749	13469	13702	
FINANCED BY						
Share Holder Funds & Retained Earnings	9695	11617	12615	13149	13469	
Profit (Loss) for the year + Gross Margin (%)	558 (2.54)	998 (3.79)	534 (2.08)	320 (1.23)	233 (0.92)	
Government Grant		2600	2600			
	10253	15215	15749	13469	13702	

* Budgets prepared Nov/Dec 1992
† Prepared by Chairman for meeting 31.3.93

Data Sheet 4 (a)　　　　　**COMPOSITION OF LABOUR FORCE**　　　　　**Jones & Sons Limited**

	1989	1990	1991	1992	1993 (Budget)
	Actual	Actual	Actual	Actual	Actual
Direct Mech	150	152	148	144	140
Direct Assy	99	102	98	96	94
Electronic Assy	–	–	–	–	–
Ind (incl Jnr Mgt)	30	30	30	28	28
Senior Mgt	9	9	10	10	10
Sales/Marketing	12	12	12	9	9
Purchasing	10	10	10	7	7
Technical	5	5	5	4	4
QC	18	19	18	17	17
TOTAL	333	339	331	315	309

Sales/employee (£000s)	65.76	77.58	75.74	82.85	81.23

© SCMG Ltd 1993

Data Sheet 5

COST BREAKDOWN OF CAR FRONT SEAT

Jones & Sons Limited

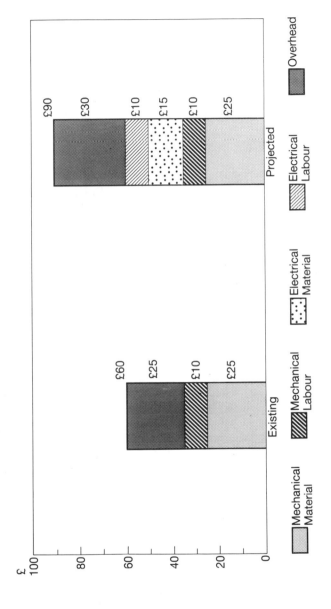

Data Sheet 1 (b)   **Jones & Sons Limited**

SALES UNITS PER MODEL & CUSTOMER
1989–1993

Model Type	Customer	1989	1990	1991	1992	1993 (Budget)	1993 (Revised)
LB60	FGM	165000	176340	171590	163380	150000	150000
HB60	FGM	81102	97670	89965	94167	90000	90000
	FGM %	67	63	61	59	57	51
HB605	UKM	100953	144255	136590	141250	140000	140000
FR90	UKM	10695	12020	14700	15276	15000	15000
	UKM %	31	35	35	36	37	33
HFR 100	Nissoto	7250	8015	15000	16000	17000	40000
HFR 150	Nissoto			455	5927	6300	(note 3) 28890
	Nissoto %	2	2	4	5	6	16
TOTAL		365000	438300	428300	435000	418300	471890
	Customer %	100	100	100	100	100	100

Notes
1. Figures for 1993 have been estimated
2. Each model type consists of a number of front and rear seat variations each at a different stage in its own life cycle
3. New Integrated Seat Assembly

© SCMG Ltd 1993

Data Sheet 2 (b)   **SALES AND INVENTORY**   **Jones & Sons Limited**

Year	Sales £m	Inventory (£000s)				
		Raw Materials	Work in Progress	Finished Goods	TOTAL	Stock Turns
1989	21.9	555	4855	2715	8125	2.7
1990	26.3	616	6507	2109	9232	2.9
1991	25.7	600	6831	2192	9623	2.7
1992	26.1	646	6471	1863	9000	2.9
1993 (Budget)	25.1	660	6600	2013	9273	2.7

1993 (Revised)	28.7	633	5100	1900	7633	3.7

Data Sheet 3 (b)

FINANCIAL RESULTS YEAR ENDED 31 DECEMBER — Jones & Sons Limited

All figures in £000s

	1989	1990	1991	1992	1993 (Budget)*	1993 (Revised)†
TOTAL FIXED ASSETS	7562	11520	13000	12500	12700	13000
CURRENT ASSETS						
Inventory (See sheets 1 and 3)	8125	9232	9623	9000	9273	7633
Debtors and Prepayments	2865	2910	2860	2903	3417	3020
Cash	9	10	15	13	14	11
	10999	12152	12498	11916	12704	10664
LESS CURRENT LIABILITIES						
Creditors and Accrual	2635	2928	2120	2737	3330	2800
Bank Loans & Overdraft	5673	5529	7529	8210	8372	6600
	8308	8457	9649	10947	11702	9400
WORKING CAPITAL	2691	3695	2749	969	1002	1264
NET ASSETS EMPLOYED	10253	15215	15749	13469	13702	14264
FINANCED BY						
Share Holder Funds & Retained Earnings	9695	11617	12615	13149	13469	13702
Profit (Loss) for the year + Gross Margin (%)	558 (2.54)	998 (3.79)	534 (2.08)	320 (1.23)	233 (0.92)	562 (1.95)
Government Grant		2600	2600			
	10253	15215	15749	13469	13702	14264

* Budgets prepared Nov/Dec 1992
† Prepared by Chairman for meeting 31.3.93

Data Sheet 4 (b)

COMPOSITION OF LABOUR FORCE

Jones & Sons Limited

	1989	1990	1991	1992	1993 (Budget)	1993 (Revised)
	Actual	Actual	Actual	Actual	Actual	
Direct Mech	150	152	148	144	140	
Direct Assy	99	102	98	96	94	
Electronic Assy	–	–	–	–	–	
Ind (incl Jnr Mgt)	30	30	30	28	28	
Senior Mgt	9	9	10	10	10	
Sales/Marketing	12	12	12	9	9	
Purchasing	10	10	10	7	7	
Technical	5	5	5	4	4	
QC	18	19	18	17	17	
TOTAL	333	339	331	315	309	

	1989	1990	1991	1992	1993 (Budget)	1993 (Revised)
Sales/employee (£000s)	65.76	77.58	75.74	82.85	81.23	

NM

Nissoto Motors (UK) Limited
Car Assembly Division
The Hale Plant
Halewood
Merseyside LP65 2DG

Mr David Jones
Managing Director
Jones & Sons Limited (Engineers)
Penarth Road
Cardiff DD2 3XY

30 March 1993

Dear Mr Jones

I am writing to confirm the substance of my conversation with you and your other executives following a visit to your facilities last week.

We are now interested to explore the possibilities of inviting your company to produce a complete assembly incorporating not only the mechanical componentry but the electrical operated actuators and associated electronic controls and connectors. This will provide a complete assembly to be delivered, on a quality assured basis, direct to our assembly lines at the Hale Plant.

I appreciate that this is a substantial development in your own business. We will, of course, offer all the services behind our group's resources to enable you to implement the full assembly production. At this stage, however, I need to know whether you consider this an appropriate development for your company and to receive your assurances that you would be prepared to commit to this future partnership.

I would be grateful if you would now consider this and to let me have your formal response no later than the end of next week.

Yours sincerely

Barry Greenwood
Supplies Manager.

WLBL

The Welsh Linen Bank Limited
Museum Place
Cardiff CD1 1AB

Personal and Confidential

Mr David Jones
Managing Director
Jones & Sons Limited (Engineers)
Penarth Road
Cardiff DD2 3XY

30 March 1993

Dear Mr Jones

I informed you some time ago about my pending move to our Head Office. I shall be taking up my new position as Regional Manager, South Wales, with effect from 20 April 1993.

It would be appropriate if I were to introduce my successor, and I would therefore like to make a firm appointment to see you in the near future. You should understand that your Company's account and the branch which is currently servicing you will remain within my jurisdiction. I will still be in close contact with you but I know that my successor would like to have an opportunity to discuss the range of services now on offer.

On a slightly less pleasant note, I am concerned to see that there has been further increase in your overdraft and loan facilities. I therefore consider that at our forthcoming meeting this would be an appropriate time to discuss your future aspirations and to consider your medium term business plan. The bank must seek assurances regarding the viability of your business due to its considerable investment in your Company.

Yours sincerely

Cyril Montague
Senior Manager.

SPEECH BUBBLES FOR THE MAIN ACTORS

Technical
- We've always made everything in house, what will this mean?
- None of my team know anything about electronics. Hugh did a bit on his HNC but that was 8 years ago!
- How can we be sure the different sub-systems will work together properly?
- How on earth are we going to cost it with no historical data, no competitive information, no technical competence to evaluate suppliers and no established friends in electronics to ask?
- Timescales are unreal! What will Manufacturing do to cock it up this time. On the last model introduction last May they decided they couldn't make it with only two weeks to go before delivery. That had cost a fortune in overtime for the design team to make changes for Manufacturing!

Manufacturing
- Technical never get it right for us, they're always late with lots of changes.
- The shop floor are really going to have to hussle to make this lot!
- It's costing us an arm and a leg to get the existing quality levels – what's it going to be like now?
- We will need to get more hardware – robots and handling equipment – to remove the people variability.
- What about the electronics – who will do that? If we buy it in that will mean more headaches for me!
- If the schedules get any tighter it's going to be hell – there won't be time for us to change the production mix to cope with any problems.
- We will need new staff for the electronics, and new storage and test equipment as well, where will it all fit in we are already short of storage space?

Materials
- How do I find reliable suppliers for the electronics – after all it's hard enough getting a good price in the mechanical market these days!
- Still we should get good leverage on prices using Nissoto's name.
- My buyers haven't any contacts in electronics.
- What about Partnership Sourcing, there was an article about that recently, now where was it?
- Our current contract terms probably won't do.
- Can we trust new suppliers when we don't trust the existing ones? Anyway we change them frequently – even if they don't go out of business.
- The time pressures on delivery are going to make it hard – I'll need expeditors!

Strategic Evaluation (a)

Jones & Sons Limited (Engineers)

TECHNICAL

ISSUE AREAS	PROBLEM AREAS	CHOICE OPTIONS	KEY INDICATORS	SOLUTIONS
Design Authority				
Core Competence/Skills				
Integration of Sub-systems				
Costing				
Timescale				

© SCMG Ltd 1993

Strategic Evaluation (a)   **Jones & Sons Limited (Engineers)**

MANUFACTURING

ISSUE AREAS	PROBLEM AREAS	CHOICE OPTIONS	KEY INDICATORS	SOLUTIONS
New Product Launch Control				
Training/Recruitment				
Factory Operations				
Quality Costs				
Production Flexibility				

© SCMG Ltd 1993

Strategic Evaluation (a)

Jones & Sons Limited (Engineers)

MATERIALS

ISSUE AREAS	PROBLEM AREAS	CHOICE OPTIONS	KEY INDICATORS	SOLUTIONS
Partnerships				
Market Intelligence				
Degree of Vertical Integration				
Component/Supplier Evaluations				
Nature of Contracts				

© SCMG Ltd 1993

REFERENCES AND FURTHER READING

Introduction

1. Womack JP, Jones DT, and Roos D, *The Machine That Changed the World,* Macmillan, 1990
2. Lamming R, *Beyond Partnership: Strategies for innovation and supply,* Prentice Hall, 1993
3. *Computervision Manufacturing Attitudes Survey* 1993, Coventry
4. *Partnership Sourcing,* Partnership Sourcing Ltd., CBI, 1992
5. de Meyer A, *Creating the Virtual Factory – report on the 1992 European Manufacturing Futures Survey,* INSEAD, 1992
6. Domino Amjet, 'Either You've Got the Chemistry or You Haven't', *Best Practice in Purchasing,* Findlay Publications for DTI 1993, 28–31.
7. Griffiths J, 'Driving Out the Old Regime' Management page *FT*, August 20 1993.

Chapter 1

1. Womack JP, Jones DT, and Roos D, *The Machine That Changed the World,* Macmillan, 1990
2. Taguchi G, 'Robust Quality', *Harvard Business Review*, Jan–Feb 1990
3. Browne J, Harhen J, Shivnan J, *Production Management Systems,* Addison–Wesley, 1988
4. BS 5750, *A Positive Contribution to Better Business,* BSI London
5. Taylor FW, *Principles of Scientific Management,* Harper and Row, 1911
6. Carlisle JA and Parker RC, *Beyond Negotiation,* John Wiley & Sons, 1989

Chapter 2

1. Hill T, *Manufacturing Strategy,* Macmillan, 1985
2. Skinner W, Manufacturing – Missing Link in Corporate Strategy, *Harvard Business Review* 47.3, 136–145
3. Porter M E, *Competitive Strategy: Techniques for Analyzing Industries and Competitors,* The Free Press, 1980
4. Ohmae K, *The Mind of the Strategist,* Penguin, 1982
5. von Hippel E, *The Sources of Innovation*, OUP, 1988
6. Morita A and Reingold EM, *Made in Japan,* Penguin, 1986

7. Jarillo JC and Stevenson HH, 'Cooperative Strategies – The Payoffs and the Pitfalls', *Long Range Planning* 24.1, 64–70

8. Womack JP, Jones DT, and Roos D, *The Machine That Changed the World,* Macmillan, 1990

9. Schonberger RJ, *Building A Chain of Customers,* Hutchinson, 1992

10. Sullivan LP, 1987 a,b, 'The Seven Stages In Company-Wide Quality', *Quality Progress,* June 1987, 77–83; 'Quality Function Deployment', *Quality Progress,* May 1987, 39–50

11. Oakland JS, *Total Quality Management*, Butterworth–Heinemann, 1993, 50

12. Taguchi G, Robust Quality, *Harvard Business Review*, Jan–Feb 1990

13. Cooper R and Kaplan R S, 'Measure Costs Right: Make the Right Decisions', *Harvard Business Review,* September–October 1988

14. *The Malcolm Baldrige National Quality Award,* American Society for Quality Control, Milwaukee, WI., 1993

15. Macbeth DK, *Advanced Manufacturing: Strategy, and Management*, IFS, 1989

16. Slack N, *'The Flexibility of Manufacturing Systems'*, *IJOPM* 7.4, 35–46

17. Goldrat EM and Cox J, *The Goal,* Creative Output Books, 1986

Chapter 3

1. Porter ME, *Competitive Strategy: Techniques for Analyzing Industries and Competitors,* The Free Press, 1980

2. Deming WE, *Out of the Crisis,* CUP 1982

3. Gilbreth FB, *Motion Study*, Van Nostrand, 1911

4. Taylor FW, *Principles of Scientific Management*, Harper and Row, 1911

5. Houlihan JB, *International Supply Chain Management,* IJPD & MM, 17.2, 51–66

6. Forrester J, *Industrial Dynamics,* MIT Press, 1961

7. Cooper R and Kaplan RS, 'Measure Costs Right: Make the Right Decisions', *Harvard Business Review,* September–October 1988

8. Scott C and Westbrook R, 'New Strategic Tools for Supply Chain Management', *IJPD & LM*, 21.1, 23–33

9. Carlisle JA and Parker RC, *Beyond Negotiation,* John Wiley & Sons, 1989

10. The Supplies Directive (#77/62/EEC); The Works Directive (#89/440/EEC); The Services Directive (#92/50 EEC); The Compliance Directive (#89/665/EEC), The Commission of the European Community, Brussels.

11. Byrne N, *Competition Law in the European Community*, EMJ 9, 2, 1991

12. Taguchi G, Robust Quality, *Harvard Business Review*, Jan–Feb 1990

13. Camp RC, *Benchmarking,* ASQC Quality Press, 1989

Chapter 4

1. Piore MJ and Sable CF, *The Second Industrial Divide,* Basic Books, 1984

2. Williamson O E, *Markets and Hierarchies,* The Free Press, 1975

3. Ford H, *My Life and Work*, Heinemann, 1922

4. Ellram L, 'Supply Chain Management: The Industrial Organization Perspective', *IJ PD & LM*, 21.1

5. Sako M, *Prices, Quality and Trust: Inter-Firm Relations In Britain and Japan*, CUP, 1992

6. Reve T, 'The Firm as a Nexus of Internal and External Contracts', in Aoki M, Gustafsson B and Williamson OE (eds), *The Firm as a Nexus of Treaties*, Sage, 1990, 155

7. Peters TJ and Waterman RH, *In Search of Excellence: Lessons from America's Best-Run Companies*, Harper and Row, 1982

8. Porter ME, *Competitive Strategy: Techniques of Analyzing Industries and Competitors*, The Free Press, 1980

9. Contractor FJ and Lorange P, *Cooperative Strategies in International Business: Joint Ventures and Technology Partnerships Between Firms*, Lexington Books, 1988

10. Gillett J, 'The Time to Market Paradigm' *European Purchasing and Materials Management*, 1.1, 67–70

11. Reve T, 'The Firm as a Nexus of Internal and External Contracts', in Aoki M, Gustafsson B and Williamson OE (eds), *The Firm as a Nexus of Treaties*, Sage, 1990, 155

12. Hakansson H and Snehota I, 'No Business is an Island: the network concept of business strategy' *Scandinavian J of Mgt*, 5.3, 187–200

13. Ford ID, (ed), *Understanding Business Markets: Interaction, Relationships, Networks*, Academic Press, 1990.

14. Lessem R, *Business as a Learning Community*, McGraw Hill, 1993

15. Senge P, *The Fifth Discipline*, , Random Century, 1991

16. Zuboff S, *In the Age of the Smart Machine*, Heinemann, 1988

17. Technology Strategies MCB, July/August 1993

Chapter 5

1. Sako M, *Prices, Quality and Trust: Inter-Firm Relations In Britain and Japan*, CUP, 1992

2. Womack JP, Jones DT, and Roos D, *The Machine That Changed the World*, Macmillan, 1990, 146

3. Hines P, 'Integrated Materials Management: a post-Porterian Paradigm?' *2nd Int Conf of PSERG*, Bath, 1993.

4. Carlisle JA and Parker RC, *Beyond Negotiation*, John Wiley & Sons, 1989

5. Axelrod R, *The Evolution of Cooperation*, Penguin, 1984

6. Dawkins R, *The Selfish Gene*, OUP, 1976

7. Lewin K, *Field Theory in Social Science*, Harper and Row, 1951

8. *Partnership Sourcing*, Partnership Sourcing Ltd, CBI, 1992

9. Johansson HJ, McHugh P, Pendlebury AJ and Wheeler WA, *Business Process Re-engineering*, John Wiley & Sons, 1993

10 SCMG *Increasing The Potential for Local Sourcing to OEMs*, Report of SERC/ACME grant GR/F68119, Glasgow, 1991

Chapter 6

1. Wilson DC, *A Strategy of Change,* Routledge, 1992
2. Hill T, *Manufacturing Strategy,* (2nd Ed) Macmillan, 1993
3. Macbeth DK, Baxter LF, Ferguson N and Neil GC, *The Customer–Supplier Relationship Audit,* IFS, 1990
4. Boddy D and Buchanan D, *The Expertise of the Change Agent,* Routledge, 1993

INDEX